# Georgia CRCT GPS Coach
# Social Studies
# Grade 8

Coach
America's Best for Student Success.

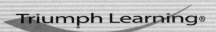

Triumph Learning®

A Haights Cross Communications ® Company

**Acknowledgments**

Photograph from Raymond Gehman/CORBIS, p. 35
Photographs from Bettmann/CORBIS, pp. 45, 70, 83, 110, 115, 126, 146, 150, 154, 162, 170, 204, 211, 233
Photograph from Lee Snider/Photo Images/CORBIS, p. 51
Photograph from William A. Bake/CORBIS, p. 59
Photographs from CORBIS, pp. 87, 99, 107
Photograph from Museum of History and Industry/CORBIS, p. 123

Photograph from Reuters/CORBIS, p. 144
Photograph from Wally McNamee/CORBIS, p. 166
Photograph from Ron Chapple Stock/CORBIS, p. 174
Photograph from Daniel Lainé/CORBIS, p. 188
Photograph from Tami Chappell/Reuters/CORBIS, p. 200
Photograph from Kevin Fleming/CORBIS, p. 215

Georgia CRCT Coach, GPS Edition, Social Studies, Grade 8
124GA

ISBN-10: 1-59823-674-1
ISBN-13: 978-1-59823-674-3

Author: Cypress Curriculum Services, LLC
Cover Images: Peach: © IT Stock Free/JupiterImages, Globe: © Creatas Images/JupiterImages

**Triumph Learning**® 136 Madison Avenue, 7th Floor, New York, NY 10016
Kevin McAliley, President and Chief Executive Officer

Printed in the United States of America.

10  9  8

# Table of Contents

Georgia Performance Standards

# Letter to the Student

Dear Student,

Welcome to the *Georgia CRCT Coach, GPS Edition, Social Studies, Grade 8*. This book will help you as you prepare to strengthen your social studies skills this year. *Coach* also provides practice with the kinds of questions you will have to answer on tests, including the state test.

The *Coach* book is divided into chapters and lessons. Before you begin the first chapter, you may want to take the Pretest at the beginning of the book. The Pretest will show you your strengths and weaknesses in the skills and strategies you need to know this year. This way, you will be aware of what you need to concentrate on to be successful. At the end of the *Coach* book is a Posttest that will allow you and your teacher to evaluate how much you have learned. We have tried to match the style of the state test in the Pretest and Posttest for better test practice.

The lessons in this book will help you review and practice your skills and get you ready to take tests. Some of the practice will be in the style of the state test. In general, you will be answering multiple-choice, constructed-response, and open-ended or extended-response questions. Questions like these may appear on your state test. Practicing with these types of questions will give you a good idea of what you need to review to triumph.

Here are some **tips** that will help you as you work through this book. Remembering these tips will also help you do well on the state test.

- Listen closely to your teacher's directions.
- When answering multiple-choice questions, read each choice carefully before choosing the BEST answer.
- Time yourself so that you have the time at the end of a test to check your answers.

We hope you will enjoy using *Coach* and that you will have a fun and rewarding year!

# Letter to the Family

Dear Parents and Families,

The *Coach* series of workbooks is designed to prepare your child to master grade-appropriate skills in social studies and to take the Grade 8 CRCT, which is the test administered each year in the state of Georgia. In your state, the grade-appropriate skills are called Georgia Performance Standards. These are the skills the state has chosen as the building blocks of your child's education in social studies, and these are the skills that will be tested on the CRCT. Your child's success will be measured by how well he or she masters these skills.

We invite you to be our partner in making learning a priority in your child's life. To help ensure success, we suggest that you review the lessons in this book with your child. While teachers will guide your child through the book in class, your support at home is also vital to your child's comprehension.

Please encourage your child to read and study this book at home, and take the time to go over the sample questions and homework together. The more students practice, the better they do on the actual exam and on all the tests they will take in school. Try talking about what your child has learned in school. Perhaps you can show your children real-life applications of what they have learned. For example, you could discuss why social studies skills are important in life and how they apply to everyday situations.

We ask you to work with us this year to help your child triumph. Together, we *can* make a difference!

## The *Coach* Guardian Involvement Pledge

As an involved guardian, I pledge to:

- promote the value of education to my child

- inspire my child to read

- discuss the skills my child needs with his or her teachers and principal

- expect my child to successfully fulfill school and homework assignments

- join in school activities and decisions

**I hereby pledge my involvement in my child's educational success!**

**Parent Signature:** _____

**Student Signature:** _____

Coach™

# Georgia Correlation Chart

| Standard | Description | *Coach* Lesson | Check When Completed |
|---|---|---|---|
| SS8H1.a | Describe the evolution of Native American cultures (Paleo, Archaic, Woodland, and Mississippian) prior to European contact. | 1 | |
| SS8H1.b | Evaluate the impact of European contact on Native American cultures; include Spanish missions along the barrier islands, and the explorations of Hernando de Soto. | 2 | |
| SS8H1.c | Explain reasons for European exploration and settlement of North America, with emphasis on the interests of the French, Spanish, and British in the southeastern area. | 2 | |
| SS8H2.a | Explain the importance of James Oglethorpe, the Charter of 1732, reasons for settlement (charity, economics, and defense), Tomochichi, Mary Musgrove, and the city of Savannah. | 3 | |
| SS8H2.b | Evaluate the Trustee Period of Georgia's colonial history, emphasizing the role of the Salzburgers, Highland Scots, malcontents, and the Spanish threat from Florida. | 3 | |
| SS8H2.c | Explain the development of Georgia as a royal colony with regard to land ownership, slavery, government, and the impact of the royal governors. | 4 | |
| SS8H3.a | Explain the immediate and long-term causes of the American Revolution and their impact on Georgia; include the French and Indian War (i.e., Seven Years' War), Proclamation of 1763, Stamp Act, Intolerable Acts, and the Declaration of Independence. | 5 | |
| SS8H3.b | Analyze the significance of people and events in Georgia on the Revolutionary War; include loyalists, patriots, Elijah Clarke, Austin Dabney, Nancy Hart, Button Gwinnett, Lyman Hall, George Walton, Battle of Kettle Creek, and siege of Savannah. | 6 | |

| Standard | Description | *Coach* Lesson | Check When Completed |
|---|---|---|---|
| SS8H4.a | Analyze the strengths and weaknesses of both the Georgia Constitution of 1777 and the Articles of Confederation and explain how weaknesses in the Articles of Confederation led to a need to revise the Articles. | 7 | |
| SS8H4.b | Describe the role of Georgia at the Constitutional Convention of 1787; include the role of Abraham Baldwin and William Few, and reasons why Georgia ratified the new constitution. | 7 | |
| SS8H5.a | Explain the establishment of the University of Georgia, Louisville, and the spread of Baptist and Methodist churches. | 8 | |
| SS8H5.b | Evaluate the impact of land policies pursued by Georgia; include the headright system, land lotteries, and the Yazoo land fraud. | 9 | |
| SS8H5.c | Explain how technological developments, including the cotton gin and railroads, had an impact on Georgia's growth. | 10 | |
| SS8H5.d | Analyze the events that led to the removal of Creeks and Cherokees; include the roles of Alexander McGillivray, William McIntosh, Sequoyah, John Ross, Dahlonega Gold Rush, Worcester v. Georgia, Andrew Jackson, John Marshall, and the Trail of Tears. | 11 | |
| SS8H6.a | Explain the importance of key issues and events that led to the Civil War; include slavery, states' rights, nullification, Missouri Compromise, Compromise of 1850 and the Georgia Platform, Kansas-Nebraska Act, Dred Scott case, election of 1860, the debate over secession in Georgia, and the role of Alexander Stephens. | 12 | |
| SS8H6.b | State the importance of key events of the Civil War; include Antietam, Emancipation Proclamation, Gettysburg, Chickamauga, the Union blockade of Georgia's coast, Sherman's Atlanta Campaign, Sherman's March to the Sea, and Andersonville. | 13 | |

| Standard | Description | *Coach* Lesson | Check When Completed |
|---|---|---|---|
| SS8H6.c | Analyze the impact of Reconstruction on Georgia and other southern states, emphasizing Freedmen's Bureau; sharecropping and tenant farming; Reconstruction plans; 13th, 14th, and 15th amendments to the Constitution; Henry McNeal Turner and black legislators; and the Ku Klux Klan. | 14 | |
| SS8H7.a | Evaluate the impact the Bourbon Triumvirate, Henry Grady, International Cotton Exposition, Tom Watson and the Populists, Rebecca Latimer Felton, the 1906 Atlanta Riot, the Leo Frank Case, and the county unit system had on Georgia during this period. | 15 | |
| SS8H7.b | Analyze how rights were denied to African Americans through Jim Crow laws, Plessy v. Ferguson, disenfranchisement, and racial violence. | 16 | |
| SS8H7.c | Explain the roles of Booker T. Washington, W.E.B. Du Bois, John and Lugenia Burns Hope, and Alonzo Herndon. | 17 | |
| SS8H7.d | Give reasons for World War I and describe Georgia's contributions. | 18 | |
| SS8H8.a | Describe the impact of the boll weevil and drought on Georgia. | 19 | |
| SS8H8.b | Explain economic factors that resulted in the Great Depression. | 19 | |
| SS8H8.c | Discuss the impact of the political career of Eugene Talmadge. | 20 | |
| SS8H8.d | Discuss the effect of the New Deal in terms of the impact of the Civilian Conservation Corps, Agricultural Adjustment Act, rural electrification, and Social Security. | 21 | |
| SS8H9.a | Describe the impact of events leading up to American involvement in World War II; include Lend-Lease and the bombing of Pearl Harbor. | 22 | |
| SS8H9.b | Evaluate the importance of Bell Aircraft, military bases, the Savannah and Brunswick shipyards, Richard Russell, and Carl Vinson. | 22 | |
| SS8H9.c | Explain the impact of the Holocaust on Georgians. | 22 | |

| Standard | Description | *Coach* Lesson | Check When Completed |
|---|---|---|---|
| SS8H9.d | Discuss the ties to Georgia that President Roosevelt had and his impact on the state. | 22 | |
| SS8H10.a | Analyze the impact of the transformation of agriculture on Georgia's growth. | 23 | |
| SS8H10.b | Explain how the development of Atlanta, including the roles of mayors William B. Hartsfield and Ivan Allen, Jr., and major league sports, contributed to the growth of Georgia. | 23 | |
| SS8H10c | Discuss the impact of Ellis Arnall. | 23 | |
| SS8H11.a | Describe major developments in civil rights and Georgia's role during the 1940s and 1950s; include the roles of Herman Talmadge, Benjamin Mays, the 1946 governor's race and the end of the white primary, Brown v. Board of Education, Martin Luther King, Jr., and the 1956 state flag. | 24 | |
| SS8H11.b | Analyze the role Georgia and prominent Georgians played in the Civil Rights Movement of the 1960s and 1970s; include such events as the founding of the Student Non-Violent Coordinating Committee (SNCC), Sibley Commission, admission of Hamilton Holmes and Charlayne Hunter to the University of Georgia, Albany Movement, March on Washington, Civil Rights Act, the election of Maynard Jackson as mayor of Atlanta, and the role of Lester Maddox. | 25 | |
| SS8H11.c | Discuss the impact of Andrew Young on Georgia. | 25 | |
| SS8H12.a | Evaluate the consequences of the end of the county unit system and reapportionment. | 26 | |
| SS8H12.b | Describe the role of Jimmy Carter in Georgia as state senator, governor, president, and past president. | 27 | |
| SS8H12.c | Analyze the impact of the rise of the two-party system in Georgia. | 28 | |
| SS8H12.d | Evaluate the effect of the 1996 Olympics on Georgia. | 29 | |
| SS8H12.e | Evaluate the importance of new immigrant communities to the growth and economy of Georgia. | 29 | |

| Standard | Description | *Coach* Lesson | Check When Completed |
|---|---|---|---|
| SS8G1.a | Locate Georgia in relation to region, nation, continent, and hemispheres. | 31 | |
| SS8G1.b | Describe the five geographic regions of Georgia; include the Blue Ridge Mountains, Valley and Ridge, Appalachian Plateau, Piedmont, and Coastal Plain. | 30 | |
| SS8G1.c | Locate and evaluate the importance of key physical features on the development of Georgia; include the Fall Line, Okefenokee Swamp, Appalachian Mountains, Chattahoochee and Savannah Rivers, and barrier islands. | 30 | |
| SS8G1.d | Evaluate the impact of climate on Georgia's development. | 31 | |
| SS8G2.a | Explain how the three transportation systems interact to provide domestic and international goods to the people of Georgia. | 32 | |
| SS8G2.b | Explain how the three transportation systems interact to provide producers and service providers in Georgia with national and international markets. | 32 | |
| SS8G2.c | Explain how the three transportation systems provide jobs for Georgians. | 32 | |
| SS8CG1.a | Explain the basic structure of the Georgia state constitution. | 33 | |
| SS8CG1.b | Explain the concepts of separation of powers and checks and balances. | 33 | |
| SS8CG1.c | Describe the rights and responsibilities of citizens. | 34 | |
| SS8CG1.d | Explain voting requirements and elections in Georgia. | 34 | |
| SS8CG1.e | Explain the role of political parties in government. | 34 | |
| S8CG2.a | Explain the qualifications, term, election, and duties of members of the General Assembly. | 35 | |
| S8CG2.b | Describe the organization of the General Assembly, with emphasis on leadership and the committee system. | 35 | |
| S8CG2.c | Trace the steps in the legislative process for a bill to become a law in Georgia. | 35 | |

| Standard | Description | Coach Lesson | Check When Completed |
|---|---|---|---|
| SS8CG3.a | Explain the qualifications, term, election, and duties of the governor and lieutenant governor. | 36 | |
| SS8CG3.b | Describe the organization of the executive branch, with emphasis on major policy areas of state programs. | 36 | |
| SS8CG4.a | Explain the structure of the court system in Georgia including trial and appellate procedures and how judges are selected. | 37 | |
| SS8CG4.b | Explain the difference between criminal law and civil law. | 37 | |
| SS8CG4.c | Describe the adult justice system, emphasizing the different jurisdictions, terminology, and steps in the criminal justice process. | 37 | |
| SS8CG4.d | Describe ways to avoid trouble and settle disputes peacefully. | 37 | |
| SS8CG5.a | Explain the origins, functions, purposes, and differences of county and city governments in Georgia. | 39 | |
| SS8CG5.b | Compare and contrast the weak mayor-council, the strong mayor-council, and the council-manager forms of city government. | 39 | |
| SS8CG5.c | Describe the functions of special-purpose governments. | 39 | |
| SS8CG6.a | Explain the difference between delinquent behavior and unruly behavior and the consequences of each. | 38 | |
| SS8CG6.b | Describe the rights of juveniles when taken into custody. | 38 | |
| SS8CG6.c | Describe the juvenile justice system, emphasizing the different jurisdictions, terminology, and steps in the juvenile justice process. | 38 | |
| SS8CG6.d | Explain the seven delinquent behaviors that can subject juvenile offenders to the adult criminal process, how the decision to transfer to adult court is made, and the possible consequences. | 38 | |

| Standard | Description | *Coach* Lesson | Check When Completed |
|----------|-------------|------|------|
| SS8E1 | The student will give examples of the kinds of goods and services produced in Georgia in different historical periods. | 40 | |
| SS8E2.a | Describe how Georgians have engaged in trade in different historical time periods. | 41 | |
| SS8E2.b | Explain Georgia's role in world trade today. | 41 | |
| SS8E3.a | Define profit and describe how profit is an incentive for entrepreneurs. | 40 | |
| SS8E3.b | Explain how entrepreneurs take risks to develop new goods and services to start a business. | 40 | |
| SS8E3.c | Evaluate the importance of entrepreneurs in Georgia who developed such enterprises as Coca-Cola, Delta Airlines, Georgia-Pacific, and The Home Depot. | 40 | |
| SS8E4.a | Trace sources of state revenue such as sales taxes, federal grants, personal income taxes, and property taxes. | 42 | |
| SS8E4.b | Explain the distribution of state revenue to provide services. | 42 | |
| SS8E4.c | Evaluate how choices are made given the limited revenues of state and local governments. | 42 | |
| SS8E5 | The student will explain personal money management choices in terms of income, spending, credit, saving, and investing. | 43 | |

## Georgia CRCT Coach, GPS Edition, Social Studies, Grade 8

# PRETEST

**Name:** _____

### General Instructions

Today you will be taking the Social Studies Criterion-Referenced Competency Test. The Social Studies test consists of multiple-choice questions. A sample has been included. The sample shows you how to mark your answers.

There are several important things to remember.

- Read each question carefully and think about the answer.

- Answer all questions on your answer sheet. Do not mark any answers to questions in your test booklet.

- For each question, choose the best answer, and completely fill in the circle in the space provided on your answer sheet.

- If you do not know the answer to a question, skip it and go on. You may return to it later if you have time.

- If you finish the section of the test that you are working on early, you may review your answers in that section only. You may not review another section or go on to the next section of the test.

## Sample Question

The sample test question below is provided to show you what the questions in the test are like and how to mark your answer to each question. For each question, choose the one best answer, and fill in the circle in the space provided on your answer sheet for the answer you have chosen. Be sure to mark all of your answers to the questions on your answer sheet.

## Sample

Which Georgia sports team completed a last to first to claim the world championship in 1991?

A.  Dawgs

B.  Braves

C.  Hawks

D.  Falcons

**PLEASE STOP! DO NOT GO ON TO THE NEXT PAGE.**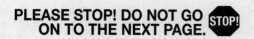

## Section 1

**Section 1 of this test has thirty questions. Choose the best answer for each question. Fill in the circle in the spaces provided for questions 1 through 30 on your answer sheet.**

1. In which geographic region of Georgia would a rich red soil MOST LIKELY be found?

   A. Blue Ridge Mountains

   B. Coastal Plain

   C. Piedmont

   D. Appalachian Plateau

2. The economic climate in Georgia has made it a favorite of start-up businesses willing to risk an investment in search of profits. What term describes this type of individual?

   A. banker

   B. inventor

   C. investor

   D. entrepreneur

3. What right does a juvenile taken into custody in Georgia have?

   A. representation by a lawyer

   B. trial by jury

   C. no school attendance requirement

   D. mandatory driver's license revocation

4. What change in the voting requirements is under consideration?

   A. voter ID

   B. age requirement of 21

   C. literacy test

   D. poll tax

**PLEASE GO ON TO THE NEXT PAGE.**

5. When Georgia changed from an agrarian society to an urban society after WWII, which industry declined?

A. technology

B. agriculture

C. real estate

D. tourism

6. During the early 1800s, what was the MOST important trade item in Georgia?

A. slaves

B. rice

C. cotton

D. indigo

7. Which Augusta company, founded in 1927, began as a small operation and is now the world's leading tissue manufacturer?

A. Merck

B. Georgia-Pacific

C. Lilly

D. Weyerhaeuser

*Use the numbered list of events in the box below to answer question 8.*

1. Arrival of the Salzburgers

2. Arrival of the Malcontents

3. Establishment of Savannah

4. Colonial Charter signed

8. Which of the following lists the events of the Trustee period in Georgia, in the chronological order in which they occurred?

A. 4, 1, 3, 2

B. 1, 2, 3, 4

C. 3, 2, 1, 4

D. 4, 3, 1, 2

**PLEASE GO ON TO THE NEXT PAGE.**

9. Which statement BEST explains the reason the expansion of Hartsfield-Jackson International Airport provides a continued boost to the state's economy?

    A. The airport offers fewer international flights.

    B. The airport brings more visitors passing through.

    C. The airport supports airline deregulation.

    D. The airport supports the easing of FAA restrictions.

10. Which governmental institution is MOST LIKELY responsible for regulating community zoning laws?

    A. Georgia Senate

    B. County Commission

    C. Regional Planning Board

    D. City Council

11. What was the goal of the reapportionment of Georgia voting districts in the 1970s?

    A. improved gerrymandering

    B. voting inequity for all

    C. voting equality for blacks

    D. voting equality for Hispanics

12. Many multinational companies have their headquarters or major facilities located in Georgia. How does this affect the state economically?

    A. The companies restrict interstate trade items.

    B. The companies open up international markets for Georgians.

    C. The companies decrease income taxes for Georgians.

    D. The companies force foreclosures and tax sales.

13. Atlanta Life Insurance Company, the largest African American stock-owned insurance company in the country, was begun by which former slave?

    A. Alonzo Herndon

    B. Booker T. Washington

    C. W.E.B. Du Bois

    D. John Burns Hope

14. Which civil rights movement leader was thrust into the national spotlight in the March on Washington?

    A. Andrew Young

    B. Maynard Jackson

    C. Dr. Martin Luther King, Jr.

    D. Malcolm X

**PLEASE GO ON TO THE NEXT PAGE.**

15. Before choosing a city for a professional sports team such as the Atlanta Braves, what are the leagues and owners MOST LIKELY to consider?

   A. local universities

   B. transportation

   C. fan base

   D. percentage of wealthy

16. Since reconstruction, Georgia has traditionally voted Democratic. With the rise of southern Republicans, who was the first Republican re-elected to the U.S. Senate?

   A. Jimmy Carter

   B. Paul Coverdell

   C. Wyche Fowler

   D. Lester Maddox

17. Which influential African American politician began as an aide to Dr. Martin Luther King, Jr., in the SCLC, and became, in 1972, the civil rights voice in the United States Senate as the first black elected from the South since Reconstruction?

   A. Andrew Young

   B. Maynard Jackson

   C. Wyche Fowler

   D. Al Sharpton

18. Which former president is matched correctly with his description?

   A. Jimmy Carter—youngest man to ever become president

   B. Theodore Roosevelt—only Georgian elected president

   C. Franklin Roosevelt—visited Warm Springs for rehabilitation

   D. Bill Clinton—addressed Congress a day after the attack on Pearl Harbor

19. What did Georgia do, in July of 1779, becoming the only one of the original thirteen colonies to do so?

   A. They defeated the British at the siege of Savannah.

   B. They boycotted the British trade of cotton.

   C. They restored allegiance to the Crown.

   D. The joined Cornwallis in Charleston.

20. What does an entrepreneur risk at the time of start up?

   A. capital

   B. health

   C. engineering

   D. nutrition

**PLEASE GO ON TO THE NEXT PAGE.**

21. The U.S. Supreme Court case of *Plessy v. Ferguson* upheld the decision of "separate but equal" in reference to

   A. voter registration.

   B. education.

   C. land title.

   D. housing rights.

22. Which major north-south artery is Georgia's commercial link for the eastern seaboard and New England?

   A. Interstate 95

   B. Interstate 20

   C. Interstate 75

   D. Interstate 24

23. In 1914, the Equal Suffrage Party of Georgia was formed. What issues were they concerned with?

   A. promoting Jim Crow laws

   B. equality in education

   C. desegregation

   D. women's voting rights

24. As chief executive for the state, the governor of Georgia is responsible for

   A. writing laws.

   B. enforcing laws.

   C. interpreting laws.

   D. overturning laws.

25. The Department of Juvenile Justice was established in 1992, with a goal to

   A. serve and protect the citizens of Atlanta.

   B. hold youth unaccountable for their actions.

   C. increase the role of the penal system.

   D. provide necessary life skills services.

26. Which Georgia statesman was a self-educated man who was appointed to the Continental Congress, was instrumental in the adoption of the Constitution, and was one of Georgia's delegates?

   A. William Few

   B. Abraham Baldwin

   C. Nathaniel Greene

   D. John Houston

27. Why was the aftermath of the 1946 election for governor so noteworthy?

   A. A Republican was elected for the first time.

   B. There were three governors running at once.

   C. The office of lieutenant governor was filled for the first time.

   D. Georgia Supreme Court ruled the election null and void.

**PLEASE GO ON TO THE NEXT PAGE.**

28. During his time in office, President Jimmy Carter established full diplomatic relations with the Peoples Republic of China, bolstered social security, formed the Department of Energy, and deregulated the airline industry. Which event helped him win the Noble Prize?

   A. Panama Canal Treaties
   B. Salt II Treaty
   C. 1980 Olympic boycott
   D. Camp David Accords

29. Which of Georgia's events is described by the phrases in the box below?

   > • Creation of almost 20,000 jobs
   > • Improvements at Hartsfield-Jackson International Airport
   > • Estimated $5.1 billion in games-related revenue
   > • Increased public financial funding commitments

   A. Super Bowl XXX
   B. 1996 Olympics
   C. Delta Airlines hub move to Atlanta
   D. Coca-Cola headquarters establishment

30. What BEST describes the duties of each house in Georgia's General Assembly?

   A. The Senate originates appropriation bills, and the House handles governor's appointments.
   B. The Senate drafts policy statements, and the House enacts each policy.
   C. The House originates appropriation bills, and the Senate handles governor's appointments.
   D. The House drafts policy statements, and the Senate enacts each policy.

PLEASE STOP! DO NOT GO ON TO THE NEXT PAGE.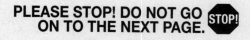

# Section 2

**Section 2 of this test has thirty questions. Choose the best answer for each question. Fill in the circle in the spaces provided for questions 31 through 60 on your answer sheet.**

31. Which industry was devastated by the boll weevil?

    A. cotton

    B. rice

    C. tobacco

    D. indigo

*Use the table below to answer question 32.*

### Georgia Statewide Employees (in thousands)

|      | Jan. | Feb. | Mar. | Apr. | May | Jun. | Jul. | Aug. | Sep. | Oct. | Nov. | Dec. |
|------|------|------|------|------|-----|------|------|------|------|------|------|------|
| 1997 | 443 | 444 | 448 | 445 | 446 | 448 | 452 | 456 | 462 | 468 | 470 | 475 |
| 1998 | 476 | 479 | 482 | 486 | 491 | 496 | 496 | 498 | 499 | 502 | 504 | 505 |
| 1999 | 507 | 512 | 515 | 523 | 523 | 528 | 523 | 524 | 525 | 527 | 530 | 530 |
| 2000 | 537 | 538 | 541 | 531 | 532 | 536 | 538 | 541 | 538 | 538 | 538 | 540 |
| 2001 | 538 | 535 | 534 | 530 | 528 | 525 | 525 | 525 | 523 | 524 | 521 | 521 |
| 2002 | 513 | 515 | 514 | 516 | 517 | 517 | 517 | 516 | 515 | 517 | 518 | 516 |
| 2003 | 488 | 488 | 488 | 487 | 485 | 487 | 490 | 491 | 493 | 494 | 496 | 498 |
| 2004 | 502 | 503 | 507 | 507 | 508 | 508 | 512 | 509 | 508 | 520 | 520 | 521 |
| 2005 | 526 | 527 | 524 | 528 | 530 | 536 | 533 | 537 | 541 | 540 | 541 | 543 |

32. According to the table, when did Georgia experience an economic downturn?

    A. January 1997 to January 2001

    B. January 1999 to January 2002

    C. January 2001 to January 2003

    D. January 2004 to January 2005

**PLEASE GO ON TO THE NEXT PAGE.**

33. How many years is the term for members of the Georgia General Assembly?

   A. 6 years

   B. 4 years

   C. 2 years

   D. 1 year

34. What BEST describes the jurisdiction of the Probate Court in Georgia?

   A. adult felonies

   B. administration of wills and estates

   C. civil cases of less than $15,000

   D. all juvenile cases except capital felonies

35. Which activity would concern a bank's loan officer?

   A. making an income

   B. opening a savings account

   C. investing in the stock market

   D. evaluating your credit

36. What was the end result of the Battle of Kettle Creek during the Revolutionary War?

   A. a loyalist victory

   B. a Tory victory

   C. a patriot victory

   D. a British victory

37. As the CEO, the governor's duties include head of state, head of the Georgia National Guard, and responsibility to negotiate foreign trade agreements. Which branch of government does the governor represent?

   A. legislative

   B. constitutional

   C. executive

   D. judicial

38. Under the Georgia Constitution, which branch holds the power to override an executive veto of an appropriation bill?

   A. judicial

   B. senate

   C. governor

   D. General Assembly

**PLEASE GO ON TO THE NEXT PAGE.**

39. The Bourbon Triumvirate, who dominated Georgia politics in the late 1800s, was led by

    A. Rebecca Latimer Felton.
    B. John Gordon.
    C. Alfred H. Colquitt.
    D. Joseph E. Brown.

40. Which group of people formed the backbone of James Oglethorpe's plan to populate the new colony of Georgia?

    A. Calvins
    B. nobles
    C. worthy poor
    D. slaves

41. Which of the following forms Georgia's western border?

    A. North Carolina and Tennessee
    B. South Carolina and the Atlantic Ocean
    C. Alabama and Florida
    D. Florida and Tennessee

42. Which term BEST describes a special-purpose government in Georgia?

    A. school district
    B. city council
    C. county commission
    D. General Assembly

43. What does the term "Three Sisters" refer to in the Woodland period of Native American evolution?

    A. rivers
    B. crops
    C. chiefs
    D. mountains

44. As a direct result of contact with the European explorers, the Native American population

    A. flourished.
    B. doubled.
    C. prospered.
    D. declined.

**PLEASE GO ON TO THE NEXT PAGE.**

45. Article 1 of the Georgia Constitution focuses on

    A.  the executive branch.

    B.  the legislative branch.

    C.  voting and elections.

    D.  the Bill of Rights.

46. Justices of the Supreme Court of Georgia serve a term of six years and are

    A.  appointed by the governor.

    B.  elected in a partisan election.

    C.  elected in a non-partisan election.

    D.  appointed by the General Assembly.

47. Who were the Salzburgers during the Trustee period in Georgia?

    A.  Scottish Catholics

    B.  English Protestants

    C.  Austrian Protestants

    D.  French Huguenots

48. What was the purpose of the Agricultural Adjustment Act?

    A.  to bring electricity to rural farms

    B.  to provide agricultural jobs for urban poor

    C.  to raise prices of staple crops by limiting supply

    D.  to provide temporary jobs in construction and education

**PLEASE GO ON TO THE NEXT PAGE.**

*Use the table below to answer question 49.*

### Coca-Cola's Annual Balance Sheet (in billions)

| | Dec. 2005 | Dec. 2004 | Dec. 2003 |
|---|---|---|---|
| **Assets** | | | |
| **Current Assets** | | | |
| **Cash** | 4,767.0 | 6,768.0 | 3,482.0 |
| **Other Current Assets** | 1,778.0 | 1,735.0 | 1,571.0 |
| **Total Current Assets** | 10,250.0 | 12,094.0 | 8,396.0 |
| **Net Fixed Assets** | 5,786.0 | 6,091.0 | 6,097.0 |
| **Other Non-current Assets** | 13,391.0 | 13,142.0 | 12,849.0 |
| **Total Assets** | 29,427.0 | 31,327.0 | 27,342.0 |
| | | | |
| **Liabilities and Shareholders' Equity** | | | |
| **Current Liabilities** | | | |
| **Accounts Payable** | 5,290.0 | 4,751.0 | 4,980.0 |
| **Short-Term Debt** | 4,546.0 | 6,021.0 | 2,906.0 |
| **Total Current Liabilities** | 9,836.0 | 10,971.0 | 7,886.0 |
| **Long-Term Debt** | 1,154.0 | 1,157.0 | 2,517.0 |
| **Other Non-current Liabilities** | 2,082.0 | 3,264.0 | 2,849.0 |
| **Total Liabilities** | 13,072.0 | 15,392.0 | 13,252.0 |
| | | | |
| **Shareholders' Equity** | | | |
| **Common Stock Equity** | 16,355.0 | 15,935.0 | 14,090.0 |
| **Total Equity** | 16,355.0 | 15,935.0 | 14,090.0 |
| **Shares Outstanding (in millions)** | 2,369.0 | 2,409.3 | 2,441.5 |

49. Which is true regarding Coca-Cola's annual business report?

    A. Coke has a positive equity to liability ratio.

    B. Coke has a negative equity to liability ratio.

    C. Assets in 2003 were greater than in 2005.

    D. Liabilities were greater in 2005 than in 2004.

**PLEASE GO ON TO THE NEXT PAGE.**

50. Where did the first wave of settlement take place in Georgia?

 A. barrier islands

 B. Savannah River

 C. Appalachian Mountains

 D. Chattahoochee River

51. What was a direct result of the invention of the cotton gin?

 A. Cotton production declined.

 B. The cotton jenny became obsolete.

 C. The need for slaves increased.

 D. The use of slavery declined.

52. Which school did Abraham Baldwin establish as the first public university in the nation?

 A. Georgia Tech

 B. University of Georgia

 C. Louisville

 D. Georgia State

53. Why did the Southern Association of Colleges and Schools remove accreditation from Georgia's public universities in 1941?

 A. World War II began.

 B. There was gross political interference.

 C. Florida universities merged.

 D. They would not use national standardized testing.

54. Which northern state was admitted to the United States as a free state as part of the Missouri Compromise?

 A. Montana

 B. Michigan

 C. Ohio

 D. Maine

55. In which form of local government does the mayor serve as the chief executive officer, but does not deal with the daily operations of the city?

 A. strong mayor-council

 B. council-manager

 C. weak mayor-council

 D. city commission

**PLEASE GO ON TO THE NEXT PAGE.**

56. Most of the rights noted within the Bill of Rights in the 1983 Georgia Constitution can be traced back to the

    A. 1861 Constitution.

    B. 1945 Constitution.

    C. 1777 Constitution.

    D. 1877 Constitution.

57. What event precipitated the Great Depression and caused the nickname the "Dust Bowl"?

    A. agricultural production increased

    B. extended drought

    C. arrival of the boll weevil

    D. pesticide production decreased

58. Which industry is experiencing a steady growth in employment as represented by the Interstate Highway System and Hartsfield-Jackson International Airport?

    A. tourism

    B. transportation

    C. manufacturing

    D. information technology

59. What was the main reason for the British interest in exploration of the Southeast, including present-day Georgia?

    A. People came to the Southeast for religious freedom.

    B. People came to the Southeast only for free land.

    C. People came to the Southeast to buy slaves.

    D. People came to the Southeast in search of gold.

60. What was the significance of the Battle of Antietam?

    A. The Confederate advance on Washington, D.C. was stopped.

    B. Union troops were defeated with heavy losses.

    C. Sherman's March to the Sea was a suprising victory.

    D. A naval blockade was in effect along the Georgia coast.

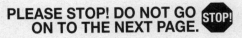

PLEASE STOP! DO NOT GO ON TO THE NEXT PAGE. STOP!

# 1 Colonization of Georgia

# 1 Prehistoric Peoples

 SS8H1.a

## Paleo-Indian Period

Thousands of years ago, people migrated to the Americas. Many scientists believe that the first *Homo sapiens* made their way to North America about 40,000 years ago. Even though people migrated, civilizations did not develop until later. These early migrants are called Paleo-Indians. Archaeologists call this time the Paleo-Indian period.

An **archaeologist** is a scientist who learns about ancient cultures by studying what ancient peoples left behind. These remains are called **artifacts. Carbon-14 dating** is a key tool used by archaeologists. By testing the amount of carbon remaining in artifacts, scientists can tell how old they are.

Paleo-Indians are the ancestors of North and South America's native people. Paleo-Indians came to the Americas from Asia in search of food. They followed big game animals, such as the woolly mammoths, mastodons, caribou, and moose. The animals they hunted traveled far in search of grasslands. These animals grazed across northern China and into Siberia. Eventually the animals made their way to the shores of the Bering Strait.

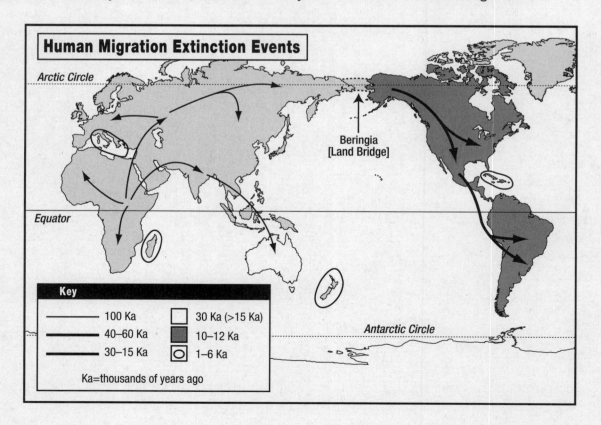

# Crossing the Land Bridge

Twenty thousand years ago, the earth experienced an ice age. During this time, frozen water formed huge glaciers that covered the northern portion of the Americas, Europe, and Asia. So much water was frozen that ocean levels lowered. Shallow bodies of water like the Bering Strait drained. This left the seafloor exposed. The Bering Strait became a huge land bridge known as **Beringia**. It connected Asia to North America. People moved back and forth across Beringia for many generations. In time, the ice age ended and water covered the land bridge again.

The new inhabitants of North and South America migrated back and forth across the land. Each group adapted to its surroundings. Their clothing, shelter, and hunting and gathering tools depended on the climate and resources available to them.

# Archaic Period

By the end of the ice age, big game animals like the wooly mammoth were becoming extinct. Their extinction might have been due to climate change or over-hunting.

The Archaic period began at this time. It lasted from about 8,000 to 1,000 BCE. The term **BCE** stands for Before the Common Era. The Common Era, or **CE**, marks the beginning of the first century. In the older Christian dating system, BCE is marked as B.C. and CE is written as A.D.

**Anthropologists** are scientists who study human life and culture. **Culture** is the pattern of behavior and thinking shared by people in social groups. Many cultural and technological advances took

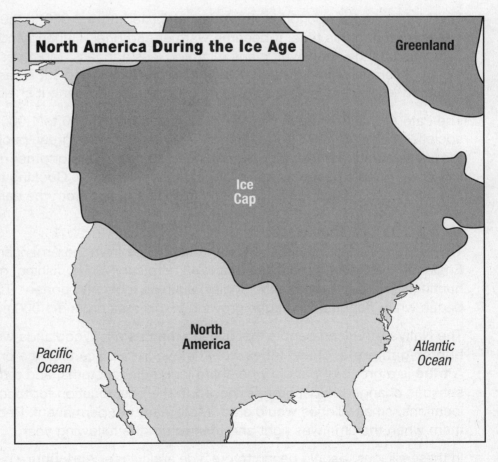

North America During the Ice Age

Greenland

Ice Cap

North America

Pacific Ocean

Atlantic Ocean

place during the Archaic period. Anthropologists divide this main period into three sub-periods. Each sub-period contains its own unique cultural characteristics.

The Early Archaic period in the Americas lasted from 8,000 to 6,000 BCE. During this time, people often traveled in small groups, or clans. A **clan** is a group of people with the same family origins. Clans worked together to gather nuts, fruits, seeds, and roots. They fished, hunted, and migrated frequently to find new sources of food. Tools used in the Early Archaic period include stone spear points that have notches at the base, serrated spears which were probably used as knives, and stone scrapers possibly used for preparing deer hides.

Early peoples hunted woolly mammoths.

The Middle Archaic period in the Americas lasted from 6,000 to 3,000 BCE. The climate changed during this time. It became warmer and drier. Hunting and gathering continued with little change. However, clans migrated less and less. Most basic needs were met locally. There was little trade between clan groups in different areas. Although clans migrated less, there is no evidence of long term or permanent shelters.

The Late Archaic period in the Americas lasted from 3,000 to 1,000 BCE. Some native societies began to build permanent structures. Societies grew, people moved less, and territories shrank further. Many groups settled near rivers or other natural resources. However, people began to travel long distances to trade. Cooking technology in the form of pottery and soapstone bowls distinguish this period from the earlier Archaic periods.

## Woodland Period

The Eastern Woodlands is a region that stretches from the American Southeast to New England. The Native Americans that lived here survived by fishing, gathering plants, and hunting. They developed technologies, such as tools and pottery. The Woodland period began when populations began growing in this area around 1,000 BCE.

The Native American people that lived in the Eastern Woodlands were **nomadic hunter-gatherers**. These tribes would move from place to place on an annual cycle. A **tribe** is a group of people who share language, customs, and territory. As the seasons changed, tribal groups moved to the best location for food and shelter. In good locations, small villages would start. Most were not permanent. People would leave them when the time was right and then return the following year.

In these villages, people began to practice agriculture. **Agriculture** is the practice of growing specific plants for food. The most common crop grown was maize, or corn. Later, beans and squash were grown. These three crops are known as the **Three Sisters** of Native American agriculture because they were the most important food crops at that time.

The Eastern Woodlands Native Americans lived in homes made of wattle and daub. This method involved building a wooden frame and covering it with reed mats and plaster. They wore clothing made of deerskin, although in warmer areas, people wore very little clothing. The Woodland peoples were tattooed and used body paint, as well.

Women held a lot of power in the Woodland culture. The basic social unit was an extended family in which all the women were related. Children were seen as belonging to the mother, not the father.

## Mississippian Period

The **Mississippian culture** existed after the Woodland period, beginning about 900 CE. The Mississippians were farmers living in the Southeast. This period lasted until Europeans made contact with Native Americans in the late 15th century. Mississippians lived in villages called chiefdoms. A **chiefdom** is a small society in which one person, a chief, makes most decisions. Mississippian chiefs controlled the distribution of all goods. Mississippians traded among themselves over a large area. This trade gave their villages access to many goods. Shell, copper, and ceramic objects were made and traded widely along the East Coast.

Native Americans began to build large mounds of earth in many parts of the Eastern Woodlands region. These mounds had different purposes. Scientists and historians are not sure how all of them were used. Some were burial mounds where special offerings were placed.

The Great Temple Mound at the Etowah Indian Mounds State Historic Site was built between 1,000 and 1,500 CE.

Temple mounds were places of worship. They were also the center of village life. The Etowah Mounds site is located in Georgia. It contains at least six mounds. Many artifacts of the Woodlands civilizations were found there. One mound that is over sixty feet tall and 300 feet wide is called the temple mound, although no one can be sure how it was used. The Kolomoki mounds are also found in Georgia. They were probably built by the Swift Creek and Weeden Island Indians between 350 to 600 CE.

## Show What You Know

Think about all you have read regarding early peoples. Write an essay about what you think it would be like to live during early periods, such as during the ice age.

_____

_____

_____

_____

_____

_____

_____

_____

_____

_____

_____

_____

_____

_____

_____

_____

_____

_____

_____

_____

_____

_____

# Lesson Practice

## DIRECTIONS
Circle the letter of the best answer for each item.

### Thinking It Through

1. How did glaciers contribute to human migration to the Americas?

   A. by making ice bridges

   B. by creating otherwise scarce water

   C. by exposing the land bridge, Beringia

   D. by growing the size of most animals

   *During the ice age, much of the world's water was frozen in glaciers. This caused sea levels to drop.*

2. During which period did people hunt mastodons?

   A. Paleo-Indian

   B. Archaic

   C. Woodland

   D. Mississippian

   **HINT** *Large game animals wxere becoming extinct by 6,000 BCE.*

3. In addition to squash, what other food crops made up the Three Sisters?

   A. peppers and corn

   B. potatoes and beans

   C. beans and maize

   D. corn and potatoes

4. Which early Native American period lasted until Europeans came to the Americas?

   A. Paleo-Indian

   B. Archaic

   C. Mississippian

   D. Woodland

# 2 European Exploration

SS8H1.b, c

Europeans traveled to the Americas in the late 15th century. Conditions there were harsh. Many Europeans died of disease or starvation. Others were killed by Native Americans. In turn, Europeans carried with them tools, goods, and diseases that would change Native Americans' way of life forever.

Europeans brought horses and guns to the Americas. These tools helped them travel across large areas and conquer people. With horses, Native Americans were able to travel and trade more easily. Guns also became important for native people. They made hunting easier and could be used as protection, too.

## Native Americans and Europeans Impact Each Other's Culture

Many European countries believed it was their duty to spread Christianity. Various Christian missionaries created settlements in the Americas to convert Native Americans. A **missionary** is someone sent by a church to a foreign country to spread its faith. The main functions of these mission settlements were to teach Native Americans "the arts of civilization" and to convert them to Christianity. For the Native Americans, the missions represented a means to help them learn English in order to trade and negotiate in an increasingly white world.

Soon after the arrival of Europeans, slavery began in the Americas. Native Americans were enslaved to work on the sugar plantations in the West Indies. However, diseases such as smallpox and measles, brought by European settlers, killed many native people. Soon, the Native American population was too small for the large amount of work on the plantations. Europeans had to look to another source of workers to enslave.

Christian missionaries tried to convert Native Americans.

It was hard for Europeans to live in the Americas. They were not familiar with local food crops. Supplies from Europe took months to arrive. Some Europeans were friendly with Native Americans.

They learned how to farm crops such as maize from the Native Americans. Many European colonies would not have survived without help from Native Americans.

# Early Spanish Missions

Most early European exploration of the American Southeast was done by the Spanish. They launched ships from bases in the Caribbean, Mexico, and Florida. They explored the coastline of the Southeast. They observed the barrier islands that line the coast of Georgia. These islands were easier for ships to access than the mainland was. Early missions were built on these islands. From those missions, the Spanish then explored the coast.

The Native Americans showed Europeans how to grow maize.

The purpose of the missions was to convert Native Americans to Catholicism. However, Natives Americans used the missions to help integrate themselves into the European world. Mission settlements usually were located in chiefdoms and contained at least one church, and a house for the missionary.

# Hernando de Soto

*Hernando de Soto* of Spain was the first European to see the interior of the American Southeast, including Georgia. De Soto landed on the coast of Florida in 1539. His party was large and well-equipped. He met many Native Americans along his way.

De Soto was looking for gold. He exploited many Native Americans in his attempt to find it. At times, this exploitation meant befriending them. Other times, it meant robbing or killing Native Americans. After a three-year campaign, de Soto died without finding any gold.

De Soto and his party were the only Europeans to see many Native American cultures before they declined. De Soto wrote of his contact with the native peoples. Today, historians benefit from de Soto's writings. Ironically, his party spread disease throughout the Native American culture, contributing to its collapse.

**Explorations of de Soto, 1540**

Atlantic Ocean

Georgia

De Soto sails from Spain.

De Soto lands in Florida.

# Causes of European Exploration

Europeans needed spices from East Asia. Asian trade goods were sold by Arab traders. Since spices were very expensive, Europeans wanted to find a safe and fast way to reach Asia and acquire the spices directly. They spent a lot of money to find this passage. The country that found the western passage to Asia would control trade between Europe and Asia. As a result of the Asian trade route explorations, the Americas were discovered.

After *Christopher Columbus* reached the Americas in 1492, rumors of the New World's wealth spread. The stories spoke of cities where the streets were paved with gold. The possibility of wealth and the power to control trade led all European countries that could afford it to spend money exploring the Americas.

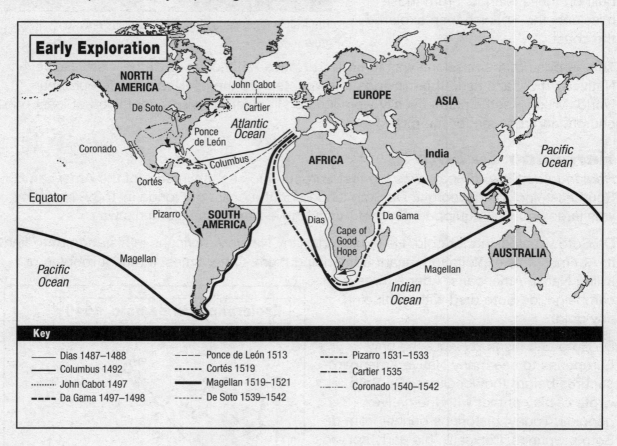

# France

In 1562, France sent explorers to North America in search of gold. The French explorers made their way to South Carolina. There, they started a colony called Charlesfort. Soon, the explorers ran out of supplies and food. A ship returned to France to get more supplies, but did not return to Charlesfort until 1565. By that time, the settlers had left. The French also founded a colony in 1564 called Fort Caroline, in Florida.

# Spain

The Spanish, like all Europeans, were looking for wealth in North America. They destroyed Fort Caroline to stop competition with the French over the wealth of the Americas. In 1568, they built the first missions in the area of Florida where Fort Caroline had been. This was the beginning of the mission period in the Southeast.

The missions were built to spread Catholicism. Missions were also used to integrate Native Americans as members of a new form of society ruled by the Spanish colonial government. This helped the Spanish control them.

Local chiefs still led Native Americans, but the chiefs were ruled by the Spanish colonial government. The Spanish colonial government used the missions to communicate with the Native Americans. Native Americans and Europeans also traded goods at missions.

Eventually, the mission system declined. Native populations in the Southeast were shrinking due to deaths. Many missions were left empty. Slave revolts and English raids destroyed the rest. The mission period ended in 1684.

# England

*Queen Elizabeth I* ruled Great Britain from 1558 to 1603. She was a Protestant, which is a Christian religion that differs from Catholicism in its practice. Great Britain was the enemy of Spain, a Catholic state. *Philip II*, the ruler of Spain, built the **Spanish Armada**, a large and powerful naval fleet, to attack the British. In 1588, the British defeated the Spanish Armada. British naval dominance enabled it to explore the Americas. It also signaled the decline of Spanish power in the Americas.

The British came to the Americas hoping to find gold. They also realized they could make money by trading other items such as copper and furs. They also traded enslaved Native Americans. Many British slaves came from Georgia's Native American population. The slave trade resulted in the deaths of many Native Americans. Many became involved in trading slaves themselves. Others moved away from the region. There are few records of what happened to most of the Native Americans who once lived in Georgia.

## Show What You Know

**The southeastern United States was explored and settled by the Spanish in the 16th and 17th centuries. What evidence of Spanish culture is left in the region today?**

_____

_____

_____

_____

_____

_____

_____

_____

_____

_____

_____

_____

_____

_____

_____

_____

_____

_____

_____

_____

_____

# Lesson Practice

**DIRECTIONS**
**Circle the letter of the best answer for each item.**

## Thinking It Through

1.  Why did European nations explore the Americas?

    **A.** They wanted to find farmland.

    **B.** They wanted to establish naval dominance.

    **C.** They wanted to search for gold.

    **D.** They wanted to meet new people.

*The first Europeans to land in the Americas were searching for a passage to Asia. What they found instead was North and South America. They returned to Europe with stories of untold riches in the newly discovered lands.*

2.  What was the most devastating effect of European exploration on Native Americans?

    **A.** the spread of disease

    **B.** the introduction of the horse

    **C.** the spread of guns

    **D.** the spread of Christianity

    **HINT** *Native Americans had never been exposed to many of the germs carried by Europeans.*

3.  How did Queen Elizabeth I create British naval dominance?

    **A.** by circumnavigating the world

    **B.** by conquering the Spanish Armada

    **C.** by enslaving Native Americans

    **D.** by spreading Catholicism

4.  What was the stated purpose of the Spanish mission system?

    **A.** to spread Spanish colonialism

    **B.** to trade European goods

    **C.** to access the American coastline

    **D.** to spread Catholicism

# 3 Trustee Georgia

 **SS8H2.a, b**

The **Trustee period** in Georgia began when King *George II* gave permission to establish the colony in 1732. For the first twenty years of Georgia's colonial history, a group of trustees governed the colony. A **trustee** is someone who oversees property on behalf of someone else. Georgia's trustees managed the colony on behalf of England and its ruler during this period, King George II. The king granted *James Oglethorpe* a **charter**, which is written permission to begin an English colony. The colony was named Georgia after King George.

Before Georgia became a British colony, there was tension between the British and Spanish over the land. This tension increased after the neighboring area of South Carolina became a British colony in 1670. Spain maintained control of Florida. The land between South Carolina and Florida remained virtually unclaimed by Europeans; however, the original boundaries of South Carolina included the land between the Savannah and the Altamaha rivers. This land eventually belonged to the Georgia colony.

## James Oglethorpe

James Oglethorpe was a British soldier and a member of British Parliament, the legislative branch of British government. Oglethorpe became interested in prison reform while he was in Parliament. He saw that many people went to prison simply because they were poor. These people were called the "worthy poor." Because the worthy poor could not afford to pay their taxes, they often ended up in debtors' prisons. Oglethorpe thought these people deserved a chance at a new life. Oglethorpe believed that their best chance for a new life was in a new American colony. He hoped Georgia would become a land where the worthy poor could thrive. He also hoped it would be a place where Protestants could practice their religion.

James Oglethorpe wanted to give the "worthy poor" a chance for a better life in America.

# Charter of 1732

On April 21, 1732, King George signed the charter to establish the colony of Georgia. This charter also established a governing board and created the **trust** to run the colony. Seventy-one men served as trustees over the course of its period. The trustees were not paid. The charter also said that trustees could not hold office or land in Georgia. The charter did not set up any type of local government, but, it said that colonists had all of the same rights as British citizens.

# Reasons for Settlement

James Oglethorpe and his supporters argued that creating Georgia was both charitable and economic. Their motto was **"Non sibi sed aliis"**, which means "Not for self, but for others." As an act of charity, the trustees paid for debtors to go to Georgia instead of prison. They also thought removing debtors would aid the economy of England. The trustees hoped the settlers would produce wine and silk to send back to England. They required new settlers to plant mulberry trees for the raising of silkworms. The trustees also argued that Georgia could help protect South Carolina from the Spanish.

# Tomochichi

Native Americans had lived in Georgia for thousands of years before the arrival of European settlers. When Europeans came to Georgia, they needed friendly relations with the Native Americans in order to establish a successful colony. The chief of the Yamacraw Indians, *Tomochichi*, played an important role in creating peace between the Europeans and Native Americans in Georgia. He helped the many different groups in the area communicate with the British. In 1734, James Oglethorpe brought Tomochichi and his family to England, where he met the royal family. Tomochichi's trip proved to be valuable to the Native Americans of Georgia. Tomochichi's efforts lead to the creation of a school for his tribe. His contributions in the peaceful negotiations between various Native American tribes and the British settlements in Georgia were celebrated with an English military funeral when he died in 1739.

Tomochichi built relationships between the Native Americans of Georgia and the British.

## Mary Musgrove

*Mary Musgrove* was also a peacemaker. She was the daughter of an English trader and a Creek Indian. She was also related to several other Creek leaders. The Creek Indians called her *Coosaponakessa*. She spent her childhood in both the Creek village of Coweta and the colony of South Carolina. Musgrove used her connections to both the British and Native Americans to help protect Native Americans and to maintain peace in the Georgia colony. She was also a trader and worked to expand her deerskin trading business. Historians have compared Mary Musgrove to other great Native American women in the history of the U.S., such as *Pocahontas* and *Sacagawea*. Musgrove claimed to have royal heritage, but few scholars have accepted this claim.

## Savannah

The city of Savannah, Georgia, was founded in 1733. It was the last British colonial capital in America. James Oglethorpe designed the city. It was very different from previous colonial towns. Its organization reflected many new European ideas about cities and buildings. Great European cities such as Paris, France, were also designed during this time using the same ideas. Savannah was built using connected neighborhoods and squares. Each neighborhood, square, ward, and garden lot was of equal size. They were also arranged in a repeating pattern. This pattern allowed the distribution of land to new settlers to be fair. Commons surrounded the city. Commons are public lands owned by the city. The commons allowed the city to expand later.

## The Salzburgers

The **Salzburgers** were a group of Protestants who were expelled from Salzburg in the early 1730s. Salzburg is a city in present-day Austria. The Salzburgers were expelled because they were not Catholic. All Protestants were expelled at that time from the region. The Georgia trustees and King George II sympathized with the Salburgers. They decided to support Protestant Salzburgers by extending an invitation for them to move to Georgia. The Salzburgers arrived in Georgia in 1734, and established the town of Ebenezer.

## The Moravians

Another group of Protestants were the **Moravians** from Bohemia, which is the present-day Czech Republic. The Moravians came to Georgia in 1735. Unlike the Salzburgers, who were expelled from the region, the Moravians came as missionaries. They wanted to unite Christians and convert non-Christians. Many other Protestants did not trust the Moravians, however. They had many new and different ideas. One of these ideas was that women could preach and hold religious offices. The Moravian community was ultimately unsuccessful and eventually dissolved. Today, there is only one Moravian community in Georgia.

## The Malcontents

Captain *George Dunbar* brought the Salzburgers to Georgia. He also brought a group of Highland Scots. The Highlanders were members of Clan Chattan in Inverness-shire, Scotland. In 1736, the Highlanders founded Darien, a town on Georgia's southern border. Later, the Highlanders would also become a group known as the Malcontents.

Most of the **Malcontents** were colonists of Scottish descent. Although the trustees aided many of Georgia's settlers, they did not aid the Malcontents. The Malcontents were wealthy enough to pay for their own voyage to Georgia. Because of this, they were not as loyal to the trustees or Britain. The Malcontents wanted to purchase land and enslaved people with their great wealth. They resented limits put in place by the trustees that prevented them from doing this.

## The Spanish in Florida

Spanish settlers in Florida were not happy that so many new settlers were coming to neighboring Georgia. The Spanish had been interested in the land that became the Georgia colony. The British built **Fort Frederica** in Georgia in an effort to protect the colony. Georgian soldiers made an unsuccessful attack on the Spanish mission of St. Augustine, Florida, in 1740. Two years later, the Spanish attacked Fort Frederica. The tension between British Georgia and Spanish Florida came to a head in the Battle of Bloody Marsh. Eventually, the Spanish retreated and never again attacked a British colony on the eastern coast. Oglethorpe waged one more attack against Spanish Florida. The attack was unsuccessful. During this campaign, Oglethorpe was requested back in England to answer misconduct charges against him. Oglethorpe was found not guilty; however, he never returned to Georgia.

Oglethorpe remained on the board of trustees until 1750. At that time, Oglethorpe disagreed with Georgia's lack of restrictions on land ownership, rum, and slavery. In 1752, the British government did not renew funding for the colony. The trustees turned over control of the colony to the British Crown. Georgia then became a royal colony.

## Show What You Know

**The trustees founded Georgia with three goals in mind: charity, economics, and defense. Write an essay about the actions the trustees took to accomplish these goals.**

_____

_____

_____

_____

_____

_____

_____

_____

_____

_____

_____

_____

_____

_____

_____

_____

_____

_____

_____

_____

_____

_____

_____

# Lesson Practice

## Thinking It Through

1. Who obtained the charter to establish the Trustee colony of Georgia?

   *James Oglethorpe had an idea to send the "worthy poor" to colonize the Americas for Great Britain.*

   A. John Dunbar

   B. Tomochichi

   C. King George

   D. James Oglethorpe

2. Which of Georgia's cities is described by the phrases in the box below?

   - built using new European ideas
   - founded by James Oglethorpe
   - made fair distribution of land possible

   A. St. Augustine

   B. Savannah

   C. Fort Federica

   D. Coweta

   **HINT** *This city was the last British colonial capital in America.*

3. What is the name of the fort designed to protect the southeastern boundary of Georgia?

   A. Savannah

   B. Fort Frederica

   C. St. Augustine

   D. Coweta

4. Which of these groups did not have a presence in Trustee Georgia?

   A. Creek Indians

   B. Japanese silk farmers

   C. Moravians

   D. Salzburgers

# 4  Royal Georgia

  SS8H2.c

Georgia did very well as a royal colony. Georgia added a great deal to the British economy. They exported rice, indigo, deerskins, lumber, beef, and pork.

Georgia officially became a **royal colony** when the Trustee period ended in 1752. This meant that the Crown of England oversaw the control of Georgia. Parliament had to pass a charter in order for Georgia to become an official royal colony. This process began in 1752, after Parliament dismissed the trustees. It took two years for the charter to go through Parliament. Georgia did not get its first official governor until 1754.

## Royal Governors

*John Reynolds* was Georgia's first royal governor. He governed from 1754 to 1757. The British Parliament recalled Reynolds in 1752 and said that he was ineffective. John Reynolds was a former naval officer and did not have the political skills to govern well. He angered his cabinet and divided the residents of Georgia. He was not good at interacting with Native Americans. This skill was especially important since his tenure began around the beginning of the French and Indian War. The **French and Indian War** was the North American phase of a war between France and Britain to control land in the colonies, lasting from 1754 to 1763. During this time, many Native American attacks plagued Georgia settlers. Many Georgians were unhappy with John Reynolds. They wrote to England and asked for his removal. Lord *Halifax* responded, and appointed a new royal governor.

*Henry Ellis* governed Georgia from 1757 to 1760. He built a solid foundation for Georgia. He had skills that Reynolds did not. He set up a budget and regulated trade with the Native Americans. He also built forts and tried to abolish slavery. Ellis's most important skill involved his communication with Native American tribes. He held on to the friendship of the Creek Nation and declared Georgia's authority to control the Indian trade. By 1760, an ailing Ellis left Georgia and the governor position.

The next royal governor was *James Wright*. James Wright was very popular and held the governor's position for sixteen years, from 1760 to 1776. Wright came to Georgia with his experience as attorney general of South Carolina. That, coupled with the benefit of having seasoned Georgians who served in the assembly, helped Wright develop Georgia during his term. The peace settlement of the French and Indian War made much more land available for settlement. This increased the size of Georgia. Georgia now had land all the way south to the St. Mary's River, and all the way west to the Mississippi River.

## Land Grants

Settlers who came to the colony by way of the Trust's charity, were limited to fifty-acre land grants. Those who paid their way could have up to 500 acres of land. Those who paid their way were required to have at least one servant or family member for every fifty acres of their grant. This rule helped ensure that enough men were available to defend the colony. At that time, only men could own land, but settlers protested. The men wanted their wives and daughters to be able to inherit their land.

## Life in Colonial Georgia

Colonial Georgia was a land of farmers. Most women worked in the home. They prepared food, cared for clothing, and planted and harvested. Children also contributed to the growth of the colony. The trustees hoped families would provide both labor and stability for the new colony. People often lived in homes made from tabby. **Tabby** is a mixture of mortar and lime that was common as a building material through the colonial period in the coastal Southeast.

Rice was a common crop in colonial Georgia.

English, Salzburgers, Germans, Scots, Irish, and Sephardic Jews were all early settlers of Georgia. When the slavery ban was lifted in 1750, life changed in the colony. Many plantation owners from South Carolina moved to Georgia to expand their slave-based economy. As a result, tens of thousands of Africans were enslaved and brought to Georgia to work on rice plantations. The beginning of African slavery changed the economy of the region. Plantation owners established socioeconomic structures and relationships that dominated Georgia's economy and government.

## Slavery

During the beginning of Trustee period, Georgia's state law prohibited slavery. However, wealthy colonists who could afford to buy enslaved people, demanded to be allowed to bring them to Georgia. In 1750, the trustees who governed Georgia at the time, lifted the ban on slavery.

Between 1750 and 1775, the number of Africans living in slavery increased from 500 to 18,000. These Africans had no rights. They were not allowed to marry, or live where they wanted, or even learn to read. They had to work and live in the harsh conditions of the Georgia rice fields. Rebellion against slave owners was almost impossible. Punishment included beatings, whippings, separation from friends or family, and even death.

In 1776, at the beginning of the American Revolutionary War, Georgia declared its independence from the British Crown along with other British colonies.

## Show What You Know

**Pretend that you live in royal Georgia. You could be a man, a woman, or a child. You could be a governor, landowner, or an enslaved person. Write a paragraph about a day in the life of this person. Use your imagination and details from this chapter to write a realistic story.**

_____

_____

_____

_____

_____

_____

_____

_____

_____

_____

_____

_____

_____

_____

_____

_____

_____

_____

_____

_____

_____

_____

_____

# Lesson Practice

## DIRECTIONS
**Circle the letter of the best answer for each item.**

### Thinking It Through

**1.** How did life in Georgia change in 1752?

*Georgia was run by a Trust until 1752. Statehood and the Union would not happen for almost 25 years.*

  **A.** It became a state.

  **B.** It became a royal colony.

  **C.** It seceded from the union.

  **D.** It divided South Carolina.

---

**2.** Which crop was produced in the royal colony of Georgia?

  **A.** olive oil

  **B.** cotton

  **C.** rice

  **D.** oranges

**HINT** *Olive oil was not common in the Americas at this time.*

**3.** How did Georgia's government respond when wealthy landowners demanded the right to own slaves?

  **A.** They explained that slavery was immoral.

  **B.** They took a vote, but did not vote to allow slavery.

  **C.** They allowed landowners to own slaves.

  **D.** The started a religious campaign against slavery.

**4.** Why were landowners required to have a servant or family member for every 50 acres of land?

  **A.** to help prevent slavery

  **B.** to make sure that there were enough people to defend the land

  **C.** to keep colonists company

  **D.** to barter with the Native Americans

# 5 Causes of the American Revolution

 SS8H3.a

The Seven Years' War was a major European conflict between France and Great Britain. In the North American colonies it was known as the French and Indian War because both sides allied themselves with different Native American groups. Britain and its allies won the war; however, peace did not last long.

## The Proclamation of 1763

At the end of the French and Indian War, France surrendered all of its North American territories east of the Mississippi to Britain. In addition, Spain gave Florida to Britain, but received the Louisiana Territory and New Orleans from France. After the war, Britain needed to deal with the growing Native American grievances against European settlers. The Proclamation of 1763 was a British decree made in favor of Britain's Native American allies. The proclamation reserved land west of the Appalachian Mountains for Native American tribes. Colonists already living in this territory were commanded to leave. However, they wanted to explore and grow their colonies. The proclamation made colonists feel betrayed by their own government.

## Taxation Without Representation

The French and Indian War left Britain greatly in debt. King *George III* raised money to pay back Britain's war debt by taxing the colonists. However, the colonists did not have representatives in Britain's government.

In 1764, Parliament passed the Sugar Act, which taxed non-British imports of sugar, textiles, coffee, wine, and indigo dye. The **Stamp Act of 1765** set a tax on all legal documents, permits, commercial contacts, newspapers, pamphlets, and playing cards. After paying a tax, these documents would receive a stamp. However, the stamps were very expensive and could only be paid in silver or gold.

Many colonists ignored the Stamp Act. They even threatened tax collectors. Many tax collectors were too afraid to enforce the law. To protest the act, colonists boycotted British goods, which hurt British manufacturers. They put pressure on Parliament to repeal the Stamp Act. Representatives from nine colonies united in the **Stamp Act Congress**, which wrote the Declaration of Rights and Grievances. It was sent to Parliament and the king. Parliament voted to end the Stamp Act in March 1766.

However, Britain continued taxing the colonies. In 1767, the Townshend Revenue Act began taxing glass, paint, oil, lead, paper, and tea. By summer 1768, protests against the Townshend Act grew violent, especially in Boston. Colonists again boycotted British goods. British merchants helped ensure the act was repealed.

In 1773, the British passed the Tea Act to help the British East India Company. The company was close to collapsing and had too much tea. The Tea Act gave the East India Company a monopoly on selling tea in the colonies by regulating tea prices. Colonist merchants feared that they would lose their businesses if the cheap British tea flooded the market. In Philadelphia and New York, colonists forced the tea ships to turn back. In Charleston, South Carolina, colonists let tea sit on the docks until it rotted. However, Boston was well-controlled by British forces. British leaders there held the tea ships in the port.

Then, on December 16, 1773, Bostonian colonists protested the Tea Act. Colonists snuck into the Boston Harbor after dark, dressed as Native Americans. They boarded the tea ships and dumped 90,000 pounds of tea into the water. This event was known as the **Boston Tea Party**.

## Intolerable Acts

The **Intolerable Acts** were four laws passed by the British. These acts were called "intolerable" because they were meant to punish the colonies. One act closed Boston Harbor as punishment for the Boston Tea Party. The second act cancelled Massachusetts's royal charter. The third act allowed British officials charged with offenses in the colonies to be tried

The First Continental Congress meets.

in England. The last act allowed British troops to live in colonists' homes. As a result of these acts, the colonists formed the First Continental Congress to discuss how to respond to the British.

## Georgia and the Revolution

Many Georgians hesitated to join the revolutionary movement. Georgia had done very well as a royal colony. Many Georgians also worried that they needed the protection of British troops against Native Americans. The First Continental Congress met in Philadelphia in 1774, but Georgia did not send a representative. The Congress asked all the colonies to form a group called the Association. The Association banned trade with Britain. In January 1775, Georgia elected representatives to the Association, but these representatives did not attend the Second Continental Congress. Georgians were divided. St. John's Parish, however, decided to send a representative independently. Their representative was *Lyman Hall*.

Georgia's loyalties were divided. Colonists who supported Great Britain were called **loyalists**, while the colonists who supported the revolution were called **patriots**. In May 1775, news of the first battles of the American Revolution reached Georgia. Many Georgians who wavered in their allegiance decided to support the revolution. These supporters gradually increased in numbers. Finally, in 1775, Georgia joined the other colonists to fight for independence from Great Britain.

On July 4, 1776, the Second Continental Congress approved the Declaration of Independence. This document announced the separation of the thirteen colonies from Britain and was signed by representatives of all thirteen colonies. Three signers were from Georgia—Lyman Hall, *Button Gwinnett*, and *George Walton*.

## Show What You Know

**Before the American Revolution, Britain imposed taxes on the colonies to pay off Britain's war debt. Make a timeline of each new tax Great Britain imposed on the colonies.**

# Lesson Practice

## DIRECTIONS
Circle the letter of the best answer for each item.

### Thinking It Through

1.  Which of the following goods were not taxed by the Stamp Act?

    A.  newspapers

    B.  playing cards

    C.  tea

    D.  legal documents

    *The Stamp Act made it illegal to own or sell any piece of paper without a stamp on it.*

2.  Which is the MOST LIKELY reason that Britain taxed goods in the colonies?

    A.  to pay for war debt

    B.  to pay to erect buildings in the colonies

    C.  to punish colonists for drinking tea

    D.  to bring more enslaved people to the colonies

    **HINT** *The French and Indian War left Britain with a large war debt.*

3.  Which of the following shows the correct order of events leading up to the American Revolution?

    A.  Stamp Act Congress, Sugar Act, Intolerable Acts, Second Continental Congress

    B.  Second Continental Congress, Sugar Act, Stamp Act Congress, Intolerable Acts

    C.  Stamp Act Congress, Sugar Act, Second Continental Congress, Intolerable Acts

    D.  Sugar Act, Stamp Act Congress, Intolerable Acts, Second Continental Congress

4.  Why were Georgians reluctant to join the colonists in revolution?

    A.  Georgia benefited from Great Britain.

    B.  Georgians were too scared to fight.

    C.  Georgia could not afford to fight.

    D.  Georgia was not a colony.

# 6 The Revolutionary War

 **SS8H3.b**

The colonists who rebelled against British rule were called patriots. They were made up of a wide variety of social groups. Some were college students. Others were farmers. Loyalists were colonists who stayed loyal to Britain. They were also called Tories. They wanted Britain to continue ruling the colonies.

## The Revolution in Georgia

Most people in Georgia thought British taxes were unfair. However, Georgia had done well under British rule. Many colonists feared that without British troops, they would be attacked by Native Americans.

People in Georgia slowly changed their minds about joining the revolution. They sent three representatives to the Second Continental Congress. First was *Lyman Hall*. The second was *Button Gwinnett*. The last was *George Walton*. These three men signed the Declaration of Independence in 1776.

Gwinnett was a planter who was elected to Georgia's Commons House of Assembly in 1769. When the Revolutionary War began, Gwinnett led opponents of the Whig Party from all parts of Georgia. He was elected by these people to command Georgia's Continental battalion in early 1776, but gave up office to join the Continental Congress in Philadelphia. He helped ensure the passage of Georgia's first Constitution, in 1777. That same year, he was appointed Georgia's president and commander-in-chief.

One of the first battles he fought was in Florida. Gwinnett led a group of soldiers into the battle, but they had to retreat. The military campaign caused a fight between Gwinnett and another military leader. The two men fought in a duel to settle the dispute. Gwinnett was shot and died on May 19, 1777. Gwinnett County, Georgia, was named for him.

Walton was a patriot, active in the revolutionary government. After signing the Declaration of Independence, Walton returned to Savannah. He was captured there by the British in 1778. By 1779, he had been released and was elected governor of the colony. Shortly afterward, he was re-elected to Congress. In the early years of the republic, he continued to serve in government—as the chief justice of Georgia, as a delegate to the Constitutional Convention, as part of the electoral college, then as governor, U.S. senator, and justice of the state superior court.

# The Battle of Kettle Creek

Loyalists thought they could recruit many supporters in the South. They believed there were loyalist groups secretly waiting to be rescued by British troops. The Battle of Kettle Creek proved them wrong.

The battle took place on February 14, 1779. Loyalist *James Boyd* and his troop of 600 were camping at Kettle Creek, on their way to Augusta, Georgia. A group of patriots half the size of loyalist forces, snuck up and attacked Boyd's troop. One of the patriot leaders in charge of the attack was *Elijah Clarke* of Georgia. The patriots killed Boyd and 19 of his troop members. Loyalist forces fled after hearing the news of Boyd's death. Twenty-two loyalists were captured, and the remaining either returned to the British army or were later captured by patriot forces.

A monument commemorating a battle of the Revolutionary War, which took place at Kettle Creek, Georgia, on February 14, 1779

Other fighters at Kettle Creek included *Austin Dabney*, an enslaved person who served under Clarke. He was the only African American soldier to fight in the battle. In recognition of his bravery, the state of Georgia gave Dabney some land. He was the only African American to receive such an honor in Georgia. *Nancy Hart*, the wife of a lieutenant who served under Elijah Clarke, also played a role at Kettle Creek. She spied on the loyalists and told the patriot soldiers what she learned. According to some accounts, she shot at least two loyalists at the Battle of Kettle Creek.

Kettle Creek gave the patriots a small victory. More importantly, it proved that the loyalists had little support in the southern colonies.

# The Siege of Savannah

In the summer 1779, Georgia's Royal Governor Sir *James Wright* returned to Georgia to restore the colony to the British Crown. Not long after Wright's return, a French fleet surprised Georgia's loyalists in the hopes of recapturing Savannah for the patriots. Soldiers from France and Haiti fought with the patriots to secure Savannah. The Battle of Savannah did not go well for the patriots. The patriots suffered around 1,000 casualties, while the British only lost 18 people.

The French retreated and Georgia's patriots followed. The siege had failed. The British controlled Savannah until the end of the war in 1782.

## Show What You Know

Look at the map below. Over the locations of major events of the Revolutionary War, write the name and date of each event. Under the map, write a sentence about each event.

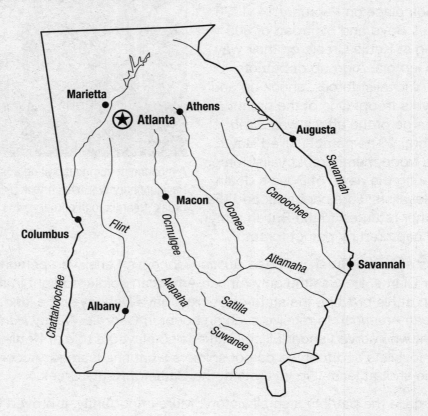

# Lesson Practice

## DIRECTIONS
Circle the letter of the best answer for each item.

### Thinking It Through

1. Why did the patriots want independence from British rule?

   *Remember that the slogan of the American Revolution was "No taxation without representation."*

   A. They wanted to have their own king.

   B. They thought that the taxes were unfair.

   C. The British government was torturing them.

   D. They wanted to be ruled by Spain.

2. Who did not represent Georgia in the Second Continental Congress?

   A. George Walton

   B. Button Gwinnett

   C. Lyman Hall

   D. Elijah Clarke

   **HINT** *One of these men was a military leader in the Battle at Kettle Creek, not a representative in Congress.*

3. Why was the Battle of Kettle Creek important?

   A. It proved that the loyalists had little support in the South.

   B. It was the beginning of a truce between loyalists and patriots.

   C. It proved the loyalists had a lot of support in the South.

   D. It resulted in the death of George Washington.

4. Which country was the patriots' ally during the Siege on Savannah?

   A. France

   B. Spain

   C. Great Britain

   D. Mexico

# 7 State and Federal Constitutions

 **SS8H4.a, b**

## Articles of Confederation

During the Revolutionary War, delegates of the colonies continued meeting as the Second Continental Congress. These men made military decisions for the colonies during the war. The Second Continental Congress adopted the **Declaration of Independence** and the Articles of Confederation. While the Declaration of Independence formally declared the colonies independent from Britain, the Articles of Confederation formally united the colonies against Britain.

The **Articles of Confederation** created one body, called Congress, with authority over all the colonies. Congress was to be made up of representatives from all thirteen colonies. They had the power to wage war, regulate the postal service, and control the affairs of Native Americans. One problem with the Articles of Confederation was that it did not give Congress the power to tax the states. This left the colonies short of money during the war. Congress also did not have enough power to enforce its new laws.

## The Constitutional Convention of 1787

The colonies won their independence from Britain, so they needed to set up their own government. The federal, or centralized, government needed to be given more power. In 1787, leaders from each state met at the Constitutional Convention. They wrote the Constitution of the United States of America to replace the Articles of Confederation. The Constitution is the basis for laws in the U.S.

There were many problems to work out during the convention. Each state wanted equal representation in the government. The **Great Compromise** solved this problem by creating a bicameral Congress, one with two houses. The number of people in the lower house, or House of Representatives, would be decided by the population of each state. States with more people would get more representatives. The upper house, or Senate, would have two representatives from each state, regardless of size, so that all states would be represented equally.

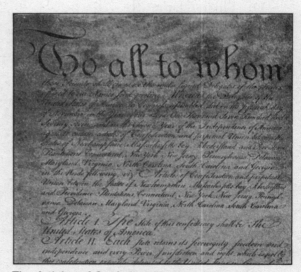

The Articles of Confederation

Slavery was another issue that had to be decided at the Constitution Convention. The delegates agreed that only three-fifths of enslaved people would be counted toward representation. This was known as the three-fifths compromise. It was also agreed that the government could not ban the international slave trade for at least 20 years. This was a way to pass the Constitution without dealing with the huge issue of slavery.

## Georgia's Role in Creating the U.S. Constitution

Two men from Georgia took part in the Constitutional Convention of 1787. *William Few, Jr.*, helped to write the Constitution of 1777 for Georgia. In 1780, he was elected to serve Georgia in the Continental Congress. Few represented Georgia during the Constitutional Convention and signed the U.S. Constitution. He was later elected to the U.S. Congress to represent Georgia.

*Abraham Baldwin* also represented Georgia at the Constitutional Convention and signed the Constitution. His vote on equal representation in the Senate played an instrumental part in the Great Compromise. Baldwin also represented Georgia in the U.S. Congress and founded the University of Georgia.

Georgia was the fourth state to ratify the Constitution. Although Georgia believed in having a strong federal government, Georgians signed the Constitution in hopes that the federal government would help them fight Native Americans in the region.

## The Bill of Rights

A fraction of the delegates in the Constitutional Convention believed there needed to be an additional document guaranteeing individual rights. The Bill of Rights is the first ten amendments of the Constitution that guarantee individual rights and limit federal and state government. For example, the First Amendment guarantees the freedom of speech, religion, and the press. **Amendments** are changes to the Constitution. In 1791, the Bill of Rights was ratified.

## The Georgia Constitution of 1777

In addition to the U.S. Constitution, each state has its own constitution. In 1777, the first Georgia Constitution was written.

The first Georgia Constitution helped the colony transition into a state. The state legislature had the most power; however, there also was a separation of powers doctrine. Certain individual rights were guaranteed, such as freedom of religion, freedom of the press, and trial by jury. Furthermore, voting rights belonged only to white men over 21 who could afford to pay taxes.

Although the Georgia Constitution was only ten years old when the U.S. Constitution was ratified, Georgia needed to rewrite it in order to conform to the laws of the new federal government. Georgia law said that only Protestant men could be legislators. But the U.S. Constitution guaranteed religious freedom. Georgia changed the law about Protestant legislators in 1789. The Georgia Constitution has been revised several times since 1789, most recently in 1976.

## Show What You Know

Fill in the chart below with information about each document in the following categories. Include how the document addresses each subject.

|  | Articles of Confederation | U.S. Constitution | Georgia Constitution of 1777 |
|---|---|---|---|
| Date Existed |  |  |  |
| Freedom of Religion |  |  |  |
| Separation of Powers |  |  |  |
| Rights of African Americans |  |  |  |
| Rights of Women |  |  |  |

# Lesson Practice

## DIRECTIONS
**Circle the letter of the best answer for each item.**

### Thinking It Through

1. Which of the following was the result of the Great Compromise?

   **A.** the formation of an upper and lower house of Congress

   **B.** the drafting of the Articles of Confederation

   **C.** the ratification of the Georgia Constitution

   **D.** war with Native Americans

*The Great Compromise was between big and small states. Both wanted equal representation in the government.*

2. How were enslaved people counted in the U.S. Constitution?

   **A.** Only enslaved males were counted.

   **B.** Enslaved people were not counted toward representation.

   **C.** Three-fifths of all enslaved people were counted.

   **D.** Slavery was made illegal.

   **HINT** *Southern states had large numbers of enslaved people.*

3. Freedoms of speech, religion, and the press were guaranteed in which amendment to the Constitution?

   **A.** First Amendment

   **B.** Second Amendment

   **C.** Three-fifths Amendment

   **D.** Sixth Amendment

4. Who were Georgia's representatives at the Constitutional Convention of 1787?

   **A.** George Washington and Abraham Baldwin

   **B.** William Few, Jr., and Abraham Baldwin

   **C.** William Few, Jr., and Austin Dabney

   **D.** Austin Dabney and Abraham Baldwin

# CRCT Review

**Choose the best answer for each question. Fill in the circle of the spaces provided on your answer sheet.**

1. Which person worked to maintain peace between Native Americans and colonists?

   A. John Dunbar

   B. John Reynolds

   C. Mary Musgrove

   D. James Oglethorpe

2. Humans began to practice agriculture during which period?

   A. Paleo-Indian

   B. Archaic

   C. Woodland

   D. Mississippian

3. Which of the following is a correct statement about the French and Indian War?

   A. Native Americans sided only with the French.

   B. Native Americans sided only with the British.

   C. The British and French joined forces to fight against Native Americans.

   D. Native Americans sided with both the French and British.

4. Why was Georgia no longer considered a royal colony in 1776?

   A. It became a Trust in that year.

   B. It declared independence from Britain.

   C. France began to rule it that year.

   D. Spain took control of the colony.

5. Why did the federal government experience financial problems while under the Articles of Confederation?

   A. It did not give states adequate taxing power.

   B. The president and Congress stole federal money.

   C. Congress lacked the power to tax U.S. citizens.

   D. The U.S. did not have adequate natural resources to generate money.

6. In addition to debtors, what other group was encouraged to settle in the Georgia colony?

   A. Native Americans

   B. Protestants

   C. enslaved people

   D. Catholics

7. Which statement BEST explains the purpose of the Spanish missions in Georgia?

   A. They were set up to spread Catholicism to Native Americans.

   B. They were set up to spread Protestantism to Native Americans.

   C. They were set up to convert Protestants to Catholicism.

   D. They were set up to teach Native Americans how to dance.

8. In addition to Abraham Baldwin, what other Georgian represented the state at the Constitutional Convention of 1787?

   A. Robert E. Lee

   B. William Few, Jr.

   C. Nancy Hart

   D. James Madison

9. Which of the following were Spanish explorers hoping to find when they first explored the Southeast?

   A. snakes

   B. Native Americans

   C. ivory

   D. gold

10. The term "loyalist" describes

    A. British naval officers.

    B. American militia leaders.

    C. Americans who supported Great Britain.

    D. Americans who supported the colonies.

11. Which European empire is described by the phrases in the box below?

    - destroyed Fort Caroline
    - built missions
    - had a navy known as the Armada

    A. England

    B. France

    C. Spain

    D. Belgium

12. How did most colonists react to the Stamp Act?

    A. They formed the Stamp Act Congress.

    B. They overthrew the Stamp Act Congress.

    C. They declared allegiance to King George III.

    D. They declared independence from Great Britain.

# CHAPTER

# 2

# Growth of Georgia and the New Nation

# 8 Spiritual and Educational Development

 **SS8H5.a**

Religion strongly influenced Georgia's growth. The Second Great Awakening swept the United States. from 1790 to 1830. During this time, interest in religion in the U.S. increased, especially for Protestantism. Baptists, Methodists, Presbyterians, and the Anglican Church participated. In the south, the religious revival fostered the development of Baptist, Methodist, and Presbyterian churches, creating the regional nickname of the Bible Belt.

## Methodists and Camp Meeting Grounds

Tent revivals were a new form of religious meeting that began during this time. A **revival** is a meeting meant to interest people in religion. Revivals happened in camp meeting grounds, which are outdoor meeting places for religious services. Most camp meetings were held by Methodist churches. The revivals helped the Methodist Church grow.

Georgia's first camp meeting on record was in Hancock County, around 1803. Thousands of people attended. Soon, many churches had built open-air shelters and cabins just for the revivals. Camp meetings continued in Georgia for several years, laying the foundation of religious importance in the state.

Methodist camp meeting; engraving, 1836

## Georgia Baptist Convention

There were many different Christian groups in Georgia at this time. Baptist leaders wanted to unite all the different Baptist groups. The groups formed the Georgia Baptist Convention. It was the largest group of Baptists in the state.

The convention brought together different types of Baptists. One type was called the Primitive Baptists. They did not like missionary work or Sunday school. They believed that life happened according to a plan set in motion by God.

Free Will Baptists were also part of the Georgia Baptist Convention. They liked missionary work and education. They believed that people had free will. Despite disagreements in their ideas, most Baptist churches joined the Georgia Baptist Convention.

Eventually, the Georgia Baptists Convention participated in the Southern Baptists Convention. Today, this group is the country's largest Protestant body.

# Anglican Church

Anglicans were another large religious group in the state at this time. The Anglican Church is an extension of the Church of England. Anglicans were among the first settlers in the state.

After the revolution, Anglicans were the biggest religious group in the state, especially in Savannah. Even though Georgia was no longer ruled by the British, Anglicans did not want to give up their British religion. In 1789, they decided to change their name to the Protestant Episcopal Church of the U.S., to mark their break from England. This church is known today as the Episcopalian Church.

# Education in Georgia

Improvements in Georgia's educational system helped the growth of the state. One of the first things the state of Georgia did after the Revolutionary War was to open a university. The state set aside a plot of land for the school. *Abraham Baldwin* wrote the plan for the school. It was named the University of Georgia.

Baldwin thought that education was necessary for a free government. He believed that everyone should have a good education, not just the wealthy. He thought that government had a duty to provide education to everyone.

Baldwin's ideas were new. Other colleges were private and too expensive for the average person. The University of Georgia was the first school open to lower-income people, and significantly, the first public university in the U.S. The University of Georgia held its first classes in September 1801. Soon afterward, other states followed Georgia's example and built public universities.

# Louisville, Georgia

After the Revolutionary War, many people moved to northern Georgia. State legislators for this region demanded that the state capital be moved further west than Savannah, where it was located at that time. In 1786, a commission, which included *William Few, Jr.*, was given the job of finding a new site for the government. The commission purchased 1,000 acres near the Ogeechee River. Louisville was named after King *Louis XVI*, a French king who helped the patriots during the revolution.

At first, Louisville did well economically. Tobacco was a big cash crop. After the invention of the cotton gin, many people in Louisville began growing cotton. The city was a popular trading area for cotton and tobacco. By the end of the 1790s, the city was booming. It had multiple newspapers, a coffeehouse, and a theater and a population of 550.

In 1796, Louisville was named Georgia's capital. However, the city began to have problems with malaria, a disease spread by mosquitoes. Trade was not as brisk in the region as some had hoped. In 1807, the state decided to move the capital to Milledgeville. Subsequently, a railroad was built, but did not pass through Louisville.

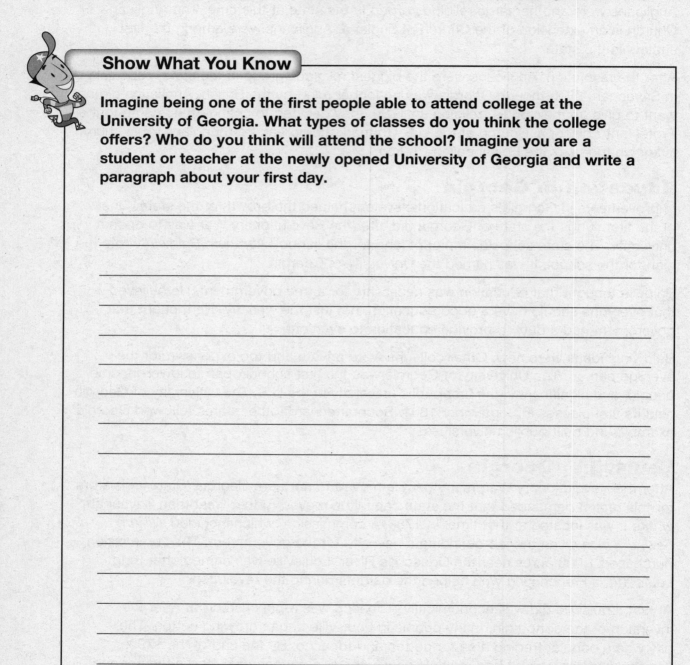

## Show What You Know

**Imagine being one of the first people able to attend college at the University of Georgia. What types of classes do you think the college offers? Who do you think will attend the school? Imagine you are a student or teacher at the newly opened University of Georgia and write a paragraph about your first day.**

# Lesson Practice

## DIRECTIONS
Circle the letter of the best answer for each item.

### Thinking It Through

1. What was the Second Great Awakening?

   A. political movement

   B. religious revival

   C. historical document

   D. pact with England

   *The Second Great Awakening swept the nation and caused a surge of interest in Protestantism. The nickname "the Bible Belt" came from this time.*

2. What did the Georgia Baptist Convention do?

   A. It unified Baptists under one organization.

   B. It changed the name of the Anglicans.

   C. It outlawed tent revivals.

   D. It wrote a religious constitution.

   **HINT** *The Georgia Baptist Convention was a union of denominations.*

3. What Georgia religious group used camp meeting grounds the most?

   A. Presbyterian

   B. Anglican

   C. Methodist

   D. Baptist

4. What is significant about the history of the University of Georgia?

   A. Its construction was the most expensive in United States history.

   B. It was built by Anglicans.

   C. It was the site of many revivals.

   D. It was the first public university in the United States.

# 9 Land Policies

SS8H5.b

Native Americans once controlled much of present-day Georgia. Against the wishes of their people, many Native American leaders sometimes gave up their land in treaties with the British. Much of this Native American land was later given to colonists.

## Headright System

Such colonists received land grants under the headright system. The **headright system** granted between 200 and 1,000 acres of land to the heads of families. By giving men land, they were able to obtain power. Farmers soon came looking for fertile farmland. Ranchers also flocked to Georgia in search of grazing areas for their livestock. These ranchers and farmers often got their businesses off the ground with land grants through the headright system. By 1782, most of the land grants were given to Revolutionary War veterans. This practice, however, quickly led to corruption.

**Southeastern United States**

## Yazoo Land Sale

The government of Georgia had been weakened by the Revolutionary War. It was not strong enough to defend settlements in the western part of the state. The Georgia government thought it had found a solution to this problem with the Yazoo land sale in 1795. In the **Yazoo land sale**, the government planned to sell 35 million acres of land in western Georgia, near the Yazoo River, to four companies for $500,000. In return for this cheap land, the companies would be able to establish a presence in the western part of the state. This presence would help keep the frontier of Georgia safe. Settlers would be more likely to move to western Georgia if the area was secure and had the jobs and products that the companies had to offer. Georgia Governor *George Mathews* signed the Yazoo Act on January 7, 1795.

The Yazoo land sale backfired. Bribes had been paid to many important Georgians in exchange for their support of the Yazoo Act. When the bribery came to light, many Georgians were shocked by the corruption. They protested in the streets and collected signatures on petitions that opposed the Yazoo land and sale. Despite the public outcry, the Yazoo land sale was completed. Georgian Senator *James Jackson* heard about the Yazoo deal and resigned his seat in the Senate. He returned home to Georgia and set out to reverse the sale. Jackson and his Jeffersonian Republican allies were soon voted into office. They used their control of the legislature to pass the 1796 Rescinding Act. This act reversed the Yazoo land sale. As part of the agreement that reversed the Yazoo land sale, the United States government promised to help remove the remaining Creek Indians from within Georgia's borders. In this way, the Yazoo land fraud led to the Trail of Tears in 1838.

## Land Lottery

After the disaster of the Yazoo land fraud, the state of Georgia implemented a lottery system to determine who could buy land. A person's age, war service, marital status, and years of residence in Georgia were all factors that determined who was eligible for the **land lottery**. The land lottery was restricted to white men, orphans, and widows. Georgia held multiple land lotteries between 1805 and 1833. During this time, Georgia sold three-fourths of the state to 100,000 families and individuals. These Georgians paid an average of seven cents per acre.

Ordinary Georgians could gain control of large areas of land through these lotteries. This led to a shift in power. As a colony, Georgia had been ruled by wealthy planter aristocrats. Through the land lottery, almost any man could become a landowner. Power and wealth began to be distributed more evenly among white men of Georgia.

Much of the land that was sold in Georgia's land lotteries was originally sold in the Yazoo land fraud. A great deal of the land sold in the lottery system had once belonged to Native Americans. Between the Yazoo land fraud and the War of 1812, the Creek and Cherokee Indians were effectively eliminated from within Georgia's borders.

Much of the land purchased through these land lotteries was used for tobacco farming. The introduction of cotton and the invention of the cotton gin would change that, and the history of Georgia. Agriculture soon shifted from small farms to large plantations. These plantations required a great deal of labor. Within twenty years of the first land lottery in Georgia, enslaved people made up 44% of Georgia's population.

## Show What You Know

**Why do you think that the people of Georgia were outraged by the Yazoo land deal? Why did they protest it? Would you feel the same as they did? If so, what would you do in response? Write an essay analyzing the Yazoo land sale that answers these questions.**

_____

_____

_____

_____

_____

_____

_____

_____

_____

_____

_____

_____

_____

_____

_____

_____

_____

_____

_____

_____

_____

_____

_____

_____

# Lesson Practice

**DIRECTIONS**
**Circle the letter of the best answer for each item.**

## Thinking It Through

1.  Two factors that contributed to the growth of the population of enslaved people in Georgia were

    A.  the Trail of Tears and the War of 1812.

    B.  the land lottery system and the Yazoo land fraud.

    C.  the introduction of cotton to Georgia and the invention of the cotton gin.

    D.  tobacco farming and the Rescinding Act of 1796.

*People were enslaved and made to do difficult labor. More people were used whenever production increased.*

2.  Which was one way Georgian politicians thought to secure western Georgia?

    A.  The Yazoo land sale opened up millions of acres to settlement.

    B.  Land lotteries made it easier for families and individuals to buy land.

    C.  The headright system gave plots of land to heads of families.

    D.  Native Americans were forced from Georgia's borders.

    **HINT** *Georgia's politicians created a system to benefit both themselves and the people that they served.*

3.  Who served as a U.S. senator of Georgia during the Yazoo land sale?

    A.  Andrew Jackson

    B.  George Mathews

    C.  Zell Miller

    D.  James Jackson

4.  Two factors that influenced who was eligible for Georgia's land lotteries of the 1800s were

    A.  religion and nationality.

    B.  gender and marital status.

    C.  political influence and wealth.

    D.  last name and date of birth.

# 10 Technological Developments

SS8H5.c

## The U.S. Grows

In 1789, *George Washington* was elected the first president of the United States. His presidency also marked the beginning of U.S. expansion. Between 1789 and 1840, the United States expanded its borders. The U.S. took land from Native Americans and then forced Native Americans to relocate to less fertile land in the West. In 1803, the U.S. completed the Louisiana Purchase, which was a huge piece of land owned by France that included present-day Louisiana, Arkansas, Missouri, Iowa, Minnesota, North Dakota, South Dakota, Nebraska, New Mexico, Texas, Oklahoma, Kansas, Montana, Wyoming, Colorado, and large portions of Canada. The purchase gave western farmers access to the Mississippi River. It also opened up new land for farming.

## When Cotton Was King

Cotton farming was the main source of money in the South. It was the largest crop that the South grew and sold. A number of inventions helped people work with cotton. Changes in the cotton industry also created changes in the development of Georgia. The fly shuttle made the thread generating process more efficient and sped up the weaving process. The spinning jenny could spin sixteen cotton threads at the same time. The old spinning wheels could only make one thread at a time. The cotton gin pulled the fiber from the seeds and separated the seeds from the lint. The machinery invented for textile and cotton production allowed more goods to be produced for less money. A common person might have owned one or two outfits before clothes started being mass produced. Now average people could afford many more clothes.

## Eli Whitney's Cotton Gin

The invention of the cotton gin changed Georgia forever. *Eli Whitney* invented the cotton gin in 1793. The cotton gin separated the seeds for the cotton plant twice as fast as a person could do it by hand. The cotton gin worked so quickly that plantation owners needed more people than before to grow and pick cotton. The South became even more dependent on slavery because there was a great need for cotton in the U.S.

The original cotton gin of Eli Whitney

If the South did not have slavery, it would not have been able to grow, produce, and profit from cotton as much as it did. Enslaved people did the hard work needed to grow the cotton, and they did it without pay. Wealthy plantation owners used enslaved people in record numbers at this time, which changed the population of the state. Soon, more than half of the population was an African living in slavery.

# Georgia Gold Rush

In 1829, gold mines were discovered in northern Georgia. This area was home to the Cherokee Indians and was known as the Cherokee Nation. Thousands of U.S. miners arrived with dreams of becoming rich quick. This began what was called the "Great Intrusion" and contributed to the forced removal of the Cherokee Indians.

The center of Georgia's gold rush was in the area of present-day Lumkin County. In 1833, the name of the county seat was changed from Licklog to Dahlonega. Dahlonega was taken from the Cherokee word "tahlonega," which means "golden." The gold pulled from these deposits was converted into currency at the Dahlonega mint, which was established in 1838. Many viewed the mint, established by the U.S. government, as a sign of Georgia's successful growth during the 1830s. The success and riches brought to Georgia by the gold rush, however, were not shared with the Cherokee Indians.

# Canals to Rails

Good transportation was necessary for the growth of Georgia. Up until the 1820s, Georgia relied on its river system to carry products long distances. Since people moved inland from the rivers, a new system was needed. In the 19th century, canals were built across the U.S. to connect waterways. Canals connected markets in the east and west. In 1825, the Erie Canal was completed, connecting Lake Erie to the Hudson River. The Erie Canal also helped New York City become a premier port and commercial city.

Many people in Georgia believed that a canal system would bring wealth to Georgia. Between 1826 and 1846, Georgia planned four major canals. After many attempts to plan the canals, however, the state decided against the plan. Instead, the state decided railroads would better satisfy the state's transportation needs. In 1840, there were still no commercial railroads west of the Mississippi, and only one was in the South (in Charleston, South Carolina). Building railroads would be a big part of Georgia's future.

## Show What You Know

The invention of the cotton gin made it quicker to remove the seeds from cotton. Think of something that you do that takes a long time. Come up with an invention that makes doing this task quicker. Describe how this new invention would change the way you do your work and what benefits you would get as a result. Consider whether others could benefit from your invention and how you would get others to use it.

_____

_____

_____

_____

_____

_____

_____

_____

_____

_____

_____

_____

_____

_____

_____

_____

_____

_____

_____

# Lesson Practice

**DIRECTIONS**
Circle the letter of the best answer for each item.

## Thinking It Through

1. Between the American Revolution and the Civil War, advances in which field contributed MOST to the growth of Georgia's economy?

   A. agriculture

   B. mathematics

   C. education

   D. entertainment

*Georgia's economy was based on cotton until well after the Civil War.*

2. The invention of the cotton gin made it necessary for plantation owners to use more

   A. enslaved people.

   B. tractors.

   C. cattle.

   D. silos.

   **HINT** *The cotton gin made the production of cotton thread from the cotton plant faster.*

3. The Louisiana Purchase gave farmers access to

   A. several gold mines.

   B. new options for crops.

   C. the Mississippi River.

   D. more enslaved people.

4. Who invented the cotton gin?

   A. John Calhoun

   B. Eli Whitney

   C. Abraham Lincoln

   D. Harriet Tubman

#  11 Indian Removal

 SS8H5.d

Near the end of the 18th century, Georgia was home to European settlers, as well as Cherokee and Creek Indians. Many settlers became rich growing cotton on plantations. The settlers viewed the Native Americans in Georgia as a barrier to further exploitation of the region's land. The Creek and Cherokee Indians viewed settlers as intruders who were stealing their land. The struggle between the two groups for control of the Georgia lasted from 1789 to 1840.

## The Creek Indians

The son of a European settler and a Creek Indian, *Alexander McGillivray* represented the Creek Nation throughout the Revolutionary War. McGillivray worked to centralize power within Creek society and to protect Creek lands more effectively.

In 1790, the Treaty of New York was signed by *George Washington*. It ceded Creek Indian lands east of the Ocmulgee River to the U.S. government in exchange for government defense of Creek territorial rights. The treaty created a formal relationship between the U.S. and the Creek Nation, giving the Creek Nation authority to punish non-native trespassers in their territories. In return, the Creeks agreed to return enslaved people who had fled and turn in Creeks who committed federal crimes. Also, agreement officially recognized the leadership of McGillivray.

From 1810 to 1820, another son of a European settler and a Native American led the Creek Nation. *William McIntosh* helped to create a police force, establish written laws, and create a National Assembly for the Creek Nation.

Meanwhile, settlers in Georgia tried to persuade the U.S. government to remove the Native Americans. In the Compact of 1802, the U.S. government agreed with the state of Georgia to end Native American ownership of lands in Georgia. In the next few years, settlers expanded into Creek Indian lands. In response, Creek tribes stole livestock and crops from the settlers. In 1814, General *Andrew Jackson* led U.S. troops against the Creek Indians. Eventually, the Creeks handed over 23 million acres to the settlers in defeat.

In 1825, Georgia agents bribed McIntosh into signing away all the Creek land in Georgia. He was later executed under the authority of the National Assembly for the Creek Nation, by the same police force he helped create. Realizing that the Georgia government would not give in to Creek territory demands, representatives from the Creek Nation ceded all remaining land to the Georgia government. By 1837, 20,000 Creeks were forced to move West, to Indian Territory in Oklahoma.

# The Cherokee Indians

The Cherokee were the quickest of the Native American tribes to take on European ways. Urged by U.S. officials, the Cherokee abandoned their traditional way of life. They adopted a republican government, and a Cherokee named *Sequoyah* created the Cherokee syllabary, a writing system that allowed the Cherokee to read, write, record laws, and publish newspapers. In 1827, *John Ross* became the principal chief of the Cherokee. Using the syllabary, he established a written constitution for the Cherokee Nation.

Sequoya made study of his own Cherokee language.

Gold was discovered in 1829, in Georgia. A flood of prospectors then began arriving in Georgia during the Dahlonega Gold Rush. The intruding prospectors paid no attention to Cherokee land ownership. The Dahlonega Gold Rush brought more whites into Georgia and increased the desire of the settlers for the removal of Native Americans from the region.

In 1828, Andrew Jackson was elected president of the United States. A major issue of his campaign was the removal of Native Americans to Indian Territory to the west. Two years later, Georgia representatives pushed an Indian Removal bill through Congress. The Indian Removal Act gave authority to Georgia to begin the removal process. It also gave the president authority to negotiate removal treaties with Native American tribes.

With the help of a handful of white missionaries, John Ross was able to appeal to the U.S. Supreme Court to protest the removals. In 1831, *John Marshall*, chief justice of the Supreme Court, wrote in a court decision that the Cherokee were a "domestic dependent nation" of the U.S. The Supreme Court decided that it could not rule on the issue in 1831.

In a case a year later, *Worcester v. Georgia,* the Supreme Court decided that the Cherokee were a sovereign nation, which should be allowed to rule itself. They should also have federal protection from other states' laws. Georgia refused to recognize the Supreme Court's ruling. President Jackson chose not to enforce the ruling. President Jackson continued to pressure the Cherokee to move West.

In 1835, a rebellious Cherokee group signed a removal treaty without the approval of Ross or other Cherokee leaders. The treaty required the Cherokee to give up their land in Georgia for a piece of land in Oklahoma and money for relocation. Ross protested the treaty to the U.S. government, but President *Martin Van Buren* responded by sending troops into Indian Territory. The army rounded up most of the Cherokee people and forced them to leave the state of Georgia.

The forced march of the Cherokee Indians from Georgia to Oklahoma in the winter of 1838 to 1839 is now known as the **Trail of Tears**. It is estimated that 4,000 people, one-fifth of the Cherokee population at that time, died from the cold or from starvation during the long march.

## Show What You Know

**Settlers and Native Americans competed for control of the state of Georgia in the years following the Revolutionary War. Imagine you are a Cherokee Indian in 1831. Write a one-page letter to the president of the United States persuading him to allow the Cherokee to stay in Georgia.**

_____

_____

_____

_____

_____

_____

_____

_____

_____

_____

_____

_____

_____

_____

_____

_____

# Lesson Practice

## DIRECTIONS
**Circle the letter of the best answer for each item.**

### Thinking It Through

1. Alexander McGillivray represented the Creek Nation throughout the

   **A.** Civil War.

   **B.** French and Indian War.

   **C.** Revolutionary War.

   **D.** Trail of Tears.

   *The Creek Nation was not part of the Trail of Tears. The Civil War did not significantly involve Native Americans. The French and Indian War was primarily fought in the Northeast.*

2. Andrew Jackson led American troops against the Creek Indians in

   **A.** 1814.

   **B.** 1798.

   **C.** 1832.

   **D.** 1802.

   **HINT** *This event took place between the Compact of 1802 and 1825, when McIntosh signed away all the Creek land in Georgia.*

3. The syllabary created by Sequoyah was a system of

   **A.** hunting.

   **B.** writing.

   **C.** fishing.

   **D.** worship.

4. In 1832, John Marshall was the

   **A.** chief of the Cherokee.

   **B.** president of the United States.

   **C.** chief justice of the Supreme Court.

   **D.** Georgia state representative.

# 12 Setting the Stage for War

 SS8H6.a

Many events led to the Civil War in the United States. The Civil War was fought over the issue of secession. **Secession** is the withdrawal of a state from the Union. The southern states (Virginia, North Carolina, South Carolina, Georgia, Alabama, Florida, Mississippi, Louisiana, Arkansas, and Texas) wanted to secede from the United States. They wanted to form a new country that was independent from the United States.

## States' Rights

Slavery was at the root of many of the problems between the North and the South. The southern states wanted to follow their own laws. They did not want federal laws to overrule the laws of states.

The people of the Missouri Territory wanted to join the United States as the next state. People in Missouri wanted slavery to be legal. However, abolitionists from the North did not want slavery to expand. An **abolitionist** is a person opposed to slavery and in favor of ending it. A compromise was reached that allowed Missouri to become a state.

The **Missouri Compromise** of 1820 was an agreement between the North and South about slavery in new states. The United States had an equal number of states where slavery was legal and illegal. The northern states wanted Missouri to be a state, but only if slavery were illegal there. Since Missourians wanted slavery, the compromise sought a balance of slave and non-slave states. Missouri joined as a slave state, while Maine joined as a non-slave state. The compromise also banned slavery above the parallel 36° 30′ north in the Louisiana Purchase.

## The Tariffs of 1828 and 1832

The Tariff of 1828 caused even more division in the country. A **tariff** is a tax on foreign goods. The tariff was put in place to protect northern factories from foreign competition. The South was buying goods from Britain, which were cheaper than those from the North. The tariff would force the South to buy northern goods.

The Tariff of 1828 led to discussions in the South about nullification. **Nullification** is the argument that a state has the right not to follow a federal law. The state of South Carolina wanted to ignore the tariff. By 1832, Congress slightly modified the Tariff of 1828 to appease the southern states. However, the people of South Carolina were still outraged with the federal government for taxing their main supply of goods.

The people of the state planned to use force to stop federal tax collectors. President *Andrew Jackson* said that he would use the army in South Carolina to collect the tariff, forcing the state to comply with federal law. Jackson called on Congress to pass a Force Bill giving Jackson the authority to use military force to collect taxes. Congress did pass the Force Bill, but it also passed a bill to reduce tariffs over a ten-year period. The compromise tariff bill satisfied South Carolina and averted crisis for a short time.

## Compromise of 1850

California and Texas both wanted to become states. Arizona, Utah, New Mexico, and Nevada would soon want to be states as well. The existing states, however, could not agree on the issue of slavery. A balance was struck again by making California a free state and Texas a slave state. This was known as the **Compromise of 1850**. A series of laws were fought in Congress for eight months and consisted of five compromises. These laws were made to keep the balance between slave and non-slave states.

In addition to the admittance of California and Texas as states, the compromise included the **Fugitive Slave Act**. This act said that all states must return enslaved people that had fled back to their owners. The compromise also prohibited the slave trade in Washington, D.C.

## Georgia Platform

The state of Georgia held a convention in Milledgeville, to debate the Compromise of 1850. A proclamation was adopted called the **Georgia Platform**. Georgians wanted the North to support the Fugitive Slave Act and to stop trying to ban slavery in new states. *Alexander Stephens* was one of three representatives from Georgia who supported the Union. He argued that the Compromise of 1850 should be upheld. Stephens's arguments led to the Georgia Platform being written in support of the Compromise of 1850. Georgia was credited by many around the country with preventing war and secession.

Alexander Stephens was Georgia's representative in Congress, and eventually, vice president of the Confederacy.

## The Kansas-Nebraska Act

The **Kansas-Nebraska Act** of 1854 was similar to the Compromise of 1850 and the Missouri Compromise. Again, the North and South argued over how slavery should be handled in new states. Kansas and Nebraska were one large territory at that time. The borders of the two new states were drawn as part of a compromise. One state would allow slavery and one would not. The vote of the people of each state would decide the issue. This policy was called **popular sovereignty**.

An election was held in Kansas to decide the issue of slavery in the state. Anti-slavery forces banded together and moved into Kansas to sway the results of the election for a slave-free Kansas. Proslavery advocates also crossed the Missouri border into Kansas to ensure slavery rights. The situation turned violent as both factions fought to control the slave vote. The crisis became known as Bleeding Kansas.

Kansas was voted to be a slave state in 1857. However, the U.S. Congress rejected the results and a new election was held in Kansas. The abolitionists won the second election. Kansas declared itself a free state, or one that would not allow slavery. It joined the United States in 1861.

## Dred Scott

The trials of *Dred Scott* increased the divisions in the United States. Dred Scott was an African American born into slavery in Virginia, in 1799. Scott traveled with his owner through Illinois and Wisconsin where slavery was illegal. He lived in free territory for over nine years. Missouri's law stated that once a man was free for any amount of time, he was free for life. In 1846, Dred Scott went to court in Missouri to win his freedom. In the famous court case *Dred Scott v. Sandford*, Scott argued that he had been a free man while traveling through Illinois and Wisconsin, so he should be able to live as a free man in Missouri.

Scott lost his first case. He appealed his case to a higher court in 1850 and won. The case was appealed again by the Missouri Supreme Court. Scott's victory was overturned there. Dred Scott and his lawyers took their case to the state of New York where they once again lost. They appealed this loss, and the case went to the U.S. Supreme Court. The Supreme Court ruled against Scott. The cases received news coverage throughout the country and caused people to debate the issue.

Dred Scott's trials divided the country before the Civil War.

# Election of 1860 and Secession

A new political party formed after the Dred Scott case, called the Republican Party. It took an anti-slavery position. In the 1860 presidential election, its candidate was *Abraham Lincoln*. He was an abolitionist and supported Dred Scott's desire for freedom. Lincoln said he would try to end the spread of slavery. Lincoln won the election in November 1860, without the support of southern states.

Lincoln's victory caused the southern states to hold conventions on secession. South Carolina was the first state to vote for secession. The Georgia Secession Convention was held in 1861, in Milledgeville. It was the fifth southern state to hold such a convention. The powers and rights of states versus the federal government were debated. *Alexander Stephens* called for the south to remain loyal to the Union. He voted against secession. However, Georgia voted to secede from the Union. On January 21, 1861, Georgia officially seceded from the United States. Georgians participated in the creation of the new southern Confederate government including Alexander Stephens who served as vice president to the new government.

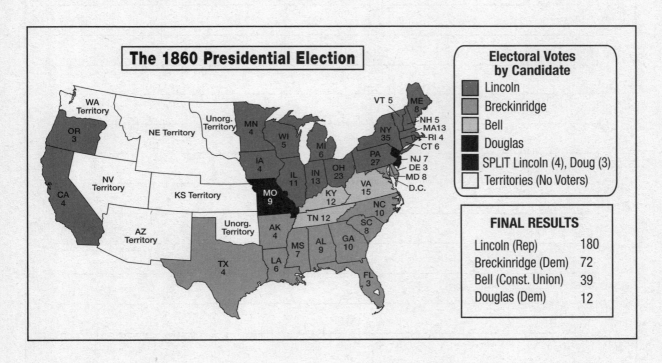

**The 1860 Presidential Election**

**Electoral Votes by Candidate**
- Lincoln
- Breckinridge
- Bell
- Douglas
- SPLIT Lincoln (4), Doug (3)
- Territories (No Voters)

**FINAL RESULTS**

| | |
|---|---|
| Lincoln (Rep) | 180 |
| Breckinridge (Dem) | 72 |
| Bell (Const. Union) | 39 |
| Douglas (Dem) | 12 |

## Show What You Know

Imagine you are at the Georgia Platform debate. Decide which viewpoint you will represent—either the North or the South. Defend your position for each of the following issues: the Missouri Compromise, the Compromise of 1850, and the Kansas-Nebraska Act. Then, write a short list of arguments for and against secession.

_____

_____

_____

_____

_____

_____

_____

_____

_____

_____

_____

_____

_____

_____

_____

_____

_____

_____

# Lesson Practice

## DIRECTIONS
**Circle the letter of the best answer for each item.**

### Thinking It Through

1. The term "popular sovereignty" describes

   **A.** abolitionism.

   **B.** the right of states to vote on laws.

   **C.** the right of the federal government to nullify laws.

   **D.** the nullification of tariffs.

*The term popular sovereignty was coined when Kansas and Nebraska had to vote to decide their position on slavery.*

2. Which of the following is described by the statements in the box below?

   > • Maine had to agree to outlaw slavery.
   >
   > • Territories wanted to become new states.
   >
   > • Abolitionists wanted to change the laws.

   **A.** Tariff of 1832

   **B.** Georgia Platform

   **C.** Kansas-Nebraska Act

   **D.** Missouri Compromise

   **HINT** *Northern states and southern states had to agree to balance slave and non-slave states.*

3. Which statement BEST describes the outcome of the Dred Scott case?

   **A.** The New York court system changed the laws of Missouri.

   **B.** Missouri granted Scott the right to be free.

   **C.** The U.S. Supreme Court decided against Scott.

   **D.** The U.S. Supreme Court sent the case back to the Missouri Supreme Court.

4. In what way is the Kansas-Nebraska Act similar to both the Missouri Compromise and the Compromise of 1850?

   **A.** Each was concerned with tariffs.

   **B.** Each decided the legality of slavery in new states.

   **C.** Each was written to end the Civil War.

   **D.** Each was written by Alexander Stephens.

# 13  The Civil War

 SS8H6.b

The first shots of the Civil War rang out on April 12, 1861, when the Confederate army attacked Fort Sumter, South Carolina. Although there was no blood shed, the Union forces surrendered the fort to Confederate troops. Upon hearing the news of the surrender of Fort Sumter, President *Abraham Lincoln* called for 75,000 men to serve in the Union army, and ordered a naval blockade of Southern ports from South Carolina to Texas on April 19, 1861.

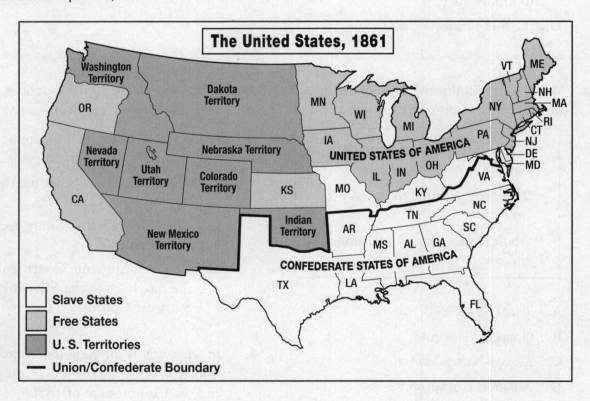

## Blockade of the Georgia Coast

Many of Georgia's ports were blocked throughout the war. These included the ports at Darien and Brunswick. Other areas were harder to block off completely. Strong Confederate forts protected some cities from falling under the blockade.

Savannah was Georgia's biggest port. It was also one of most important cities in the Confederacy. Fort Pulaski protected the city. It was a very strong fort that took eighteen years to build. Some of the best army engineers from both the North and the South believed that the fort would not crumble from artillery fire. In April of 1862, Union artillery bombarded the fort and caused the Confederate forces to surrender.

As a result, the Union troops used the fort to block ships from entering Savannah. Savannah fell under the blockade. The blockade made it difficult for farmers and merchants to sell their wares. It also made it hard for the Confederate army to receive new supplies from their allies in other countries. Confederate forces in the North were experiencing difficulties of their own in their pursuit of gaining military supplies and capturing the Union capital of Washington, D.C.

## Battle of Antietam

After his victory at the Second Battle of Bull Run, Confederate General *Robert E. Lee* moved his troops to Maryland. From there he planned to capture Washington, D.C. However, his troops were stopped by Union troops commanded by *George B. McClellan* at Antietam Creek, Maryland. On September 17, 1862, George B. McClellan and his troops stopped the Confederate army from advancing on Washington, D.C. The Battle of Antietam proved to be one of the bloodiest single days in the war. Confederate casualties were about 13,700, while the Union lost about 12,400 men. Although McClellan protected the capital from Confederate forces, he allowed Lee's army to escape to Virginia.

## Emancipation Proclamation

In 1862, four slave-owning states—Maryland, Delaware, Missouri, and Kentucky—were still loyal to the Union. Abraham Lincoln was careful when talking about slavery. He wanted these four states to remain part of the Union. Therefore, when he decided to emancipate, or free slaves, he emancipated slavery only in Confederate states.

Abraham Lincoln announced the emancipation of slavery in rebellious states on January 1, 1863. This decree was known as the **Emancipation Proclamation**. Northern states could now feel that they were fighting not only to save the Union, but also to end slavery. Yet as far as the Confederate government was concerned, the new law held no power. Confederate states had already seceded from the Union and no longer followed Union laws.

Abraham Lincoln led the country through this difficult time with diplomacy.

The proclamation officially signified the intentions of the United States government concerning slavery. European countries were reluctant to support a government that promoted slavery and thus more likely to assist the Union cause. In addition to freeing enslaved people, the Emancipation Proclamation allowed the Union to recruit African Americans from the Confederacy to fight in the army. By 1865, nearly 180,000 African American soldiers had enlisted in the Union army.

## Battle of Chickamauga

The Battle of Chickamauga took place September 18–20, 1863. Control of the railroad in nearby Chattanooga, Tennessee, was at stake. After three days of fighting, most of the Union forces retreated in disorder to Chattanooga. Casualties numbered more than 16,000 for the Union and more than 18,000 for the Confederates. It was the bloodiest battle fought in Georgia. The battle was considered a Confederate victory because Confederate forces pushed Union forces back to Chattanooga rather than letting them proceed into Georgia. However, Union forces captured Chattanooga which was the campaign's goal.

## Sherman's March to the Sea

In May 1864, Union General *William Tecumseh Sherman* began his March to the Sea in Georgia with 100,000 soldiers. After fighting off a much smaller force of Confederates, Sherman and his troops entered the city of Atlanta. General Sherman told the people of Atlanta they had five days to leave the city. Five days later, General Sherman had his troops burn Atlanta to the ground. After this, Sherman started his March to the Sea with 60,000 men, marching through Georgia and South Carolina. The plan was for the army to feed itself with what it found in its path. Sherman's troops took everything they could use and destroyed what they could not use. Because of the blockades, Southern farmers had a surplus of what they could not sell. Many animals were slaughtered but not eaten. Stored crops like rice, flour, cotton, and corn were emptied onto the ground. Houses were looted and burned to the ground. Railroads were destroyed. When Sherman's troops reached South Carolina, they burned down most of the capital city of Columbia. Sherman's March to the Sea generated bad feelings between the North and South even years after the war was over.

Sherman's March to the Sea destroyed Georgia.

The Confederate army was destroyed. On April 9, 1865, Lee surrendered the Confederate army of Northern Virginia to *Ulysses S. Grant* at the Appomattox Court House in Virginia. This marked the end of the Civil War. The Union was preserved and slavery was outlawed.

## Andersonville Prison

In February 1864, the Confederates opened a prison camp to house Union soldiers. Andersonville Prison was located in Georgia and held the largest amount of prisons than any other camp at the time. During the Civil War, tens of thousands of Union soldiers were imprisoned there. Conditions were very bad. Unhealthy sanitation conditions, malnutrition, and overcrowding led to mass amounts of casualties. Out of 45,000 men that were imprisoned at Andersonville, almost 13,000 died. Today, the prison is part of Andersonville National Historic Site, a memorial for all American prisoners of war.

The surrender at the Appomattox Court House was the end of the war.

Many Union soldiers were held at Andersonville Prison.

## Show What You Know

**What did the Emancipation Proclamation accomplish? What did it not accomplish? How did it help the Union? How did it affect enslaved people? Write your answers in the space below.**

_____

_____

_____

_____

_____

_____

_____

_____

_____

_____

_____

_____

_____

_____

_____

_____

_____

_____

_____

_____

# Lesson Practice

## DIRECTIONS
**Circle the letter of the best answer for each item.**

### Thinking It Through

1. What was at stake in the Battle of Chickamauga?

    **A.** access to ammunition

    **B.** the fate of Washington, D.C.

    **C.** control of the railroad center in nearby Chattanooga

    **D.** access to the port city of Savannah

    *Union forces wanted to control the railroad lines leading into the South. A major railroad station was located outside of Chattanooga.*

2. Why was the Union victory at Antietam important?

    **A.** It stopped Confederate forces from advancing to Washington, D.C.

    **B.** It cut the Confederate forces off from their supplies.

    **C.** The Confederate forces lost thousands more soldiers than the Union forces.

    **D.** It put an end to the war.

    **HINT** *Antietam Creek, Maryland, is not far from Washington, D.C.*

3. Why did General Sherman burn Atlanta and destroy everything in his path on his March to the Sea?

    **A.** His armies were large and they needed all of the resources they found.

    **B.** He couldn't control his armies anymore.

    **C.** He was ordered to by President Lincoln.

    **D.** He wanted to destroy the resources of the South.

4. Which Georgia port city did Fort Pulaski protect?

    **A.** Brunswick

    **B.** Savannah

    **C.** Darien

    **D.** Atlanta

# 14 Reconstruction

 SS8H6.c

After the Civil War, the South was left in ruins. Cities and farms had been burned to the ground. **Reconstruction** was the time period when rebuilding began. During this time, the South was ruled by the Union army. Southern states began to rejoin the Union.

## Presidential Reconstruction

President *Abraham Lincoln* believed that the Southern states should be admitted back into the Union following some initial steps. Only 10% of the voting population in each state needed to promise to be loyal to the Union. Also, the state had to outlaw slavery. Many Northerners believed Lincoln was too lenient with the South and desired that the South be punished for the war.

A group of anti-slavery activists called the **Radical Republicans** thought that more needed to be done. They wanted the Confederates to be punished. The Radical Republicans created a stricter bill called the Wade-Davis Bill that provided military leaders to govern the Confederate states until a series of actions allowed the states to return to the Union. Although Congress passed the bill, Lincoln vetoed it.

When President Lincoln was assassinated, shortly after the end of the war in April 1865, *Andrew Johnson* became president. He continued with Lincoln's moderate Reconstruction plan, however, he believed that some extreme measures needed to take place. Johnson did not let former Confederate officers and wealthy landowners vote. He also made reconciling states ratify the **Thirteenth Amendment** to the U.S. Constitution. This amendment officially ended slavery in the U.S.

Angered by his moderate stance on Reconstruction, Congress impeached President Johnson after he tried to fire a Radical Republican. **Impeachment** occurs when an elected person is formally accused of doing something wrong. The Radical Republicans were not able to kick President Johnson out of office. The impeachment was acquitted, but much of Johnson's power was taken away.

## Congressional Reconstruction

After Johnson's power was depleted by Congress, Congress took it upon itself to come up with a Reconstruction plan for the South. During Congressional Reconstruction, lawmakers created the **Freedmen's Bureau**. It helped the people who were enslaved. It provided food and clothing. It also built schools for African Americans. In Georgia, the bureau helped white landowners create contracts so that African Americans could be paid for their labor.

Congress also passed the Fourteenth and Fifteenth Amendments. The **Fourteenth Amendment** defines U.S. citizenship and includes newly freed slaves.

The **Fifteenth Amendment** ensures that the right to vote cannot be denied to any U.S. citizen on account of "race, color, or previous condition of servitude." At that time, women still could not yet vote, and the voting age was 21.

African Americans' support in Georgia helped to elect *Henry McNeal Turner*, an African American, to state legislature. Another African American politician in Georgia was *Tunis Campbell*. He was elected to the U.S. Senate. Campbell worked hard to protect African Americans, but he was eventually voted out of office. He was harassed and eventually jailed by white opponents in Georgia.

## White Backlash

Most white Southerners were angry that African Americans were freed. Those in power passed state laws to control African American people. These laws were called the **black codes**. Georgia's black codes were less strict than those in other states. African Americans in the state had the right to buy and sell property. They also were able to sue people in court. However, they were not allowed to serve as jurors and could not testify against whites in court. Georgia and other states also limited the rights of African Americans to vote, despite the Fifteenth Amendment.

Southern whites created a policy of **segregation**, which is the separation of the races. The Supreme Court said segregation was legal as long as different races had "separate but equal" accommodations. Schools, restaurants, theaters, bathrooms, and all public facilities were segregated.

Many whites also used violence to regain control of the South. The Ku Klux Klan (KKK) was a terrorist group that targeted blacks and often went out in robes and hoods. KKK members killed many African Americans and also beat and killed whites who helped African Americans. African American politicians like Georgia's Tunis Campbell and Henry McNeal Turner were often targeted by the Klan.

A group of poor sharecroppers harvest cotton in the fields of Georgia.

## Farming after Slavery

After the Civil War, farming continued to be the main source of income for Southerners. Now that slavery was illegal, planters had to pay workers for their labor. Some paid their former slaves a wage for their work. Many planters did not have money to pay their workers. This led to **sharecropping**, the most commonly used agricultural working relationship between African Americans and whites in the South. Under this system, a person planted crops on a landowner's land and paid the landowner a share of the profit. Most of the time there was little or no money left for the sharecropper after the debts, or money owned to the landowner, had been paid.

Renting small plots of land to individual farmers was another type of farming. This was called tenant farming. It was not as popular as sharecropping because most people did not have enough money to buy the seeds and equipment needed to plant crops.

## Show What You Know

**Divide the space below into two sections. In one section, brainstorm ways in which life was different for African Americans after the Civil War. In the other section, think of ways in which life was the same. Compare and discuss the two lists. Are any of the answers surprising?**

# Lesson Practice

## DIRECTIONS
Circle the letter of the best answer for each item.

### Thinking It Through

1. Which of the ideas below did the Radical Republicans believe in?

   A. more freedoms for African Americans

   B. leniency for former Confederate soldiers

   C. slowing down Reconstruction

   D. preventing African Americans from holding office

*The Republican Party was founded as an anti-slavery party. The Radical Republicans wanted enslaved people to be free.*

2. How were landowners compensated by sharecroppers?

   A. Sharecroppers collected rent from landowners.

   B. Sharecroppers let landowners use their equipment.

   C. Sharecroppers paid a portion of their profits.

   D. Sharecroppers and landowners worked for no profit.

   **HINT** *The word "sharecropping" describes how the profit from the harvest was split up.*

3. Which person was one of the first African Americans elected to the U.S. Senate?

   A. Tunis Campbell

   B. Austin Dabney

   C. Henry McNeal Turner

   D. Andrew Johnson

4. Why did the Supreme Court allow Southern states to practice segregation?

   A. They decided it was an issue of states' rights.

   B. They allowed it if accommodations were "separate but equal."

   C. The justices said black codes were illegal and banned them.

   D. They believed it would decrease violence.

Choose the best answer for each question. Fill in the circle of the spaces provided on your answer sheet.

1. Which of the terms below is the right of a state not to follow a federal law?

   A. slavery

   B. secession

   C. nullification

   D. abolition

2. How did the cotton gin make processing cotton faster?

   A. It separated the seeds from the cotton plant.

   B. It spun cotton into thread.

   C. It pulled many cotton plants out of the ground very quickly.

   D. It made the cotton plant grow twice as fast.

3. What did General Sherman do to destroy the resources of the South?

   A. He blockaded the ports.

   B. He imposed a curfew.

   C. He closed the churches.

   D. He launched the March to the Sea.

4. Which of the following shows the correct order of events in the removal of Native Americans in Georgia?

   A. Treaty of New York, Compact of 1802, Trail of Tears, Dahlonega Gold Rush

   B. Dahlonega Gold Rush, Treaty of New York, Compact of 1802, Trail of Tears

   C. Trail of Tears, Dahlonega Gold Rush, Treaty of New York, Compact of 1802

   D. Treaty of New York, Compact of 1802, Dahlonega Gold Rush, Trail of Tears

5. Which statement BEST explains the importance of the Georgia Baptist Convention?

    A. It helped unify the Baptist church.

    B. It drew divisions between Baptist groups.

    C. It unified the Baptists and the Anglicans.

    D. It nominated the first Baptist president of the U.S.

6. What is the practice of providing "separate but equal" public accommodations for different races?

    A. nullification

    B. segregation

    C. sharecropping

    D. reconstruction

7. Why did the Yazoo land sale end with the 1796 Rescinding Act?

    A. The sale was ruled unconstitutional.

    B. The land was sold to the wrong people.

    C. Government officials had accepted bribes.

    D. Yazoo decided he wanted his land back.

8. Georgia experienced tremendous growth in its enslaved population after 1793. What created the demand?

    A. the invention of the cotton gin

    B. slaves were becoming cheaper

    C. improved land distribution

    D. government corruption

9. When Cherokee Indians were forced to leave Georgia, what is the MOST LIKELY reason that their journey is known as the Trail of Tears?

   A. Cherokee women cried for the Native Americans killed by the army.

   B. Cherokee men were not allowed to cry.

   C. Many Cherokee people lost their lives on the journey.

   D. The Cherokee killed many soldiers along the way.

10. What is the name of the system that granted land to the heads of families of white settlers?

    A. Rescinding Act

    B. lottery system

    C. Yazoo land sale

    D. headright system

11. The Missouri Compromise was an agreement between the northern and southern states about

    A. the right to own slaves.

    B. slavery in new states.

    C. slaves' rights.

    D. the obligation to return runaway slaves.

12. Which Civil War battle is described by the phrases below?

    - Confederate forces won
    - fought over a railroad
    - took place over three days in September 1863

    A. Gettysburg

    B. Antietam

    C. Chattanooga

    D. Chickamauga

# CHAPTER

## 3 Post-Reconstruction Georgia

# 15 The End of Reconstruction

 SS8H7.a

## End of Republican Rule in Georgia

In 1868, the Republican Party gained control of the Georgia government. *Rufus B. Bullock* was elected governor. Bullock wanted equal rights for African Americans. Most Democrats in Georgia did not. A campaign began to remove the Republicans from power. During this time, the Ku Klux Klan (KKK) attacked many African Americans in Georgia.

As a part of Radical Reconstruction, federal troops were sent to Georgia to restore order. After they withdrew, in 1870, the Democrats regained control of the Georgia government. The Republican Party was referred to as the Party of Lincoln, and southern states associated it with anti-South policies.

## Bourbon Triumvirate

From 1872 to 1890, the Bourbon Democrats controlled the Georgia government. Bourbon Democrats were conservative Democrats. The **Bourbon Triumvirate** led the Bourbon Democrats. The Bourbon Triumvirate were *Alfred Colquitt, Joseph Brown*, and *John Gordon*. They wanted Georgia's economy to be industrialized, not based solely on agriculture. During their time in power, the cotton textile industry grew. Production of cottonseed oil, cattle feed, and fertilizer began. Atlanta became prosperous again.

## Henry Grady

*Henry Grady* was a journalist from Georgia who was called the "Spokesman of the New South." Through his speeches and writings, he promoted industry and crop diversification as a means to help the economy in Georgia, particularly in Atlanta. He encouraged northern investors to develop industries in Georgia. Grady spoke about unity and trust between the North and South.

## International Cotton Exposition

The International Cotton Exposition was held in Atlanta, in 1881. It was a fair to bring money to Atlanta's cotton textile business. The exposition displayed equipment for making textiles. Southern products such as sugar, rice, and tobacco were shown. Because of the exposition, millions of dollars were invested in Atlanta. New jobs were created. Similar expositions would be held there in 1887 and 1895. Atlanta became known as the center of the New South.

## Thomas Watson and the Populists

Small farmers in Georgia were upset because they were not prospering during this time. Prices of farm products were dropping. Farmers owed many loans and were charged a great deal of money by railways to ship their products. Farmers formed groups to help one another. The Farmers' Alliance was one of these groups. The formation of these groups was called **populism**. Together, these groups formed a political party called the People's Party. *Thomas Watson* was a leader of the populists. Under Watson's leadership, the People's Party became powerful in Georgia. The Democrats worried that the People's Party might take control. To avoid this, the Democrats won the election by breaking the law, or "stealing" the election.

## Rebecca Latimer Felton

*Rebecca Latimer Felton* was a writer, teacher, and reformer. With her husband's political career, Felton entered the public eye. She was an early supporter of women's **suffrage**, the right to vote. Through making speeches and writing, Felton was able to help women win the right to vote. She pushed social reform at the state level by helping to instate Prohibition and end the convict lease system, a system of leasing convicts to private businesses as cheap labor. At the age of 87, Felton became the first woman to serve in the U.S. Senate, in 1922. The governor appointed her to the position in order to temporarily fill a vacated seat. Felton lived until she was 94.

Rebecca L. Felton, the first female United States Senator, sits at her desk in the Russell Senate Office Building in Washington, D.C.

## The 1906 Atlanta Riot

The Atlanta Riot of 1906 was a string of violent events by whites against African Americans. Such an event is known as a race riot. Dozens of African Americans were killed and many more were wounded. The riot began because of stories of African American men attacking white women. These stories later proved to be untrue. Racial tension had been increasing in Atlanta at that time because of competition between African Americans and whites for jobs. Also, whites were worried that the African American upper class was becoming too powerful. News of the riots circulated the country and focused the eyes of the nation on the problems of Atlanta. Many African Americans began turning to aggressive tactics in order to achieve equality and justice.

## Leo Frank Case

*Leo Frank* was a Jewish man from Georgia who was lynched, or hung, by a mob because of anti-Semitism. **Anti-Semitism** is a belief system against Jewish people. Frank was a factory manager who was accused of murdering a young girl employee. Frank's case went to trial and he was found guilty. However, much of the evidence against Frank was faulty and suspicious. The governor of Georgia, *John Slaton*, reviewed Frank's case and eventually decided that Frank was innocent. However, anti-Semites refused to accept his innocence. A group of citizens lynched Frank before he could enjoy his freedom.

## County Unit System

In 1917, Georgia established the **county unit system**. This was a way of giving votes in primary elections. Each county was given a certain number of votes, called unit votes. The counties were divided into three categories—urban, town, and rural. The candidate who received the most votes in a county won all of the unit votes given to that county. The problem with this system was that it did not always represent what the population wanted. There were more rural counties than the other counties, but not as many people lived in those counties. As a result, the county unit system was eventually abolished.

### Show What You Know

Think about what happened before and during Reconstruction. What do you think are the positives and negatives of Reconstruction?

_____

_____

_____

_____

_____

_____

_____

_____

_____

# Lesson Practice

### Thinking It Through

1. The term "populism" describes

   A. southern farmers working together.

   B. the belief in southern states that African Americans deserved equal rights.

   C. the idea that races could be kept separate as long as there were equal facilities for both.

   D. a movement of violence or unfairness against Jewish people.

   *Populism is a term that refers to people. The People's Party was part of this movement.*

---

2. Henry Grady was known as the

   A. leader of the Confederates.

   B. journalist from Georgia.

   C. great emancipator.

   D. spokesman of the New South.

   **HINT** *Grady was an excellent public speaker.*

3. All of these were reasons for Georgia farmers to join the Farmers' Alliance EXCEPT

   A. dropping prices of farm products.

   B. loan burden.

   C. segregation of railway cars.

   D. increased charges by railways to ship their products.

4. Anti-Semitism is associated with

   A. *Plessy v. Ferguson.*

   B. Leo Frank.

   C. Rufus B. Bullock.

   D. Rebecca Latimer Felton.

# 16 Jim Crow South

 SS8H7.b

The Thirteenth, Fourteenth, and Fifteenth Amendments increased the rights of African Americans after the Civil War.

When formerly Confederate states rejoined the Union, they had to first agree to honor the amendments. Most, however, only followed the Thirteenth Amendment. The southern states did not honor the others because they feared equal rights for African Americans. Southern states regularly denied rights to African Americans.

## Jim Crow Laws

Georgia and other southern states passed state and local legislation called Jim Crow laws. **Jim Crow laws** mandated the segregation of African Americans and whites. Signs were hung in public places designating "Whites Only" for some public places and "Colored Only" for others. African Americans were commonly called "colored" at that time.

### *Plessy v. Ferguson*

Some African Americans challenged the Jim Crow laws in court. The most famous challenge was between *Homer Plessy* and a railroad company in Louisiana. The company tried to make Plessy move from a "Whites Only" passenger car. Plessy, however, refused and was arrested.

Segregated drinking fountains were used in the South.

In the case of *Plessy v. Ferguson*, in 1896, the U.S. Supreme Court disagreed with Plessy. The court ruled that segregation was not against the Constitution. This idea became known as "separate but equal," which meant that it was legal for states to keep the races separate as long as there were equal facilities for both races. Most public facilities, however, such as hospitals and schools, were not of the same quality for African Americans as those for whites.

For example, money that was set aside for African American schools often went to white schools instead. Some African American schools often did not have enough books for all students. Some schools did not even have chalkboards.

# Disenfranchisement

Formerly enslaved men were given the right to vote by the Fifteenth Amendment. Many southern whites felt this right was a threat to their way of life. Southern states made it more difficult for African American men to vote. The act of denying a person the right to vote is called **disenfranchisement.** Furthermore, all women were disenfranchised because none of them were allowed to vote.

Disenfranchisement of African Amerian men was accomplished partly by poll taxes, property tests, and literacy tests. A **poll tax**, which was adopted in Georgia, was a fee that a voter had to pay in order to vote. A voter also had to demonstrate that he owned property. Poll taxes and property tests prevented many poor people, including African Americans, from voting. In addition, voters were required to pass a **literacy test**, which determined their ability to read and write. Most African Americans could not pass this test because under slavery, they had not been allowed to learn to read and write.

These laws also prevented poor, uneducated whites from voting. Southern lawmakers did not want to lose the votes of whites. They passed a law called the **grandfather clause**. The grandfather clause stated that if a person had an ancestor who had been allowed to vote before 1867, he was permitted to vote. Since 1867 was the first year that African Americans were allowed to vote, the grandfather clause only helped whites.

**White primaries** also denied African American men the right to vote. A primary is an initial election in which the voters of a political party nominate candidates. In many states, the Democratic Party would not allow African Americans to be members. When primaries were held, only male members of the Democratic Party, who were all white, were allowed to participate.

# Racial Violence

Race riots and the terrorist activities of the KKK increased at this time. As African Americans gained more power, whites reacted with fear and violence. Often, whites would attack African Americans in groups, such as in the race riots in Atlanta in 1906. Such events occurred throughout the South. This violence continued for decades, with lynchings becoming an increasingly common event throughout the South. Not until the civil rights movement of the 1960s, would violence against African Americans slow in the region.

## Show What You Know

**List some of the methods used by southern states to keep the lives of African Americans and whites separate. Discuss disenfranchisement and the ways that southern states limited African Americans' right to vote. Why do you think that southern whites feared equal rights for African Americans and took such actions to prevent it?**

_____

_____

_____

_____

_____

_____

_____

_____

_____

_____

_____

_____

_____

_____

_____

_____

_____

_____

_____

_____

# Lesson Practice

**DIRECTIONS**
Circle the letter of the best answer for each item.

## Thinking It Through

1. The term "separate but equal" describes

   A. the way that land was apportioned among farmers in the South after the Civil War.

   B. the belief in southern states that African Americans deserved equal rights.

   C. the idea that races could be kept separate as long as there were equal facilities for both.

   D. a method of voting used in the South during Reconstruction.

*When the Jim Crow laws were tried in the Supreme Court, they were found to be constitutional, as long as "separate but equal" facilities were maintained.*

2. Who was Homer Plessy?

   A. governor of Georgia during Reconstruction

   B. inventor of the cotton gin

   C. a lawmaker who helped to draft the Fourteenth Amendment to the Constitution

   D. an African American who refused to move to a segregated railway car

   **HINT** *In the case of Plessy v. Ferguson, in 1896, the U.S. Supreme Court ruled that segregation was not against the Constitution.*

3. How did southern states limit the rights of African Americans after the end of Reconstruction?

   A. redrawing state boundaries

   B. passing Jim Crow laws

   C. educating illiterate whites

   D. hosting cotton expositions

4. All of these methods were used for the disenfranchisement of African American men EXCEPT

   A. amending the Constitution.

   B. property tests.

   C. literacy tests.

   D. poll taxes.

# 17 Civil Rights Advocates

SS8H7.c

During the years between 1877 and 1918, many significant changes in civil rights took place in the state of Georgia. Many civil rights advocates of this period were educators, however, businesspeople also played a role. In the approximately fifty years following the Civil War, colleges in Georgia had begun to serve African Americans. The availability of education for former slaves was a great advance in civil rights.

## Booker T. Washington

*Booker T. Washington* was born into slavery. He grew up during Reconstruction and was educated by a freedmen's school. That experience motivated him to later champion education for other African Americans. Washington headed the Tuskegee Institute in 1881 in Alabama. It was a teaching college that prepared African Americans for agricultural and domestic work.

Booker T. Washington (1856–1915)

Washington became a well known educator and thinker. His idea of **accommodationism** was explained in a widely acclaimed speech at the 1895 Cotton States and International Exposition in Atlanta. Many historians believe the speech is one of the most significant in United States history.

Washington's speech focused on what he called the "Negro problem." The poor social and economic conditions of African Americans concerned him. Racial relations in the economically unstable South were another of his concerns. He encouraged African Americans to embrace jobs in agriculture, mechanics, commerce, and domestic service. He asked African Americans to "dignify and glorify common labor." This idea was greeted happily by southern whites. Washington argued that, for African Americans, seeking social equality was a mistake. He believed progress for African Americans would come gradually and could not be forced.

Washington stated that both whites and African Americans could "be as separate as fingers, yet one as the hand in all things essential to mutual progress." This speech also called for whites to take the initiative in improving social and economic relations between the races. His ideas of shared responsibility and the importance of education over equality came to be known as the **Atlanta Compromise**.

# W. E. B. Du Bois

There were critics of accommodationism. *W. E. B. Du Bois*, a prominent professor at Atlanta University in 1897, recognized the speech's importance, but was not satisfied with the gradual nature of Washington's ideas. He viewed the accommodationist approach as simply accepting the racism of southern whites. Because of this, Du Bois founded the Niagra movement. According to Du Bois, "Mr. Washington represents in Negro thought the old attitude of adjustment and submission." Du Bois thought that African Americans should fight for total racial equality.

Dr. W. E. B. Du Bois (1868–1963), sociologist, historian, educator, editor, and writer

After writing *The Souls of Black Folk*, Du Bois founded the Niagara movement. Civil rights activists gathered at Niagara Falls to assemble a list of demands, which included the end of segregation and discrimination. Eventually the activists involved in the Niagara movement founded the National Association for the Advancement of Colored People (NAACP). Du Bois took a leadership position in the organization and was the editor of their publication, *Crisis*. After spending years with the NAACP, Du Bois went back to Atlanta University to conduct more research.

# John and Lugenia Burns Hope

Two more African American educators played roles in advancing civil rights for African Americans in the South. *John and Lugenia Burns Hope* devoted their time and efforts to educating African American people.

John Burns Hope became the first African American president of Morehouse College in 1906. Twenty-three years later he became the first African American president of Atlanta University. Under his leadership, Atlanta University became the first college in the nation to offer graduate education for African Americans. Hope supported public education, healthcare, job opportunities, and recreational facilities for African Americans.

Hope supported a number of civil rights associations. He embraced Du Bois's **Niagra movement** and the **National Association for the Advancement of Colored People (NAACP)**, as well as the southern-based **Commission on Interracial Cooperation**.

Lugenia Hope was also a prominent civil rights advocate of her time. She worked for many community organizations to assist African American people in Georgia. Hope created the first woman-run social welfare agency for African Americans in Georgia. She also was a member of the **National Association of Colored Women (NACW)**, created in 1896. Lugenia Burns Hope also championed universal suffrage.

# Alonzo Herndon

Businesspeople also became civil rights advocates during this time. *Alonzo Herndon* was, by the time of his death in 1927, the wealthiest African American in Atlanta. He was involved in and supported many local institutions and charities devoted to advancing African American life in Atlanta.

By 1904, Herndon's barbershops were known as the best in America. Herndon's business success allowed him to purchase a failing mutual aid association. Herndon established the Atlanta Mutual Insurance Association (AMIA). The AMIA grew in assets from $5,000 in 1905 to over $400,000 in 1922.

Herndon was one of the founding members of the National Negro Business League, which was started by Booker T. Washington in Boston. In 1905, he was also among the twenty-nine men who founded W.E.B. Du Bois's Niagra movement.

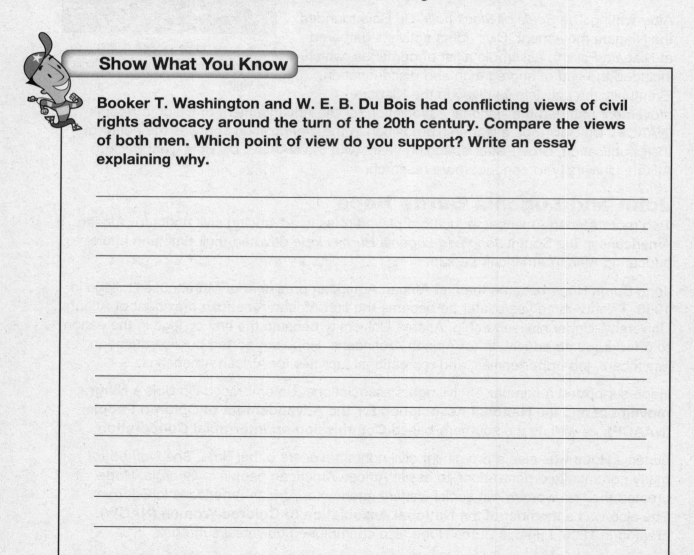

## Show What You Know

**Booker T. Washington and W. E. B. Du Bois had conflicting views of civil rights advocacy around the turn of the 20th century. Compare the views of both men. Which point of view do you support? Write an essay explaining why.**

# Lesson Practice

**DIRECTIONS**
**Circle the letter of the best answer for each item.**

## Thinking It Through

1. The African American leader who supported a gradual approach to civil rights and racial equality was

   A. W. E. B. Du Bois

   B. Martin Luther King, Jr.

   C. Alonzo Herndon

   D. Booker T. Washington

   *Dr. W. E. B. Du Bois worked against the accommodationist ideas of this leader. Dr. Martin Luther King, Jr., was a civil rights leader in the 1960s.*

2. W. E. B. Du Bois established the civil rights movement known as the

   A. Atlanta Compromise.

   B. Niagara movement.

   C. Equality Now movement.

   D. National Association for African Americans.

   **HINT** *The Atlanta Compromise was an idea of Booker T. Washington.*

3. John Burns Hope was the first African American president of Morehouse College and Atlanta University. Atlanta University was the first

   A. university to allow African Americans into the student body.

   B. university to integrate classes.

   C. to focus on the graduate education of African Americans.

   D. African American-led university to receive funds from the government.

4. Alonzo Herndon owed his leadership role and involvement in Du Bois's Niagara movement primarily to his

   A. business success.

   B. charity involvement.

   C. academic achievement.

   D. accommodationist view.

# 18 World War I

**SS8H7.d**

In June 1914, Archduke *Franz Ferdinand*, heir to the throne of Austria-Hungary, was assassinated by Serbian nationalists. Soon after, Austria-Hungary declared war on Serbia. Within a few months, the allies of these countries had joined the war. World War I had begun. As with almost all wars, there were several causes for World War I. These included ethnic and ideological conflicts, nationalism, and political and economic rivalries.

## Ethnic Conflicts

An **ethnic group** is a group of people that shares a common and distinctive culture. Usually, they also share the same language and religion. Ethnic conflicts are often the cause of wars, as each side of the conflict has allies and enemies that also become involved. This is what happened prior to World War I.

A major ethnic conflict existed in what was called the **Austro-Hungarian Empire**. This large empire consisted of many ethnic groups, but only the Austrians and the Hungarians had the right to vote. Other ethnic groups in the empire had their own form of nationalism and bitterly resented their loss of political freedom.

## Ideological Conflicts

An **ideology** is a system of ideas that guides individuals, social movements, or groups of people. The ideology of **weltpolitik** in Europe in the early 20th century led to many problems in the world and became another cause of World War I. This German word means "world politics." The Germans believed they deserved to be equal partners with other leading world powers such as Great Britain.

Initially, Germany formed a series of peaceful alliances with other powers. Then, starting in the late 19th century, German leaders became more aggressive and wanted to build up their influence throughout the world. Germany had conflicts with all the other major European powers except Austria-Hungary.

## Nationalism

Nationalism is devotion and loyalty to one's own ethnic background or country of origin. In the 19th century, many nationalist movements led to a widespread struggle for independence. This was especially true in the Balkans. Serbia was at the center of the nationalist movements in the Balkans. Austria-Hungary was considered an enemy of Serbia because of the desire of the Serbs in Austria-Hungary to unite with Serbia and create a larger Serbian state.

# Political and Economic Rivalries

Russia was the largest European country and had the most people. This country wanted to expand in all directions, especially to the south, into the Balkans. Great Britain considered this a threat. The Balkans bordered the Mediterranean Sea and Great Britain wanted to remain the leading naval power there. If Russia controlled the Balkans, then Great Britain's trade and economic interests would be threatened.

Other than the concern in the Balkans, Great Britain did not want to be involved in Europe's problems. It was most concerned with controlling its empire—from Canada, to Australia, to India—and trade. It did this through its navy, which was the largest in the world.

Germany's growing navy began to threaten Great Britain. France was also threatened by Germany. France wanted to reclaim two provinces that had been lost to Germany. France made important alliances with Great Britain and other countries in order to prevent another defeat by Germany. Like other world powers, France had overseas colonies. However, these colonies put them into conflict with other world powers that were also trying to build colonial empires, such as Italy. Italy wanted an area that was under the control of the Austro-Hungarian Empire, even though most of the people in the area were Italians. Germany and Austria-Hungary allied and Italy eventually sided with Great Britain and France against them.

Balkan Peninsula, 1914

# Georgia's Contributions during World War I

Initially, Georgians were less than enthusiastic about the prospect of America entering World War I. Even before America had declared war on Germany and its allies, the Georgian economy had begun to suffer. Shipments of cotton, timber, and tobacco were unable to reach the European market. However, Georgia's attitude quickly changed when America declared war on April 6, 1917. Thereafter, Georgia played a crucial and patriotic role in America's war effort. During the war, over 100,000 Georgian men and women contributed to the Allied victory.

Georgia was a key state for the United States military. Before the war, Georgia already housed five large federal military installations. These bases became vital to the United State's war effort. By the end of the war, Georgia had more military training camps than any other state in the country. The largest of these camps was Camp Gordon. It was completed in 1917 and was located in Chamblee, Georgia. Camp Gordon became widely known for training a famous division of soldiers. This division, the **Eighty-second All-American Division**, was staffed mainly by native Georgians.

World War I was the first war that used airplanes as weapons. An air force flight school was housed in Georgia. Over 2,000 combat pilots were trained on Georgian soil. These pilots went on to fly missions in Europe. Additionally, Georgia housed a prisoner of war camp that eventually held over 4,000 prisoners.

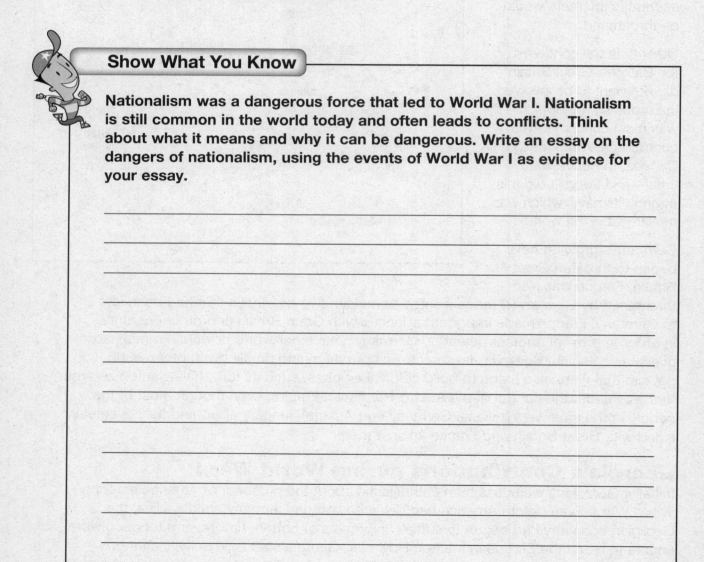

## Show What You Know

**Nationalism was a dangerous force that led to World War I. Nationalism is still common in the world today and often leads to conflicts. Think about what it means and why it can be dangerous. Write an essay on the dangers of nationalism, using the events of World War I as evidence for your essay.**

# Lesson Practice

## DIRECTIONS
**Circle the letter of the best answer for each item.**

### Thinking It Through

1. Which region of Europe sparked World War I?

   **A.** the Balkans

   **B.** England

   **C.** Spain

   **D.** the Alps

   *This region of Europe shares borders with the former Austria-Hungary and Russia.*

2. Which was a major contribution of Georgia during World War I?

   **A.** Several coast guard training bases were located there.

   **B.** Factories where airplanes were built were located there.

   **C.** Many army bases were located there.

   **D.** Georgians baked a record number of pies for the troops.

   **HINT** *The efforts of Georgia during World War I continue to impact the region today.*

3. Both Great Britain and Italy

   **A.** fought against each other in World War I.

   **B.** contributed money but not armies to World War I.

   **C.** wanted to merge to form one country.

   **D.** fought as allies in World War I.

4. Which of the following was a result of the assassination of Archduke Franz Ferdinand?

   **A.** His wife took his place in the government.

   **B.** His government collapsed.

   **C.** World War I began.

   **D.** World War I ended.

# 19 Drought and the Great Depression

SS8H8.a, b

## The Boll Weevil

Cotton has always been an important crop in Georgia. It is because of the cotton crops that agriculture thrived in Georgia in the 19th and early 20th century. However, the end of World War I brought the severe fall of cotton prices. The cotton industry suffered again in 1921. Nearly half of the cotton crop was destroyed by the boll weevil.

The boll weevil is a small beetle, which most likely came from Mexico. It spread to the southern United States and devastated the cotton crop in 1922. Adult boll weevils puncture cotton buds and lay eggs inside. The larvae hatch inside the bud and feed on the cotton bolls. Because the larvae stay inside the buds, insecticides cannot kill boll weevils.

## Drought

During World War I, farmers were encouraged to expand and produce as much as possible. In states such as Oklahoma and Texas, overworking of the soil combined with strong winds and low rainfall led to the creation of the Dust Bowl. In Georgia, drought was not a problem, but the increase in cotton production meant an overuse of the land. Eventually, the soil was exhausted and would not yield crops.

The boll weevil punctures cotton buds with its long snout.

A combination of exhausted soil from overuse, and the destruction by the boll weevil forced many farmers to leave their farms. Some of the poorer farmers even left the state completely. Even before the Great Depression, Georgian agriculture was suffering from a farm depression that would change farming in Georgia from then on.

## The Great Depression

In the United States, it is normal for the economy to go through highs and lows. When the economy is at a high point, it is called a peak. A low point in the economy is called a trough. When a trough is extreme, the economy is said to be in a **depression**. During times of depression, unemployment is high and people cannot afford many goods and services. Businesses suffer greatly or fail altogether.

The worst depression in the United States occurred in the 1930s. It was caused by a chain of events beginning after World War I. The countries involved in World War I faced several different trials and accomplishments. Great Britain had trouble providing employees with enough money for them to prosper. Germany had trouble paying the debt it owed to the winning nations for the damage the fighting caused. In the United States, many were very optimistic and the economy prospered.

The era preceding the depression is known as the Roaring Twenties. During this time, many people were not postponing purchases, but were buying things on credit instead. As businesses made large profits, average consumers actually plunged into debt. Consumers were confident in national businesses, which led to investment in these companies. This consumer support helped the economy to grow quickly. Unfortunately, such swift growth is not always a good thing. In this case, it led to a stock market crash.

## The Stock Market Crash

Consumer confidence led to investment. People thought they could make a profit when the stock's value increased. Many people borrowed money in order to buy shares.

However, the value of the stocks dropped considerably on October 29, 1929, a day now known as Black Tuesday.

Many people tried to sell their stock at the same time when they thought the shares they owned would not increase in value. Soon, banks could not collect on loans because the people had no money to pay them back. The banks ran out of money and many lost their savings from their accounts. This meant they could no longer make payments on their possessions bought by credit.

A shantytown, also called a Hooverville, in Seattle, Washington, during the Great Depression

Many Americans were forced to sell all of their possessions in order to pay for necessities like food, clothing, and heat. Many had to sell their homes and farms for their best offer. Soon, businesses were suffering because people could no longer afford luxury goods, and unemployment increased. The businesses that did survive had to cut their production drastically because there were so few left who could afford to buy anything but the essentials. This period of over ten years in which the economy was slow, unemployment was high, and everyone suffered is known as the **Great Depression**.

## Show What You Know

There were several factors which led to the Great Depression. Choose one of the following factors and explain how it contributed to an economic depression in the 1930s. Could this factor alone cause a depression? Why or why not?

- Drought and overuse of farmland
- Consumer overconfidence
- Reliance on credit

_____

_____

_____

_____

_____

_____

_____

_____

_____

_____

_____

_____

_____

_____

_____

_____

_____

_____

_____

_____

# Lesson Practice

## Thinking It Through

1. Which of the following illustrates the farming trends in Georgia after World War I?

   A. farming alternate fields each year in order to keep the land fertile

   B. overworking the land in order to keep up with demand

   C. using lots of pesticides in order to rid the crops of insects

   D. introducing machinery to replace workers

*The Dust Bowl happened as a result of planting the same crop in a field year after year. This farming practice leads to the eventual destruction of the soil.*

2. Which of the following is not a result of the stock market crash in 1929?

   A. People were forced to sell their homes.

   B. Banks ran out of money.

   C. Savings accounts were emptied.

   D. Businesses increased production.

   **HINT** *The stock market crash of 1929 led to a widespread economic downturn.*

3. An extreme low point in the economy is known as

   A. a peak.

   B. a trough.

   C. a depression.

   D. inflation.

*Use the numbered list of events in the box below to answer question 4.*

---

1. Black Tuesday
2. drought
3. sharp economic growth
4. World War I

---

4. Which of the following lists the correct order of events leading up to the Great Depression?

   A. 3, 1, 4, 2

   B. 4, 2, 1, 3

   C. 3, 4, 2, 1

   D. 4, 3, 1, 2

# Lesson

# 20 Eugene Talmadge

 **SS8H8.c**

*Eugene Talmadge* was one of Georgia's most charismatic and controversial politicians. He lived from 1884 to 1946 and spent 20 of those years in service to the government of Georgia. Because of his personality and actions, many voters in the state were divided into Talmadge and anti-Talmadge groups. Some saw him as a political hero. Others viewed him as a racist bully.

## Early Career

Talmadge began his career as commissioner of agriculture. He supported an economic policy that benefited farmers. He was very popular with farmers and people in rural areas. Conflicts about government money caused Talmadge trouble during his time as commissioner. He was accused of plotting to illegally raise the price of hogs. He was also accused of using government money to take his family to the Kentucky Derby. The Georgia legislature talked of impeaching him. Others threatened to sue him for misspending funds. In the end, none of the charges against him were pursued. He was elected to three terms as commissioner of agriculture before being elected governor in 1932.

## The Governor

During Talmadge's first two terms, he proved to be a strong governor. To fulfill his campaign promise to lower the price of automobile registration tags, he invoked an executive order. An **executive order** is an act by a governor or president that does not have to be approved by the legislature. The state legislature had voted not to lower the tag's price. Talmadge overruled their decision with his executive order. When the Public Service Commission refused to lower the price of utilities, Talmadge fired them, although they were elected by the public. He then appointed new people to the commission who would lower prices.

Governor Eugene Talmadge of Georgia (left) listens as Assistant Solicitor Dan Duke of Fulton Superior Court waves a heavy leather lash to emphasize his opposition to mercy for six convicted KKK members of East Point, Georgia. The governor took the pleas under advisement.

A similar conflict took place between the governor and the highway board. When the highway board resisted Talmadge's efforts, he once again fired and replaced the members of that board. Once, he even had the state treasurer and comptroller general physically removed from their offices in the state capitol.

Talmadge was an outspoken critic of President *Franklin D. Roosevelt*. He especially did not agree with Roosevelt's New Deal programs. Talmadge did what he could to keep New Deal programs out of Georgia.

## The Third Term

Because the law would not let him run for governor three times in a row, Talmadge ran for United States Senate in 1936. He lost to the incumbent, the senator who had already been serving as one of Georgia's senators. Two years later, he ran against Georgia's other U.S. senator and lost that race as well.

Talmadge was eligible to run for governor again in 1940. He won and began his third term as governor of Georgia. This era of Talmadge's governorship is probably best remembered for what is called the **Cocking Affair**.

*Walter Cocking* was the dean of the College of Education at the University of Georgia. He was hired into that position to improve academic standards, a goal which he accomplished. In May of 1941, Talmadge met with the Board of Regents, the committee that runs the university. Talmadge accused Cocking of supporting racial integration. Talmadge and other members of the board were firmly opposed to integration and they voted not to rehire Cocking.

The president of the university heard about the Board of Regents' decision and threatened to quit unless Cocking was given a chance to defend himself and save his job. Many other college professors came out in support of Cocking. At a June meeting of the Regents, Cocking was reappointed as the dean of the College of Education.

Talmage was furious and began to attack Cocking in the newspapers, for his background and political beliefs. Once again, Talmage replaced members of a committee with people who agreed with his point of view, this time it was the Board of Regents. When another vote was taken at a July meeting of the Regents, Cocking was again voted out of his job.

This began a chain of events that seriously damaged the state's university system. Over the next year, ten excellent educators were fired, the libraries suffered, the Board of Regents became less powerful, and academics began to have a low opinion of Georgia's universities.

An investigation by the Southern Association of Colleges and Schools declared that "gross political interference" had damaged the state's colleges. As a result, they removed accreditation, or official approval, from the public universities for white people. This disaster caused Talmadge to lose the next gubernatorial election.

In 1946, however, he was elected governor for a fourth term. His victory was largely due to his opposition to the Supreme Court decision to allow black people to vote in primary elections. He died before taking office, but his son went on to serve in Georgia's government for many years. However, his career ended when the Senate denounced him for pocketing money from his supporters.

## Show What You Know

**In Georgia, there is a bridge named after Eugene Talmadge and also a statue of him at the state capitol. Do you think Talmadge is worthy of these honors? Why is Talmadge's career important to the history of Georgia? Write your ideas in a paragraph.**

_____

_____

_____

_____

_____

_____

_____

_____

_____

_____

_____

_____

_____

_____

_____

_____

_____

_____

# Lesson Practice

## DIRECTIONS
Circle the letter of the best answer for each item.

### Thinking It Through

1. Eugene Talmadge often got things done by overruling the state legislature. This is known as invoking

   *The U.S. president and most governors have the right to make a new law by using this privilege.*

   A. the Board of Regents.

   B. impeachment.

   C. the New Deal.

   D. an executive order.

2. What was the event that marked Talmadge's third term as governor and most likely caused him to lose the next election?

   A. the Board of Regents

   B. impeachment

   C. the New Deal

   D. the Cocking Affair

   **HINT** *Talmadge used his power and even went beyond the powers allowed to him to achieve his goals.*

3. Before becoming governor, Talmadge served three terms as

   A. a Georgia representative.

   B. a member of the Board of Regents.

   C. the commissioner of agriculture.

   D. a United States senator.

4. Why was Talmadge unable to serve his fourth term as governor?

   A. The law prohibited it.

   B. He became a senator.

   C. He died before taking office.

   D. He had been impeached.

# 21 The New Deal

 SS8H8.d

*Herbert Hoover* was president at the beginning of the Great Depression. Many criticized Hoover for the way he managed things. People thought he depended too much on the individual states. These states were too poor to create any new programs to ease the burden of its people. During the Depression, people started to believe that the only way the economy would prosper again was if the government stepped in to help the states. When President *Franklin Delano Roosevelt* took office in 1933, he set up a national plan called the **New Deal**.

When Roosevelt took office, American agriculture was suffering. Unemployment was high as well. The New Deal was an attempt at fixing the economy. Roosevelt hoped that by creating jobs and national relief programs, the economy would grow.

## The Agricultural Adjustment Administration (AAA)

Within his first 100 days in office, Roosevelt created the Agricultural Adjustment Act. The purpose of the act was to raise the price of staple crops by limiting supply. In Georgia, farmers were paid to plant less cotton in order to drive the price up. The act also formed the Agricultural Adjustment Administration (AAA). This administration had many goals. They hoped to raise the prices of farms and vary the crops farmers grew. They also wanted to protect the soil that farmers had overworked.

## The Rural Electrification Administration (REA)

Before 1935, very few rural areas in Georgia and all over the country had electricity. Many people lived next to power lines. However, private electric companies would not offer service to them. Roosevelt created the Rural Electrification Administration (REA) in 1935. The Rural Electrification Act was signed in 1936. It created an agency that provided loans to states. The loans were meant to improve electric service to rural areas. The money was used to build power plants and power lines. This changed the power companies' control over service. Within four years, Georgia was leading the country in the number of Rural Electrification Administration groups.

## The Civilian Conservation Corps (CCC)

The Civilian Conservation Corps (CCC) was a New Deal relief program that created jobs for thousands of young men. Many of these men were war veterans who were suffering from job loss and poverty. In exchange for work, the men received housing, food, and money. Soil conservation, reforestation, fire prevention, and park building were just some of the jobs they did. The government even provided educational classes of all levels and training for the workers. Their labor helped to build many of Georgia's parks. For example, the CCC workers built many structures in the Indian Springs State Park during the Depression.

# Works Progress Administration (WPA)

The Works Progress Administration (WPA) was a very important agency of the New Deal. Created in 1935, it provided jobs for people. It was the largest work relief program in U.S. history. The program temporarily employed both men and women with jobs in construction and education. With the WPA's creation, Roosevelt hoped to repair the spirit of the people.

One example of WPA projects is the Georgian library system. Over one hundred libraries received assistance from the WPA from 1936 to 1943. The program provided pay for workers and technical services to libraries in Georgia.

# The Social Security Act

In 1935, the Social Security Act was passed by Congress. People wanted a permanent plan to protect them from losing their wages. This act was a response to that wish. This act provided two social insurance programs. The first was a

The WPA provided many jobs.

system of old-age benefits for retiring workers, which would support them monetarily when they could no longer work. This system was run by the federal government. The federal and state governments ran the second system together. This system offered insurance for the unemployed and disabled. This act helped provide workers with a sense of security in their jobs. With both measures in place, the government hoped that the severe poverty could be remedied and prevented in the future.

# Labor and the New Deal

A new way of looking at labor came about with the New Deal programs. The idea of employee payment being "time paid for time worked" was over. Unions had greater power now and began asking for benefits beyond better wages and working conditions. Unions started demanding better welfare packages. The New Deal gave those who suffered the most during the Depression security and power.

## Show What You Know

Imagine you are a business owner during the Great Depression. Why might you have a problem with the New Deal? Do the programs help or hurt you? Be specific.

_____

_____

_____

_____

_____

_____

_____

_____

_____

_____

_____

_____

_____

_____

_____

_____

_____

_____

_____

_____

_____

# Lesson Practice

Circle the letter of the best answer for each item.

## Thinking It Through

**1.** Which of the following New Deal Programs helped raise the price of cotton in Georgia?

  **A.** the Social Security Act

  **B.** the Civilian Conservation Corps

  **C.** the Agricultural Adjustment Administration

  **D.** the Rural Electrification Administration

*Social Security created an economic safety net for seniors and the disabled. The CCC built new infrastructure in regions that needed it. Many rural regions of the country did not yet have electricity in the 1930s, but received it through a New Deal program.*

**2.** All of the following are true about the Rural Electrification Act EXCEPT

  **A.** it provided money for alternative fuel research.

  **B.** it took the power away from privately owned electric companies.

  **C.** it provided loans to states.

  **D.** it helped build power plants.

**HINT** *The Rural Electrification Act was only trying to help rural areas receive electricity.*

**3.** Why was the Works Progress Administration so important?

  **A.** It gave farmers a chance to grow different crops.

  **B.** It was the first time money was ensured for retired workers.

  **C.** It gave people a chance to start their own businesses.

  **D.** It was the largest emergency work relief program in U.S. history.

**4.** During the Great Depression, President Herbert Hoover was criticized for

  **A.** putting too much responsibility on individual state governments.

  **B.** giving too much money to federally funded programs.

  **C.** creating unemployment insurance.

  **D.** investing in banks.

**CRCT Review**

**Choose the best answer for each question. Fill in the circle in the spaces provided on your answer sheet.**

1. Which African American leader called for the expectation that civil rights will come only gradually to African Americans?

   A. Booker T. Washington

   B. W. E. B. Du Bois

   C. John Burns Hope

   D. Alonzo Herndon

2. The term "race riot" describes

   A. a series of several running contests used to decide elections in early Georgia.

   B. a type of African American dance common in the late 19th century.

   C. a series of physical confrontations between two or more groups of different races.

   D. a march by the KKK through the center of town.

3. Which Georgian is described by the phrases in the box below?

   - elected governor four times
   - ran for U.S. Senate twice
   - often used executive orders

   A. W. E. B. Du Bois

   B. Eugene Talmadge

   C. Rebecca Latimer Felton

   D. Jimmy Carter

4. Which statement BEST explains the effect of the boll weevil on Georgia's economy?

   A. It is beneficial to the soil.

   B. It kills weeds but helps peaches.

   C. It cannot be killed by pesticide.

   D. It is uniquely able to destroy cotton crops.

5. Which of the following made the Great Depression worse?

   A. World War II

   B. drought and over farming

   C. colonization

   D. racism

6. World War I created the growth of a new type of institution in Georgia. What type of institution created this growth?

   A. steel mills

   B. peach orchards

   C. computer manufacturing

   D. army bases

7. Which statement BEST explains the impact of the New Deal on Georgia?

   A. The Indian Removal Act caused thousands of Native Americans to move out of the region.

   B. The Rural Electricity Act caused many rural regions to receive electricity for the first time.

   C. The fourth governorship of Eugene Talmadge was a period of enlightenment for the region.

   D. King George III released Georgia from its obligations to the crown.

8. The term "Jim Crow law" describes

   A. racist public policy common in the South after Reconstruction.

   B. the special favors given to members of the Crow family throughout Georgia.

   C. executive orders issued by Governor Jim Crow over a series of years.

   D. the decision to commemorate World War I veterans of Georgia.

9. Which Georgian and his description are matched correctly?

A. Eugene Talmadge—one-term governor

B. W. E. B. Du Bois—civil rights leader

C. Lyman Hall—signer of the Georgia Constitution

D. Booker T. Washington—radical socialist

10. The Republican Party was formed as an anti-slavery party just before the Civil War. In the South, the Democrats remained popular. The Bourbon Democrats were conservative democrats who were led by the Bourbon Triumvirate, which was

A. a coalition of three bourbon-producing states.

B. three leading Democrats.

C. a plan for the Confederacy to overtake the Union.

D. a plan to bring back slavery in only three states.

11. Which person ran twice for U.S. senator, but lost?

A. W. E. B. Du Bois

B. Booker T. Washington

C. Eugene Talmadge

D. Zell Miller

12. Which of the following was a characteristic of the agricultural disaster of the 1930s?

A. overplanting

B. too much rain

C. severely cold winters

D. long heat waves

CHAPTER

**World War II and the Struggle for Rights**

#  World War II

SS8H9.a, b, c, d

World War II resulted from the growth and combination of two regional conflicts on opposite sides of the globe, in Europe and East Asia. During the 1930s, both Germany and Japan sought to expand their borders. To expand, they had to conquer other countries. With each neighboring country they invaded and occupied, the area of conflict expanded. Eventually, all industrialized countries became involved in one of the regions of conflict. Either they defended their own borders, or acted in defense of an **ally**. World War II lasted from 1939 to 1945. Eventually, the two sides of the war were the **Allied powers** (Britain, France, and later, the Soviet Union and the United States) and the **Axis powers** (Germany, Italy, and Japan).

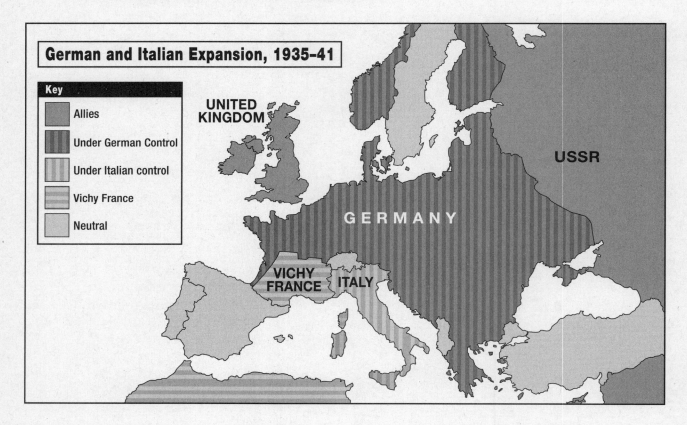

## Germany's Third Reich

*Adolf Hitler* brought the National Socialist German Workers' Party (the Nazi Party) to power in 1933. He immediately began to build up the army. In 1936, Germany formed alliances with Japan and Italy. Each country wanted more resources.

They felt the other major powers—France, Great Britain, and the United States—had more than their share. In 1938, Germany took over Austria to create what Hitler called "Greater Germany." Next, Germany took over Czechoslovakia. Hitler then eyed Poland to become the next part of the German empire that he called the **Third Reich**. At this point, both France and Great Britain declared that they would defend Poland's independence.

Hitler realized that neither France nor Great Britain could move their troops quickly enough to Poland in order to stop Germany's invasion. The British let Germany know that if it did not stop its attack on Poland, that it would declare war. When Germany disregarded Great Britain's warning, the British declared war. In September 1939, World War II started as one country after another was brought into the war either as an ally or defeated nation.

In less than a year, Germany had conquered almost all of Europe. Denmark, Norway, the Netherlands, Belgium, and France were all defeated. The German armies overrunning one country after another did so in a **blitzkrieg**, a German word meaning "lightning war." The Germans had fast moving tanks and other motorized equipment that made it possible for them to complete their blitzkrieg attack on the European continent.

## The Holocaust

During this time, news of Hitler's policies against the Jews reached the states. Even before Hitler came to power in 1933, he wrote about his hatred for the Jewish religion in his book, *Mein Kampf*. When Hitler came to power, he began to systematically discriminate against German Jews. At first, Jewish businesses were boycotted and Jews were fired from civil service jobs. Jewish children were forbidden in German schools. Thousands of Nazi students and professors burned all non-German and anti-Nazi books in over 30 libraries. The **Holocaust** was Nazi Germany's systematic killing of Jews, Gypsies, communists, intellectuals, and political dissenters.

On the evening of November 9, 1938, anti-Jewish rioters began looting, burning, and destroying Jewish synagogues, businesses, and homes. The rioters broke the windows of over 7,500 Jewish businesses. This event was called Kristallnacht, or "Night of Broken Glass." Nazi police arrested over 30,000 Jewish men and sent them to concentration camps. Concentration camps were Nazi prison camps. This marked the beginning of millions of Jewish men, women, and children being sent to concentration camps throughout the course of World War II. Hitler's ultimate goal, the Final Solution, was to eliminate all Jewish and minority groups in Germany.

At the same time they learned of the atrocities in Europe, Jewish communities in the U.S. faced increased discrimination at home. Though the U.S. was not officially engaged in the war, local communities organized support efforts. Atlanta's Jewish social service agencies raised funds to combat discrimination abroad. Their successful fundraising continued throughout the war. The Holocaust ended in 1945, when the Allied powers won the war and freed the people held captive in the camps.

## Japan Builds an Empire in the East

Japan invaded China in 1937, for the second time during that decade. Japan's plan was to capture as much of China as it could, and control the resources of Southeast Asia. When Germany defeated France, Japan was successful in gaining control of the French colonies in Southeast Asia. The United States opposed Japan's aggression. It threatened to cut off Japan's oil supplies.

## U.S. Involvement

Throughout the 1930s, the United States maintained that Europe's problems were its own, and not those of the United States. It followed a policy of **isolationism** in which it kept itself politically and militarily apart from the rest of the world. One reason for this approach was that the United States was still recovering from the Great Depression.

President *Franklin D. Roosevelt*, however, was concerned with the effect that the fighting in Europe and Asia could have on the United States if it continued to grow. In 1940, he announced that the United States would become the "great arsenal of democracy." He meant that the U.S. would sell weapons to its allies—Great Britain and France. This arrangement benefited the United States. It created new jobs for unemployed U.S. workers. Many of these jobs would directly benefit the people of Georgia.

As the war grew, the U.S.'s European allies soon found it hard to pay for the weapons they needed. Roosevelt encouraged the U.S. to continue supplying weapons to allies without charging them. He compared this to giving a garden hose to a neighbor whose house was on fire, to keep the fire from spreading to your house. In 1941, Congress passed the Lend-Lease Act. The act gave Roosevelt the right to send weapons to allies who were fighting a common enemy, but could not pay.

Diplomacy between Japan and the United States was failing. Japan believed that if it could cripple the United States naval fleet, it could then continue its efforts at controlling Southeast Asia. Japan attacked the U.S. Pearl Harbor naval base in Hawaii, on December 7, 1941. Japan also attacked the Philippine Islands, where the United States maintained a major air force facility.

The U.S. waged war after the Pearl Harbor bombing.

What the Japanese did not count on was that instead of a limited war, the United States waged a full out, total war once it had recovered from the sudden bombing of Pearl Harbor.

The attack on Pearl Harbor led to the U.S. entrance into World War II. The U.S. dropped atomic bombs on two Japanese cities in August 1945. Furthermore, the Soviets declared war against Japan in that same month. These events motivated Japan to end the war. Japan surrendered and the Allies won the war.

## Georgia During the War

Before World War II, Georgia was mostly a rural state. Most people worked on farms and were having a difficult time recovering from the Depression. U.S. involvement in the war brought economic opportunities to Georgia. In turn, Georgia played a significant role in the war effort. Three men in particular shaped Georgia's experience during the war—Carl Vinson, Richard B. Russel, Jr., and President Franklin D. Roosevelt.

## Carl Vinson

Congressman *Carl Vinson* helped to build the U.S. navy in the years leading up to World War II. From 1934 until the war began in 1941, Representative Vinson wrote many bills that expanded the U.S. Navy. This expansion enabled the U.S. to ship supplies to Allies during the Lend-Lease Act, to overcome the attack of Pearl Harbor, and to eventually send troops into battle.

Hundreds of ships built during this expansion were built in the shipyards of Savannah and Brunswick, Georgia. The importance of these ports as economic and military centers continues today. In gratitude for his contributions to the navy, Vinson's peers called him "Admiral."

## Richard B. Russel, Jr.

Senator *Richard Russel* served on the Senate Naval Affairs Committee. He worked to bring wartime opportunities to Georgia. He helped to bring over a dozen military bases to Georgia, including the largest infantry base in the United States. Over 300,000 Georgians would serve during the war, but troops from all over the country trained in Georgian camps. Every major city in Georgia had a military base, bringing jobs and resources to the state.

Senator Russel traveled to both Europe and the Pacific region during the war, and became an expert in military strategy.

## Franklin D. Roosevelt

By the time World War II began, President Roosevelt had a close relationship with Georgia. Since the 1920s, he had visited Warm Springs regularly in hopes of curing his polio. He had spent a lot of time campaigning in the state and had many friends there. His close relationship with the state led to the building of the Bell Aircraft plant in Marietta. The plant produced military planes and created jobs for over 28,000 Georgians. Once the war ended, plant employees used their skills to find other industrial jobs instead of returning to the farm. Many attribute the growth of Georgia's industry in the 20th century to the funds and resources brought into the state during this time.

Roosevelt continued to visit Warm Springs throughout the war. He died there in 1945, while he was still president.

## Show What You Know

**Write an essay explaining how Georgia recovered from the Great Depression during World War II.**

_____

_____

_____

_____

_____

_____

_____

_____

_____

_____

_____

_____

_____

_____

_____

_____

_____

_____

_____

_____

_____

_____

# Lesson Practice

## DIRECTIONS
**Circle the letter of the best answer for each item.**

### Thinking It Through

1.  Which statement BEST explains Georgia's military importance during World War II?

    **A.** Its economy was historically agricultural.

    **B.** Many factories that built war technology were built there.

    **C.** It had several natural ports.

    **D.** It had a large Jewish population.

    *Georgia's economy was agricultural but this fact did not make it important during World War II. The same is true of its natural ports. Georgia has never been home to a large population of Jewish people.*

2.  In 1941, the Lend-Lease Act was created to

    **A.** create jobs for the sluggish economy.

    **B.** improve U.S. relations with Japan.

    **C.** protect the U.S. by arming Allies that could not afford weapons.

    **D.** end U.S. isolationism.

    **HINT** *The U.S. wanted to lend or lease weapons instead of selling them.*

3.  What is one significant result of Carl Vinson's work?

    **A.** The U.S. naval base Pearl Harbor was bombed by the Japanese.

    **B.** President Roosevelt was re-elected.

    **C.** Vinson was appointed admiral of the navy.

    **D.** The U.S. Navy increased its strength and size.

4.  What was U.S. isolationism?

    **A.** a policy by which the U.S. kept its affairs separate from other countries

    **B.** a system in which certain populations were kept apart

    **C.** a period of U.S. foreign policy that continues today

    **D.** a policy that called for U.S. entry into World War II

# 23 Post–World War II Developments

SS8H10.a, b, c

Georgia remained a farming state until after World War II, which ended in 1945. The number of people living in the country remained about the same from 1920 to 1960. In 1920, there were 2.1 million people living in rural areas. In 1960, there were 1.98 million living in rural areas. By 1990, however, the percentage of the population living in the country would drop to only a quarter of those in Georgia. Georgia's cities had begun to grow. Today, less than 2% of Georgians are involved with farms—either living on them or working on them. Most Georgia farms sell less than $10,000 in products a year.

## William B. Hartsfield

*William B. Hartsfield* (1890–1971) served as mayor of Atlanta for longer than any other mayor in the city's history—six terms, from 1937 to 1961. During his tenure, Atlanta's population multiplied by ten times—from 100,000 to 1 million. Another important change was the laws governing people of color. Hartsfield promoted the idea of Atlanta as "A City Too Busy to Hate."

Hartsfield's political career began at the age of 32, when he was elected to the Atlanta City Council. There, he worked to build Atlanta's aviation industry. At the time that he began this campaign—in the 1920s—people did not yet fly on airplanes for travel as they do today. In 1928, he was named Atlanta's "father of aviation" by the Atlanta Chamber of Commerce.

A Delta jet flies past the control tower at Hartsfield International Airport in Atlanta, Georgia.

In 1924, Hartsfield ran for the Georgia House of Representatives, but lost. He ran again in 1932 and was elected to represent Fulton County. In 1936, Hartsfield was elected as Atlanta's mayor. The Great Depression had hurt Atlanta's economy a great deal by that time. He secured donations from Coca-Cola for the city's funding. Hartsfield's strict budgeting helped the city recover from the Great Depression by 1938.

Hartsfield was defeated as mayor in 1940. However, when the U.S. joined World War II in 1941, the sitting mayor joined the military. A special election was held in 1942 and Hartsfield won again. He was elected in four more elections.

In 1952, Atlanta tripled its size from 37 to 128 square miles, adding 100,000 people to its population. Hartsfield presided over the construction of expressways and parks throughout the city.

In 1961, Hartsfield chose not to run for office again, and was named mayor emeritus of the city. He died in 1971, and the Atlanta airport was renamed in his honor.

## Ivan Allen, Jr.

*Ivan Allen, Jr.* (1911–2003) served in World War II. Then, he worked for the governor and then in his father's business. When Hartsfield left office, he won the following election and served as mayor from 1962 to 1970. Many people thought Allen kept the city calm during the civil rights movement.

As mayor, Allen was politically liberal. When he took office, it was still common to see signs on public facilities, like water fountains, saying "White Only." Allen's first act as mayor was to order these signs removed from City Hall. Before he took office, black police officers could not arrest white people and there were no black firefighters. Allen ended these rules.

Allen worked with civil rights leaders such as *Martin Luther King, Jr.* He was the only politician from the South to speak in favor of the Civil Rights Act in the U.S. Congress. By 1964, Allen was able to bring desegregation to all public facilities in Atlanta.

Unfortunately, Allen was also mayor during the construction of a concrete wall intended to keep black people away from a white area. This incident was called the Peyton Road Affair. The wall was later found to be unconstitutional and was torn down.

Allen worked to bring the Atlanta Braves to the city. He worked to build the Atlanta Stadium for a team and then convinced the team to move from Milwaukee, Wisconsin. He also helped to bring major league football and basketball teams to the city in the late 1960s.

## Atlanta Braves

When the Braves moved to Atlanta, they were the first professional sports team to be located in the South. In 1966, the baseball team played its first season. In 1969, they won the Western Division of the National League. Throughout the 1970s, however, the Braves continued to be one of the worst professional teams. One player, however, *Hank Aaron*, set the 1974 record for the most home runs, in front of a television audience of millions.

In 1976, entrepreneur and billionaire *Ted Turner* bought the Braves. Turner owned a cable network and he wanted to play the team's games on his channel. This was the beginning of the well known cable television station, TBS. The station televised Braves games throughout the country.

Through the 1980s, the Braves continued to play poorly. In 1991, the team hired new players. The season ended with the team winning the Western Division title. Through the early 1990s, the numbers of fans attending games rocketed to 3 million. Finally, in 1995, the Braves won the World Series. It was the first time a major league team in Georgia had won a national title. The Braves made it to the World Series two more times, in 1996 and 1999. Both times, however, they lost to the New York Yankees.

## Atlanta Falcons

In 1965, the Atlanta Falcons football team joined the National Football League. *Rankin M. Smith* of the Life Insurance Company of Georgia purchased the team for $8.5 million.

Like the Braves, the Falcons played their first game in 1966, at Atlanta Stadium. Through the mid-1970s, the Falcons were not a particularly strong team. Beginning in 1977, the team began to improve. They reached the play-offs three times, but continued to play losing seasons through 1997.

In 1998, they played in the Super Bowl for the first time, but lost. Since 1998, the team has continued to struggle for wins. Today, *Arthur Blank* and *Rich McKay* of The Home Depot own the Falcons.

## Atlanta Hawks

The Atlanta Hawks, a basketball team that plays in the National Basketball Association, moved to Atlanta in 1968. They play at the Philips Arena. The team moved to Atlanta from St. Louis, Missouri.

Georgia real estate developer *Thomas Cousins* and former Georgia Governor *Carl Sanders* purchased the team for Atlanta. The team went through several seasons of unsuccessful play, however. Then in 1977, Ted Turner purchased the team. In 1980, the team won the Central Division title. Although many players and coaches have strong records as individuals, the team has never won a major championship. The Hawks are currently owned by Atlanta Spirit, a company with nine owners that also controls the Philips Arena, where they play. The Hawks are currently coached by *Mike Woodson*, the team's tenth head coach since the Hawks moved to Atlanta in 1968.

## Atlanta Thrashers

The Atlanta Thrashers is a hockey team that plays in the National Hockey League. It came to Atlanta in 1999 when it was purchased by Ted Turner. Today, Atlanta Spirit owns the team. Atlanta Spirit bought the Hawks, the Thrashers, and the Philips Arena for $250 million. Although the Thrashers have yet to play a winning season, they are active in community service.

# Ellis Arnall

*Ellis Arnall* (1907–1992) served as governor of Georgia from 1943 to 1947. During his tenure, Arnall aggressively reformed Georgia government and paid off the state debt.

He was elected to represent Coweta County in the Georgia House of Representatives when he was just 25 years old. At only 31, he was appointed attorney general of the state, the youngest attorney general in the country at that time. In 1942, at the age of just 35, Arnall defeated *Eugene Talmadge* and became governor, also the youngest in the nation.

Arnall worked to bring progressive reform to the state. Georgia's universities had fallen out of accreditation, which Arnall worked to restore. He also reformed the state prisons, tax system, and constitution and lowered the state's voting age. Arnall also backed a liberal candidate who was unpopular in Georgia, in the 1944 presidential election.

In addition, Arnall's reforms allowed black voters to vote in the state's white-only primary elections. Court rulings had already held that such primaries were unconstitutional. Other states had avoided enforcing such rulings, but Arnall did not. The politically powerful Eugene Talmadge unseated Arnall in the next governor's race.

Governor Ellis Arnall, 1943

## Show What You Know

**What do Georgia's professional sports teams mean to you? Do you attend games with your family and friends? Write a short paragraph to explain why Georgia's sports teams are or are not important to you or your family.**

_____

_____

_____

_____

_____

_____

_____

_____

_____

_____

_____

_____

_____

_____

_____

_____

_____

_____

_____

_____

# Lesson Practice

**DIRECTIONS**
Circle the letter of the best answer for each item.

## Thinking It Through

1. Which statement BEST explains William B. Hartsfield's importance to aviation in Georgia?

   A. William Hartsfield enjoyed riding on planes.

   B. William Hartsfield was afraid to fly.

   C. William Hartsfield worked to make planes safer.

   D. William Hartsfield was the father of aviation in Georgia.

*The Atlanta airport is named to honor Hartsfield. He began promoting aviation in Georgia in the 1920s. He worked to build airports in the region.*

2. Which statement BEST explains Ellis Arnall's political point of view?

   A. He was a conservative.

   B. He was not a politician.

   C. He was a progressive reformer.

   D. He was the founder of the progressive movement.

   **HINT** *Ellis Arnall worked to change laws to benefit working class people.*

3. Which event brought the only national championship win in Georgia's professional sports?

   A. the World Series of 1995

   B. the Super Bowl of 1974

   C. the NBA Championships of 1998

   D. the Rose Bowl of 1983

4. Ted Turner has owned

   A. the Braves and the Falcons.

   B. the Falcons and the Hawks.

   C. the Braves and the Hawks.

   D. the Falcons and the Thrashers.

# Segregation

SS8H11.a

From its founding in 1733 until 1865, Georgia was dependent on slavery for the economic stability of the state. Change came slowly to the state. In the 1940s and 1950s, Georgia saw a great deal of social change. These changes set the stage for the modern civil rights movement.

## Slow Beginnings for the Civil Rights Movement

*Herman Talmadge* was governor of Georgia from 1948 to 1951. His father, *Eugene Talmadge* died shortly after winning his fourth campaign in 1946, but before being sworn in. The Georgia General Assembly then voted to make Herman Talmadge governor. In 1956, he was elected to the U.S. Senate. The people of Georgia re-elected him to the Senate three more times. He served in the Senate until 1980. As a senator, Talmadge also championed laws that aided rural regions.

In the 1940s, public schools were segregated by the color of people's skin—white students in one school, black students in another school. Like his father, Herman Talmadge resisted the desegregation of public schools. While governor, however, he started the first sales tax in the state. This money was used to improve the public school system. Nevertheless, Talmadge continued to fight desegregation and was a staunch critic of the 1954 Supreme Court decision ruling segregation unconstitutional.

The Reverend Dr. Benjamin E. Mays wrote four books, including *The Negro's God* and *Seeking to Be Christian in Race Relations.*

Reverend Dr. *Benjamin E. Mays* was a distinguished African American minister, educator, scholar, and social activist. He is best known as the president of Morehouse College in Atlanta. While president of Morehouse, he had great influence on events in the history of the United States. Many social activists went to Morehouse, but the most famous was Dr. *Martin Luther King, Jr.* Throughout his tenure at Morehouse, Mays emphasized two main ideas. The first was the inherent dignity of all human beings. The second was the differences between American ideals of democratic government compared to America's actual social practices. These ideas became central to the language used by Dr. King and the civil rights movement. In 1957, Mays published his ideas in the book, *Seeking to Be Christian in Race Relations.*

## Brown v. Board of Education

In the 1950s, many people in the U.S. were opposed to the desegregation of schools. The country was divided over the issue of how people of different skin colors should be treated in society. Several cases about school segregation came to the courts in the 1950s. In 1954, the U.S. Supreme Court ruled against the Board of Education of Topeka, Kansas in the case now known as *Brown v. Board of Education*. The court ruled that schools must be desegregated. The Supreme Court decided that segregation denied equal opportunity to all groups in the U.S. Even after the Supreme Court ruling, it took many years for segregation to end. However, *Brown v. Board of Education* helped launch the modern civil rights movement. This led to changes in the U.S. that eventually ended legalized segregation and discrimination.

## 1956 Georgia Flag

In 1955, Georgia's Democratic Party leader, *John Sammons Bell*, raised the issue of changing the state flag. Bell wanted the new flag to contain the Confederate battle flag's symbols of stars and bars. Without any resistance, the General Assembly of Georgia voted to change the Georgia state flag in 1956. Many people in the U.S. viewed this decision as a statement by Georgia's politicians against the Supreme Court's decision on *Brown v. Board of Education.* Georgia's political leaders did not support the Brown decision and believed that the state government should impose "massive resistance" to federally forced integration of schools. Georgia Representative *Denmark Groover* said that the new flag "will show that we in Georgia intend to uphold what we stood for, will stand for, and will fight for." The past that Groover refers to is the Civil War, when Georgia fought, among other causes, to continue legalized slavery.

## Dr. Martin Luther King, Jr.

Dr. Martin Luther King, Jr., was a principal leader of the U.S. civil rights movement. He was a clergyman and an advocate of nonviolent protest. He entered Morehouse College at the age of 15. There he earned a degree in sociology and graduated in 1946. King's time at Morehouse helped shape his political beliefs. He was a gifted speaker and leader. King went on to earn a Ph.D. in systematic theology from Boston University. By 1954, he was pastor of his own church in Montgomery, Alabama.

King was instrumental in the social and political advancement of African Americans. His career in the civil rights movement began in December 1955, after the arrest of Rosa Parks. *Rosa Parks* was an African American woman who refused to give up her seat on a bus. Police arrested Parks for violating a city segregation law. After the arrest, the African American community in Montgomery proposed boycotting the bus company. King allowed the use of his church as a meeting place to discuss the boycott. From then on, King committed himself to the civil rights movements at the cost of his family's safety and ultimately his life.

King led and participated in marches and protests calling for equal rights for all Americans. King believed that many of the problems African Americans faced resulted from economic inequalities in society. His last campaign was a dramatization of the problems of poverty in America. In April 1968, Dr. King was assassinated in Memphis, Tennessee. Today King's legacy is remembered and his birthday in January is a national holiday.

## Show What You Know

**Social problems still exist in the U.S. between people of different races and gender. Write a one-page essay on your experience with this complex problem.**

_____

_____

_____

_____

_____

_____

_____

_____

_____

_____

_____

_____

_____

_____

_____

_____

_____

_____

# Lesson Practice

## DIRECTIONS
Circle the letter of the best answer for each item.

### Thinking It Through

**1.** In 1956, the Georgia state flag was changed to include

   **A.** the Board of Regents.

   **B.** a skull and crossbones.

   **C.** three cornstalks.

   **D.** the Confederate battle flag.

*The change in the flag followed the* Brown v. Board of Education *decision. The decision mandated that school districts around the country find a way to desegregate schools. Lawmakers in Georgia did not support this decision.*

**2.** Who influenced and helped shape the ideas of Dr. Martin Luther King, Jr.?

   **A.** Herman Talmadge

   **B.** Benjamin Mays

   **C.** Abraham Lincoln

   **D.** Dr. W. E. B. Du Bois

**HINT** *Dr. Martin Luther King, Jr., attended Morehouse College.*

**3.** After serving as governor, Herman Talmadge served four terms as

   **A.** a United States senator.

   **B.** a member of the Board of Regents.

   **C.** the commissioner of agriculture.

   **D.** a federal judge.

**4.** What brought about change in the way children are educated in the U.S.?

   **A.** Georgia changing its flag in 1956

   **B.** Rosa Park's refusal to give up her seat

   **C.** *Brown v. Board of Education* decision

   **D.** Martin Luther King, Jr.'s bus boycott

# 25 The Civil Rights Movement

 SS8H11.b, c

Even though the U.S. Congress had passed laws that protected civil rights in 1964 and 1965, the struggle for civil rights continued well into the 1970s.

## The SNCC

The Student Nonviolent Coordinating Committee or SNCC (called "Snick"), was one of the main groups fighting for civil rights in the 1970s. The group formed during April 1960, when students at Shaw University in Raleigh, North Carolina, met with Ella Baker. *Ella Baker* was the executive secretary of the Southern Christian Leadership Conference (SCLC). SNCC encouraged young people to join the fight for civil rights by using nonviolence and direct action. SNCC also helped plan the 1963 March on Washington.

Standing, sitting, and marching in groups are forms of nonviolent protest. During a **sit-in**, protestors would occupy segregated restaurants and businesses and refuse to leave. **Freedom riders** protested by riding on segregated buses. Social protest was much more common during the 1960s and 1970s than it is today.

## Sibley Commission

The General Assembly Committee on Schools, known as the Sibley Commission, gathered information about how individuals felt about desegregation. The Sibley Commission formed in 1960 when Georgia's Governor *Ernest Vandiver* had to choose between closing schools and following a federal order to desegregate them. The report decreased resistance against the desegregation of schools. However, it also provided local school boards with methods to slow down the desegregation process. Not until the late 1960s did desegregation of schools begin in Georgia.

John Lewis, head of SNCC, and other members of the group stage a sit-in protest at the state capitol building in Jackson, Mississippi, in 1965.

## African Americans Enter University of Georgia

*Hamilton Holmes* and *Charlayne Hunter* were the first African American students to go to the University of Georgia. They started classes in 1961, marking the end of segregation at the university. Hunter's dormitory was the site of many riots against her attendance. In 2001, the building where Holmes and Hunter registered for school was renamed the Hunter-Holmes Academic Building.

## Albany Movement

The Albany movement began in 1961. The goal of the Albany movement was to desegregate the Albany, Georgia region. A group of SNCC volunteers joined efforts with a number of other civil rights groups working in the Albany community, including the Youth Council of the National Association for the Advancement of Colored People (NAACP), the Baptist Ministerial Alliance, the Federation of Women's Clubs, and the Negro Voters League.

SCLC leader Dr. Martin Luther King, Jr., was part of the Albany movement. Hundreds of black protestors, including King, were arrested during their work on the Albany Movement.

## March on Washington

The March on Washington for Jobs and Freedom took place on August 28, 1963. This was the event where Dr. Martin Luther King, Jr., gave his well-known **"I have a dream" speech.**

The 1963 march was the second March on Washington for Jobs and Freedom. The first was in 1941. The first march was planned by African Americans. The 1963 march was planned by a broader coalition. The organizers of the 1963 march wanted to bring attention to the following goals:

- Meaningful civil rights laws

- Massive federal works program

- Full and fair employment

- Decent housing, the right to vote

- Adequate integrated education

## Civil Rights Act

These goals came together in the passage of the Civil Rights Act of 1964. This act guaranteed equal voting rights, prohibited segregation in public places, banned segregation by trade unions, schools, and employers that were involved in interstate commerce or do business with the federal government, called for the desegregation of public schools, and assured nondiscrimination in the distribution of federal funds. In 1972, an amendment called the Equal Employment Opportunity Act was added to this law, to extend protection against discrimination to women in the workplace.

## Lester Maddox

*Lester Maddox* became governor of Georgia in 1967. Maddox was popular with many Georgians who supported segregation. Maddox had forcibly turned away black activists who challenged segregation at his restaurant. When he became governor, many Georgians were afraid that he would return widespread segregation to the state.

Maddox moderated his views, but his career as governor remained controversial. After the assassination of Dr. Martin Luther King, Jr., in 1968, he ordered a massive police presence at the funeral, which prevented some of the public from taking part. He also worked against the civil rights aims of the Democratic Party at the Democratic National Convention that same year.

## African Americans Take Office

*Maynard Jackson* was elected mayor of Atlanta in 1973. He was the first African American mayor of a major southern city. Jackson encouraged a number of **affirmative action** programs, which helped African Americans move into higher status jobs. The number of African Americans and other people of color in the city's work force increased. Jackson was mayor from 1974 to 1982 and was elected again in 1990.

*Andrew Young* was an aide to Dr. Martin Luther King, Jr. He was also the executive director of the SCLC. In 1972, Young won Georgia's Fifth District seat in the U.S. House of Representatives. He was the first African American from Georgia to be elected to Congress since the 1860s.

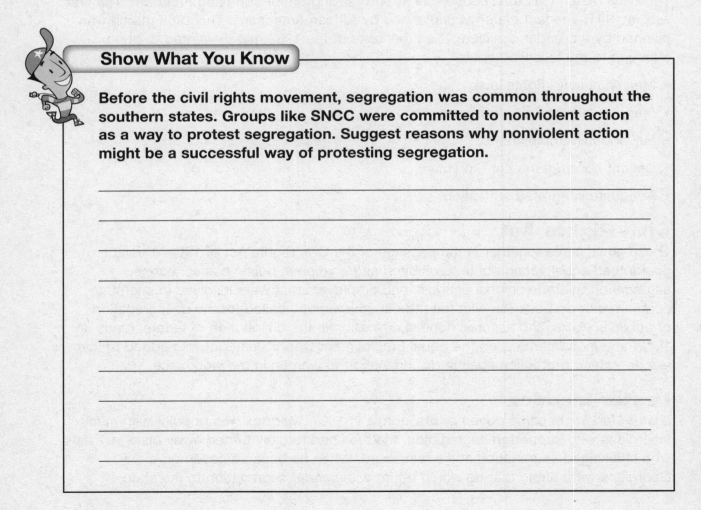

### Show What You Know

Before the civil rights movement, segregation was common throughout the southern states. Groups like SNCC were committed to nonviolent action as a way to protest segregation. Suggest reasons why nonviolent action might be a successful way of protesting segregation.

_____

_____

_____

_____

_____

_____

_____

_____

_____

_____

# Lesson Practice

## DIRECTIONS
**Circle the letter of the best answer for each item.**

### Thinking It Through

1. How did participants of the SNCC voice their opinions?

   A. by using nonviolent, direct actions

   B. by using force and violent means

   C. by writing their members of Congress

   D. by joining politics and making a difference

   *The SNCC subscribed to the same point of view as Dr. Martin Luther King, Jr. The group joined forces with the SCLC and NAACP for many protests and campaigns.*

2. Why was the Sibley Commission formed?

   A. to find out how people felt about taxes

   B. to tell people about the March on Washington

   C. to organize freedom rides

   D. to help determine how Georgians felt about desegregation

   **HINT** *The findings of the Sibley Commission helped in the desegregation of Georgia schools.*

3. Which of the following was a goal of the Albany movement?

   A. to bring new residents to Albany, Georgia

   B. to bring residents of Albany, Georgia, to the integrated cities of the northeast

   C. to end segregation in Albany, Georgia

   D. to end segregation in Albany, New York

4. Why was the Civil Rights Act of 1964 passed?

   A. to ensure segregation in schools and businesses

   B. to guarantee protection from segregation and discrimination

   C. to allow African Americans to move to Canada

   D. to prevent a third March on Washington by protesters

**Choose the best answer for each question. Fill in the circle of the spaces provided on your answer sheet.**

1. Which of the following teams won a major sports championship in 1995?

   A. Atlanta Braves

   B. Atlanta Thrashers

   C. Atlanta Hawks

   D. Atlanta Falcons

2. Which Georgian and his description are matched correctly?

   A. Maynard Jackson—led the Albany movement

   B. Lester Maddox—founded Morehouse College

   C. Franklin Roosevelt—voted in favor of *Brown v. Board of Education*

   D. Dr. Martin Luther King, Jr.—led the March on Washington

3. Why are Georgians less likely to own farm animals today than before World War II?

   A. Owning farm animals has become too expensive.

   B. There is a higher tax now on farm animals than before World War II.

   C. Most Georgians live in cities today.

   D. The population of rural communities in Georgia has continued to grow.

4. Since the Civil War, advances in which field have contributed MOST to the growth of Georgia's economy?

   A. consumer products

   B. manufacturing

   C. tourism

   D. agriculture

5. Which person was known as "Admiral"?

   A. Carl Vinson

   B. Martin Luther King, Jr.

   C. Richard Russell

   D. President Jimmy Carter

6. Which of the following characteristics was shared by Ellis Arnall's tenure as a representative, attorney general, and governor?

   A. He was impeached from each position.

   B. He resigned from each position.

   C. He was the oldest person ever to serve in each position.

   D. He was the youngest person ever to serve in each position.

7. In 1972, Andrew Young became the first African American from Georgia to be elected to the U.S. Congress in over 110 years. The most likely reason for his success was

   A. his work on behalf of farmers.

   B. his work on behalf of historic preservation districts.

   C. his work with Dr. Martin Luther King, Jr.

   D. his opposition to equality in civil rights.

8. Which of Georgia's attractions led President Franklin Roosevelt to spend so much time in the state?

   A. the barrier islands

   B. Warm Springs

   C. the state capitol

   D. Stone Mountain

9. Which program allowed European powers to have access to American weapons without purchasing them?

   A. Lend-Lease Act

   B. Lending Loan Program

   C. Free Weapons Act

   D. Weapon Leasing Act

10. Which Georgian and his description are matched correctly?

    A. Herman Talmadge—CEO of the Coca-Cola Company

    B. Benjamin Mays—industrial innovator

    C. Dr. Martin Luther King, Jr. —civil rights leader

    D. Ted Turner—Georgia governor

11. Today Georgia is home to many military bases and military technology factories. When did these industries come to the state?

    A. 1880s

    B. 1910s

    C. 1940s

    D. 1970s

12. Ellis Arnall worked to allow all Georgians over age 18 to vote in primary elections. Which statement BEST explains why this work was necessary?

    A. Women were not allowed to vote in Georgia primaries.

    B. Only those over age 25 were allowed to vote in Georgia primaries.

    C. Atlanta was the only city allowed to vote in Georgia primaries.

    D. Only white people were allowed to vote in Georgia primaries.

# CHAPTER 5

# Georgia in Recent History

# 26 County Unit System

SS8H12.a

The state of Georgia has had many important political, economic, and social developments since 1970. Many of these changes began at the end of the county unit system. The county unit system started as an informal election system in 1898. This informal system became legal in 1917, when the **Neill Primary Act** was passed. Before 1962, Georgia did not allow each individual to cast a vote. The winner of the **popular vote** in each county received the "unit" votes for that county. This system was found to be unconstitutional in 1962 and was ended by the Supreme Court.

The county unit system gave each county a given number of voting "units" based on the size of the population. **Urban** counties with large cities, received as many as eight voting units, town counties received up to four voting units and **rural** counties with mostly farms received at least two voting units each. This caused a problem because there were more rural areas than urban and town areas.

Thousands of African Americans turn out to the polls in Marietta, Georgia.

Therefore, smaller rural areas had more voting units per person than the large city areas. A candidate could easily win an election in the state of Georgia without winning the popular vote. Candidates often campaigned more in the rural counties to win the greatest number of county voting units. Even though the cities had a greater population, the cities did not have enough county voting units needed to win an election.

The county unit system helped to keep many **inequalities** in place in the state of Georgia. Many African Americans and whites who wanted to see change were living in the cities. Cities did not have as many county unit votes, so their vote did not count as much as the people who lived in rural, or country areas of the state. Districts were segregated to increase the voting power of white citizens. This protected segregation and slowed the progress of **civil rights** throughout the state.

Political change began in 1962. That year, *James O'Hear Sanders* sued *James Gray*, the head of the state Democratic Party. Sanders lived in Atlanta where there were fewer county unit votes per person. Gray lived in a rural area with more unit votes per person. Mr. Sanders said his vote was worth less than Mr. Gray's vote. Judge *Griffin Bell* decided that Mr. Sanders was right and declared that each person should have one vote. This became known as the one man, one vote rule. The governor called the state legislature together to reorganize the voting system within Georgia.

The next year, the United States Supreme Court said each person should have one vote and that vote should be counted. This is a right of each person because of the equal protection clause of the Fourteenth Amendment. The Supreme Court also ordered the reapportionment of the congressional districts in Georgia. **Reapportionment** means to reorganize. The **congressional districts** in Georgia had to be reapportioned so they would represent the people of Georgia in a better way.

Civil rights leaders fought to make sure that the boundaries of the voting districts made sure that all voters had an equal vote. Under this new system, a new political party began to grow. The new districts increased the number of legislators that represented the mostly African American areas in Fulton County and Atlanta. In 1965, the Georgia General Assembly had ten new African American legislators. These were the first African Americans to serve in the legislature since 1907.

Society changed after the end of the county unit system and reapportionment. Before the end of the county unit system and reapportionment, many African Americans were not able to vote. Laws were in place that set different standards for African Americans and whites to register to vote. Most African Americans in Georgia lived in city areas with only a few unit votes. The unit votes they had did not add up to enough to make a change. When the county unit system ended, African Americans and other liberals looking for change were able to speak out and vote for change. People living in cities had more influence on the votes because each vote was counted and each vote was equal. Groups like the NAACP helped African Americans register to vote. The people began to vote for changes to help decrease segregation in public places and integrate the schools. Soon, it was illegal to segregate lunch counters or other public places, to require different standards for black and white voters, and to stop anyone from voting.

The economy in Georgia changed also after the end of the county unit system. *Carl Sanders*, the first governor elected by popular vote under the new system, helped Georgia shift from an agricultural economy to a more industrial economy. The legislature increased the minimum wage. Minimum wage is the smallest amount of money a person can be paid for doing a job. Laws were also made to protect African American workers from other racist practices. These changes helped many African Americans make more money and live a better life.

## Show What You Know

Use the table below to answer the question.

### Distribution of County Voting Units in Georgia in 1960

| County | Population | Number of Voting Units |
|--------|-----------|------------------------|
| Echols | 1,876 | 1 |
| Fulton | 556,326 | 3 |
| Glascock | 2,672 | 1 |
| Quitman | 2,432 | 1 |

**Explain why the county unit voting system was considered unfair and did not provide equal protection to all voters within the state.**

_____

_____

_____

_____

_____

_____

_____

_____

_____

_____

_____

_____

_____

_____

_____

_____

# Lesson Practice

## DIRECTIONS
**Circle the letter of the best answer for each item.**

### Thinking It Through

1. The Neill Primary Act supported discrimination by

   *The Neill Primary Act occurred in 1917. It legalized the system of voting that had been in place since the 1800s. This system was ended in 1963.*

   **A.** requiring minorities to pass tests in order to vote.

   **B.** legalizing the county unit system.

   **C.** encouraging blacks to vote in the cities.

   **D.** reorganizing the voting system in Georgia.

2. The county unit voting system was declared unconstitutional by the Supreme Court because it violated the

   **A.** Civil Rights Act.

   **B.** Voting Rights Act.

   **C.** Fourteenth Amendment.

   **D.** Equal Rights Protection Act.

   **HINT** *One man, one vote is protected because of this.*

3. Which term and definition is matched correctly?

   - amendment—a change made to the U.S. Constitution
   - legislator—the executive head of a state
   - reapportionment—sharing funds with all citizens equally
   - segregation—racial equality in public spaces

   **A.** amendment

   **B.** legislator

   **C.** reapportionment

   **D.** segregation

# 27 Jimmy Carter

SS8H12.b

James Earl Carter, known as *Jimmy Carter*, was born on October 1, 1924 in Plains, Georgia. Carter went to public schools in Plains and then later attended Georgia Southern College and the United States Naval Academy in Annapolis, Maryland. He served in the navy from 1946 until 1953. In 1953, he returned to Plains to manage the family business following his father's death. The family business thrived under Carter's management and during this time, Carter gave much of his time to public service. Although he was respected by many in Plains, his views on **racism** differed from most people living in Plains. Carter did not approve of the segregation laws throughout the South. These views have shaped many of his policies and actions during his life.

Jimmy Carter, 39th president of the United States

## State Senator and Governor

Jimmy Carter was elected to the Georgia Senate in 1962, and again in 1964. Carter worked hard to improve education during this time. He ran for **governor** of Georgia in 1966 and lost in the primary election. He ran for governor again in 1970 and won. Carter surprised many with his **inaugural address** when he said: "I say to you quite frankly that the time for racial discrimination is over. No poor, rural, weak, or black person should ever have to bear the additional burden of being deprived of the opportunity of an education, a job, or simple justice."

As governor, Carter set up task forces to study every state agency. He then combined some 300 state agencies and boards into about 30 agencies. This restructure of the state government saved time and money for the state. Carter also passed a law that made the state give the same amount of money to schools in the wealthy and the poor areas of the state. Laws were passed to protect the environment and keep historical sites. Carter also changed the way judges and state officials were chosen. The people earned their jobs based on things they had done, not the political influence they held. One of the greatest changes Carter made was the appointment of women and people of color to important jobs in the state government. Carter appointed more people of color to positions than all of the governors before him combined.

# United States President

Carter won the presidential election in 1976. He was known as a casual president who worked hard. His daughter, *Amy Carter*, attended public schools in Washington, D.C., and children from her school often came over to play at the White House.

During his time in office, President Carter had great political impact on the United States and the world. He helped develop peaceful relationships between countries. President Carter developed and signed Panama Canal treaties, the **treaty** of peace between Egypt and Israel, the **SALT II** treaty to reduce nuclear arms with the Soviet Union, and he established U.S. **diplomatic relations** with China. Carter also took steps against countries that violated **human rights** by decreasing or ending U.S. aid to those governments. The United States did not attend the 1980 Summer Olympics in Moscow after the Soviet Union invaded Afghanistan in 1979. President Carter also asked the United States Senate to wait before approving the SALT II treaty with the Soviet Union because of this invasion.

One major crisis that occurred during Carter's presidency was the **Iranian hostage crisis**, in 1979. The crisis began as a result of Carter allowing the former shah of Iran to see a doctor in the United States after being removed from power by *Ayatollah Khomeini*. Angry Iranians seized a group of Americans in Iran and held them as hostages for 444 days. One attempt to rescue the hostages was made and failed. The American people were very disappointed in the way the crisis was handled. This contributed to Carter's loss in the 1980 presidential election. The hostages were released the day after President Carter left office.

Carter's presidency had many economical problems as well. The price of oil, one of the largest problems, remained high. High oil prices caused problems for many Americans, including a soaring inflation rate. Inflation went from 6% to about 15% during Carter's presidency and unemployment was high as well. President Carter developed a plan to cut federal spending, placed a tax on imported oil, and put restrictions on consumer credit. Congress approved the national energy program and the new Department of Energy, but Carter's popularity and the economy kept getting worse.

Social developments during the Carter presidency included creating the Department of Education. The Department of Health, Education, and Welfare was reorganized and renamed the Department of Health and Human Services.

# Jimmy Carter: Life After the Presidency

Jimmy Carter returned to Plains after losing the presidential election in 1980. Since that time, he has continued to work for human rights and peace throughout the world. Carter founded the Carter Presidential Center and the Carter Center at Emory University. He established the International Network Council, the Jimmy Carter Work Project, and the Atlanta Project to help low-income families. These organizations all work to increase peace and to improve health around the world. He has also worked as a carpenter for Habitat for Humanity to build homes for those in need.

Carter has written several books and continues to work with leaders around the world to build peaceful relationships. Since his presidency, Carter has helped solve conflicts in Ethiopia and Eritrea (1989), Bosnia (1994), Haiti (1994), Liberia (1994), North Korea (1994), Sudan (1995), the Great Lakes region of Africa (1995–96), Sudan and Uganda (1999), and Venezuela (2002–2003). Carter also works with the Carter Center to improve healthcare and agriculture in poor countries.

President Carter has represented the United States around the world in efforts to maintain peace. In 1999, President Clinton awarded him the highest civilian honor in the United States, the **Presidential Medal of Freedom**. In October 2002, he received the **Nobel Peace Prize** for his efforts to find peaceful solutions to problems around the world.

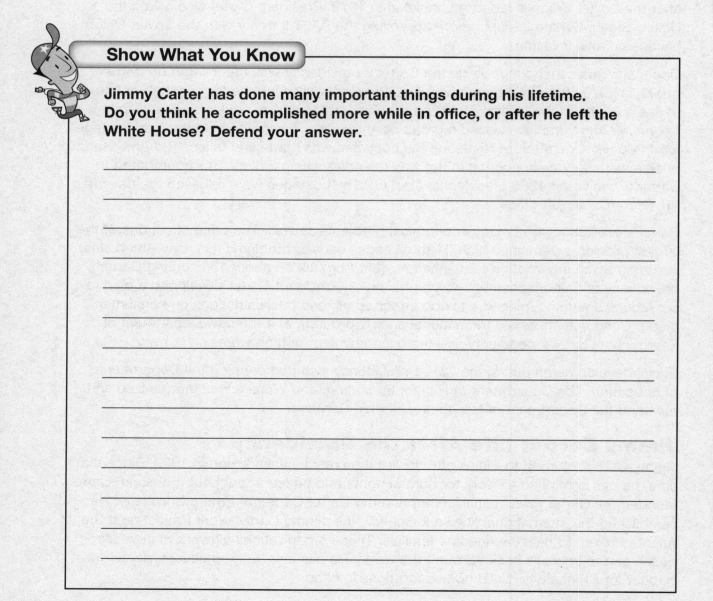

### Show What You Know

**Jimmy Carter has done many important things during his lifetime. Do you think he accomplished more while in office, or after he left the White House? Defend your answer.**

_____

_____

_____

_____

_____

_____

_____

_____

_____

_____

_____

_____

# Lesson Practice

## DIRECTIONS
Circle the letter of the best answer for each item.

### Thinking It Through

1. How did Jimmy Carter personally help to end racial discrimination and segregation as governor of Georgia?

   **A.** Carter appointed more people of color to government positions than ever before.

   **B.** Carter made funding for education equal for students in low-income and wealthy areas.

   **C.** Carter merged about 300 state agencies and boards into about 30 agencies.

   **D.** Carter appointed judges and state government officials based on accomplishments and merit.

*Jimmy Carter made a promise to help stop racial discrimination in his first speech as governor. His actions proved that he kept his promise.*

2. Which international award did President Carter receive for his efforts to find peaceful solutions around the world?

   **A.** the Walter Mondale Peace Prize

   **B.** the United Nations Service Award

   **C.** the Nobel Peace Prize

   **D.** the Presidential Medal of Freedom

   **HINT** *This award is given each year in Stockholm, Sweden.*

3. Which economic development was the biggest cause of inflation during Jimmy Carter's presidency?

   **A.** the Iranian hostage crisis

   **B.** the Soviet invasion of Afghanistan

   **C.** high prices on foreign oil

   **D.** decreasing aid and exports to foreign countries

4. In which branch of the armed forces did Jimmy Carter serve?

   **A.** army

   **B.** navy

   **C.** air force

   **D.** marines

# 28 Georgia's Two-Party System

SS8H12.c

From the early 1900s until the early 1970s, Georgia could be considered a one-party state. Politics were controlled by the predominately white Democratic Party and elections were decided at the primary level. A **one-party system** allows only one political party to have political power. Even though Georgia was a **democracy** with at least two political parties, the county unit system kept white supremacy policies and the Democratic Party in charge. The shift in power started with the end of county unit voting system and the beginning of the Voting Rights Act in 1965. However, the Democratic Party was still very strong in Georgia until the 1970s.

## Political Developments Since 1970

The Voting Rights Act in 1965 encouraged many blacks to vote. Eight African Americans were elected to the Georgia House of Representatives and two African Americans were elected to the Senate in 1965 and 1966. African Americans continued to win public office. One early sign of change occurred when *Julian Bond*, an African American civil rights leader, won a seat in the Georgia state legislature in 1965. Other members of the state legislature refused to let Representative Bond be a member. They told the Supreme Court that Bond spoke against the United States during the Vietnam War. The Supreme Court ruled that the Georgia state legislature had denied Julian Bond his freedom of speech and upheld Bond's election victory. Bond served as a Representative in the Georgia state legislature.

Maynard H. Jackson, mayor of Atlanta, became the first black mayor of a large southern city.

African Americans began to use their right to vote as a way to make changes. The power of the Democratic Party was being tested. Many of the policies the county unit system had once protected were now illegal and had to be changed. African Americans no longer had to pass tests to become registered voters. They were no longer held back from polling places. The popular vote in the urban areas began to out vote the rural counties. African Americans organized groups like Georgia Legislative Black Caucus (GBLC) to help African American legislators make changes. The Georgia Legislative Black Caucus (GBLC) began in 1975. The GLBC has worked to appoint more African American judges, hire more African American state workers in management positions, create an Office of Fair Employment Practice, increase aid to poor families with children, give more money to the African American state colleges, give more state jobs to minority businesses, and start a state minority business enterprise program.

During this time, African American politicians were elected in city government as well. *Maynard H. Jackson* was elected mayor of Atlanta in 1973. He became the first African American governor of a large southern city. He served as the mayor of Atlanta for three terms.

Other African American leaders since 1970 include *Calvin Smyre*. Smyre was appointed by Governor *Joe Harris* as the assistant floor leader in 1983, and became floor leader in 1986. A floor leader promotes the governor's interest in the Georgia House of Representatives. *Gene Walker* was elected as the Senate majority whip in 1989. *Bob Holme*s was appointed to the House budget subcommittee in 1990. *Al Scott*, Commissioner of Labor, was the first African American to hold a statewide constitutional office.

## Georgia's Political Changes Affect the Economy

The Democratic Party was run by rural farming communities during the 1960s. The political push for state funds was toward the farmers in Georgia. Cities did not have the money they needed for improvements. They also lacked political power to push for the money they needed. The cities had mostly black and liberal voters. As the number of voters in the cities grew, so did the number of new companies and jobs. As Georgia's election laws changed, voters in the two-party system were able to get legislation passed to attract new companies. The minimum wage was raised and the standard of living increased. The two-party system also helped make affirmative action stronger. Affirmative action helps women and people of color get jobs or contracts. More people of color were given jobs that paid more. Companies owned by people of color were given more contracts and were able to increase profits.

Farming is still important for the state, however, more **industry** has come to the urban areas of the state. Many people also work in **tourism**, the **service industry**, and **manufacturing**. Georgia's leading manufactured goods are now chemicals, food products, textiles, and transportation equipment.

## Social Developments Since 1970

The strength of voters in urban areas helped to improve the standard of urban living. White supremacy decreased, and equality began to increase. Schools in black urban areas improved. State money given to schools in wealthy and poor areas was equal, so all children had the same opportunity. Standards in education were raised and education improved. Since 1970, there has been an increase in aid given to poor families and public housing has also improved. Public education has been enhanced for the handicapped and for young children. Black colleges have received more financial support and have been able to grow in size and numbers. The state now helps minority businesses get started. Public transportation has also improved.

By having a two-party system, the state of Georgia has given its people a chance to make changes for the better.

### Show What You Know

**Julian Bond was elected by popular vote in 1965, but the other legislators did not allow him to serve as a member of the state legislature. Is this the result of a one-party system, a two-party system, or the period of change between the two? Explain your answer.**

_____

_____

_____

_____

_____

_____

_____

_____

_____

_____

_____

# Lesson Practice

**DIRECTIONS**
**Circle the letter of the best answer for each item.**

## Thinking It Through

1. Which politician is correctly matched with his position?

   A. Julian Bond—Georgia legislator in 1965

   B. Maynard H. Jackson—mayor of Savannah in 1973

   C. Gene Walker—House majority whip in 1989

   D. Al Scott—Commissioner of Education

*The first southern African American mayor of a major city was elected in Atlanta, Georgia. In 1965, the Supreme Court decided that Georgia violated a representative's freedom of speech and made the government reinstate the representative.*

2. How has the economy in Georgia changed since 1970?

   A. Farming is the largest industry in the state.

   B. Industries have become the state's largest income.

   C. Not much has changed since the 1970s.

   D. Entertainment is now the largest industry in the state.

   **HINT** *More people live in urban areas than in rural communities.*

3. A person who supports a one-party system would most likely agree with which of these statements?

   A. All people, no matter what their education, should be able to vote.

   B. There is only one good choice, do not get people confused.

   C. People of color need to have a voice.

   D. Everyone's opinion and vote counts.

4. Which of the following is a direct result of the Voting Rights Act of 1965?

   A. Segregation was made illegal at election polls.

   B. Black legislators were elected.

   C. Many new black voters registered in 1966.

   D. Julian Bond's right to free speech was upheld.

# 29 Changing Communities

 **SS8H12.d, e**

## 1996 Olympic Summer Games

The Olympic Summer Games came to Georgia in 1996. The idea started nine years earlier with *Billy Payne*, an Atlanta lawyer, and grew with the help of Georgia business and political leaders. Business leaders wanted to bring the Olympics to Atlanta to show the world that the city was ready to be part of worldwide business. Together with the Atlanta mayor at that time, *Andrew Young*, Payne had to sell the idea first to local leaders, then the U.S. Olympic committee, and finally to the International Olympic Committee. Two things that impressed the Olympic committee were Georgia's mild climate and the city's history as a center of the United States' civil rights struggle in the 1960s.

The 1996 Summer Olympics were played throughout Georgia. Atlanta was the main location, where the opening and closing ceremonies and many other events were located.

It took a lot to get the state ready for this huge event. The **federal** government paid to replace sidewalks, put in street signs, and plant trees to make the Olympic sites more beautiful. This cost the country millions of dollars. The streets and highways also had to be fixed and enlarged to handle all the traffic that would come to town during the seventeen days of the Olympics.

More than 72 million visitors came to Atlanta during the Olympics. Hotels added 7,500 new rooms. Restaurants and shops were built. Sports **venues**, or sites, were added as new ones were built and older venues were expanded. The money needed for these projects came from the government and from the sale of tickets and advertising opportunities. For example, a company could pay to have the Olympic symbol on its products or to have the company's name on signs at one of the venues. During the Olympics, many booths and tents were set up in the areas around the sports venues, where people sold goods, food, and drinks.

The games were held throughout Georgia. Most of the events were in Atlanta, but the games were held in Savannah, Columbus, Athens, Gainesville, and Cleveland. Transportation to the different locations was hard and sometimes created problems.

The Olympics' effect on Georgia was good. During the five years following the games, Atlanta hosted more conventions than previous years. The expanded sports venues continue to bring in more tourists from around the United States and the world.

The Olympics also affected housing around Georgia, especially in Atlanta. In downtown Atlanta, some housing areas were replaced with new apartment buildings. Dormitories at Georgia Tech University were improved and used to house Olympic athletes.

After the Olympics were over, people were asked how they felt Georgia handled the Olympics. Most people thought they were well done. The international Olympic committee liked the events and the number of people who went to the games. One thing that many people did not like was the amount of commercialism going along with the games. **Commercialism** means being very concerned with how much money can be made from an event. When the Olympics ended, people had mixed feelings about how well the games had gone. Overall, people enjoyed the games and visiting Atlanta and the other sites.

# Immigrants Coming to Georgia

New people move to Georgia each year. Many of these people move to Georgia from other countries. They are called **immigrants.** Immigrants come from countries all around the world. Most of the immigrants come to the United States for better jobs and a chance to better their lives.

In 1965, a large number of immigrants began coming to the United States. By the 1970s, large amounts of people immigrated to the U.S. Almost 4.5 million people legally entered the country. In the 1990s, almost 9 million people came, which was the largest number up to that time. Many of these people were already illegally living in the United States and they decided to apply for legal citizenship. In the 1990s, the United States government thought that many of the immigrants would come from Europe. However, about 80% came from Asia, the Caribbean, or Latin America.

Since the 1980s, there has been a lot of concern about immigrants coming to the United States illegally. Congress has passed laws to try to slow down the illegal immigration. The Immigration Reform and Control Act of 1986 created penalties, or punishments, for companies that hire illegal immigrants. However, this has not stopped immigrants from coming to the United States.

Throughout history, there have been times when there were not enough workers. Immigrants solved this problem by filling jobs. They have raised the amount of money in an area and the amount of work that is done. The added workers mean added money spent in the surrounding stores and on housing. Many immigrants have come to Georgia from Mexico and other Latin American countries. They have helped fill jobs in farming and manufacturing. Dalton, Georgia has many immigrants that work in the carpet mills. Other towns have immigrants working in the chicken farms.

During the 1970s, many international businesses moved to Atlanta. Fifty-two different countries have offices in Georgia to help their businesses in the United States. Georgia works to bring businesses from other countries to its cities. This brings more jobs for people in Georgia. Georgia's deepwater ports help attract businesses because they make it easier to move goods internationally. The international companies that moved to Georgia and other cities have brought immigrants that have gone to college and are professionals.

## Show What You Know

**Pretend that you are Billy Payne or Andrew Young. Write a letter or speech to Georgia's business leaders explaining why it would be good for Georgia to host the Summer Olympics. Include at least three improvements that the Olympics will bring to the state.**

_____

_____

_____

_____

_____

_____

_____

_____

_____

_____

_____

_____

_____

_____

_____

# Lesson Practice

**DIRECTIONS**
**Circle the letter of the best answer for each item.**

## Thinking It Through

1. Which of the following BEST states why Georgia's business leaders wanted to host the Olympics?

   A. to make money for themselves

   B. to provide educational opportunities for Georgia's children

   C. to show the world that Georgia is a city for international business

   D. to enjoy the games in their home state

   *Atlanta lawyer, Billy Payne, and Mayor Andrew Young saw the benefit of bringing the Olympics to Georgia. Many visitors from around the world would visit the state. The business leaders believed that this would get companies in other countries to begin doing business in Georgia.*

2. Much of the money needed to host the Olympics came from

   A. the federal government.

   B. the International Olympic Committee.

   C. foreign governments.

   D. local businesses.

   **HINT** *It cost the United States a lot of money to host the Summer Olympics.*

3. A way in which immigrants help the economy is by

   A. bringing money into the country.

   B. sending money to the country from which they came.

   C. running for political office.

   D. filling jobs when there aren't enough workers.

4. Many of the immigrants who come to Georgia are from

   A. Asia.

   B. Mexico.

   C. Europe.

   D. Canada.

# 30 Regions and Features

 SS8G1.b, c

## The Five Geographic Regions of Georgia

Georgia is divided into five geographic regions. The first three regions are in the mountains and foothills of the state and form part of the Appalachian Mountain range. The other two regions include the coastal areas, farming areas, and a mid-state area including some of the large cities in Georgia.

## The Blue Ridge Mountains

You will find the Blue Ridge Mountains in the northeast part of Georgia. In this area, electricity is created through hydroelectric power. Hydroelectric power is created by damming river water and using its energy to make electricity. These dams make many beautiful lakes in this area, like Allatoona Lake, Lake Lanier, Lake Hartwell, and Lake Oconee.

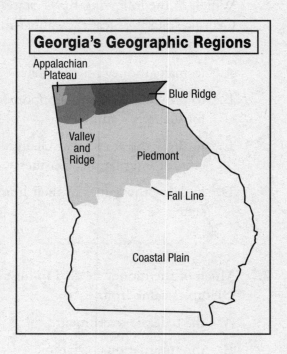

**Georgia's Geographic Regions**

Appalachian Plateau
Blue Ridge
Valley and Ridge
Piedmont
Fall Line
Coastal Plain

## Appalachian Valley and Ridge

The valley area is known for rich soil in which fruits, grains, and vegetables are grown. Beef cattle graze in the broad valleys. This area is also known for **textile** and carpet manufacturing. The ridge areas are made of sandstone rock and separate the valleys.

## Appalachian Plateau

The Appalachian Plateau is a very poor farming area because of its sandy soil. Located in the northwest corner of the state, it is wooded with thin valleys. It is made up of two flat topped mountains that form the Chickamauga and Lookout valleys. At the bottom of both of the mountains are cliffs that are 200 to 300 feet high.

## Piedmont

The Piedmont region is in the central area of Georgia. It is where almost half of the people live. Major cities located here are Atlanta, Athens, Augusta, Columbus, and Macon. There are a lot of businesses in the Piedmont region. The land in this area is rolling hills sloping toward the south. Its southern boundary, the fall line, meets with the Coastal Plain.

## Coastal Plain

The southern area of Georgia is the Coastal Plain which makes up almost half of the state. It lies along the Atlantic Ocean and the Gulf of Mexico. It contains two different coastal areas: the Atlantic Coastal Plain and the East Gulf Coastal Plain. Both of the Coastal Plain areas are good farming regions. The East Gulf Coastal Plain has rich soil and many crops are grown here including soybeans, peanuts, and tobacco. In the Atlantic Coastal Plain onions, peanuts, sweet potatoes, tobacco, and watermelons are grown.

This region has 100 miles of coast on the Atlantic Ocean. Some of Georgia's coastal islands are popular beach resorts and deep harbors. Many people vacation at the Cumberland Island National Seashore, St. Mary's, and Tybee or Jekyll Island.

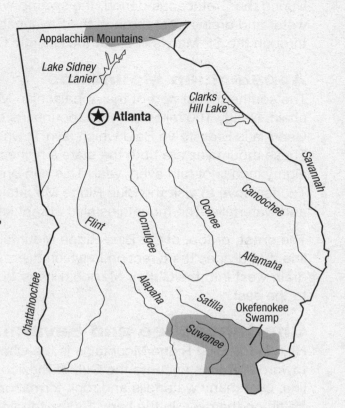

## The Fall Line

There is a boundary about 20 miles wide that separates Georgia's Piedmont region from the Coastal Plain region. This boundary is called the fall line because of the number of waterfalls along the rivers of the Coastal Plain. During the 1700 and 1800s, the falls got in the way of river travel throughout that area. Major cities developed along the fall lines of rivers. Columbus, Macon, Milledgeville, and Augusta became centers of business because of their position along the fall line and the rivers that ran through them. The geography is very different north and south of the fall line. North of the fall line are crystal rocks, while in the south are sedimentary rocks. In the north there is clay soil, but the southern soil is sandy. There are different plant and animal species on either side of the fall line.

## Okefenokee Swamp

Home to more than 400 species of animals, the Okefenokee Swamp is the largest swamp in North America. Almost 700 miles of the southeast corner of Georgia are covered by the swamp, which the Seminole Indians called "land of the trembling Earth." In 1937, President *Franklin Roosevelt* created the Okefenokee National Wildlife Refuge. This act made the swamp protected land and stopped logging companies from cutting down trees. Since 1910, logging companies had cut down trees including some of the largest and oldest in the nation. Now the swamp exists in its natural state without roads. This helps keep the **ecosystem** healthy.

During the Cretaceous period, the swamp was a part of the ocean floor. It is now fresh water and drains west through the Savannah River to the Gulf of Mexico, and east through the St. Mary's River to the Atlantic Ocean.

## Appalachian Mountains

The southernmost part of the Appalachian Mountain chain is the Blue Ridge Mountain chain. Nearly 100 miles of these mountains extend into Georgia. The highest peak in Georgia is Brasstown Bald which is in Towns County. It is 4,786 feet above sea level. These mountains are both the state's highest and wettest areas, getting more than eighty inches of rain every year. This rain brings much of Georgia's drinking water. Tourists love to visit the Blue Ridge Mountains for the beautiful views of mountain tops and waterfalls. The mountains also attract kayakers, canoeists, and whitewater rafters.

The **crest**, or top, of the Blue Ridge Mountains forms the Continental Divide. This is a line that divides the direction in which rivers drain. Rivers west of the Continental Divide drain west into the Gulf of Mexico. Rivers to the east drain to the Atlantic Ocean, to the east.

## Chattahoochee and Savannah Rivers

High in the Blue Ridge Mountains is the Chattahoochee River which flows southwest toward Alabama and into the Gulf of Mexico. The Chattahoochee goes through the fall line, over many waterfalls and rock formations. The fall line is a natural barrier to boat traffic on the river. In the early 1800s, the first steamboat ran from Columbus, Georgia to the Gulf of Mexico, making Columbus a center for the cotton industry. The waterfalls kept boats from going north on the Chattahoochee most of the year. The river in the area just north of Atlanta was a fast moving creek that powered mills during the Civil War era.

After World War I, the Chattahoochee's fast water was used to create hydroelectric power through dams. Several other dams were built to control flooding in nearby towns. Now the Chattahoochee River is important to Georgians for both drinking water and recreational purposes.

The Savannah River is the natural boundary between Georgia and South Carolina. The river begins at Lake Hartwell and flows southwest toward Savannah. It finally empties into the Atlantic Ocean, just south of the city of Savannah. The Savannah River is the shipping channel for Port of Savannah, one of the nation's busiest ports for ocean-bound ships.

The Savannah River is important to life in Georgia. Hydroelectric dams give power to the area. The river is a source of drinking water for Augusta and Savannah and smaller towns nearby. People in some South Carolina towns also get drinking water from the Savannah River. Pollution is a concern for the health of the river and steps are being taken to keep it clean and healthy.

# Barrier Islands

**Barrier islands** form a barrier between the mainland and the ocean. Georgia's coastline is guarded by a row of these islands which are constantly being formed by the wind, waves, and currents. On Georgia's barrier islands, also called the Golden Isles, are beautiful resorts and beaches. Here, many people spend their vacations playing on the beaches. Jekyll, Sea Island, St. Simons, and Tybee islands are connected to the mainland by bridges and are the most developed. Tourists can only get to the other barrier islands by boat. In addition to tourism, other industries on the barrier islands include paper production and fishing.

St. Simons Island, off the Georgia mainland, has much to offer citizens and tourists.

## Show What You Know

Draw and label the following features on the map below: the fall line, the Okefenokee Swamp, the Appalachian Mountains, the Chattahoochee and Savannah Rivers, and the barrier islands.

# Lesson Practice

## DIRECTIONS
**Circle the letter of the best answer for each item.**

### Thinking It Through

1. Which of the following regions is a poor farming area?

   A. Appalachian Valley and Ridge

   B. Blue Ridge Mountains

   C. Appalachian Plateau

   D. Coastal Plain

   *The Coastal Plain is known for its rich soil and many crops. The Appalachian Ridge is known for beef cattle and crops of fruits, grains, and vegetables. The Appalachian Plateau has sandy soil in which it is difficult to grow crops.*

2. Which of the following geographic regions has the most people?

   A. Piedmont

   B. Blue Ridge Mountains

   C. Coastal Plain

   D. Appalachian Valley and Ridge

   **HINT** *Piedmont is home to many of the largest cities in Georgia.*

3. Which of the following is true of the Coastal Plain?

   A. Its main source of power comes from hydroelectric dams.

   B. It is known for carpet manufacturing.

   C. It has many major cities.

   D. It has rich soil for growing peanuts.

4. Which of the following physical features made it difficult to travel by river?

   A. the Okefenokee Swamp

   B. the fall line

   C. the Appalachian Mountains

   D. the barrier islands

# 31 Location and Climate

 SS8G1.a, d

## Georgia in Relation to the Rest of the World

Georgia is one part of a very large world. It is important to understand the state's relationship to the rest of the world. Georgia is located in the Northern Hemisphere, in North America.

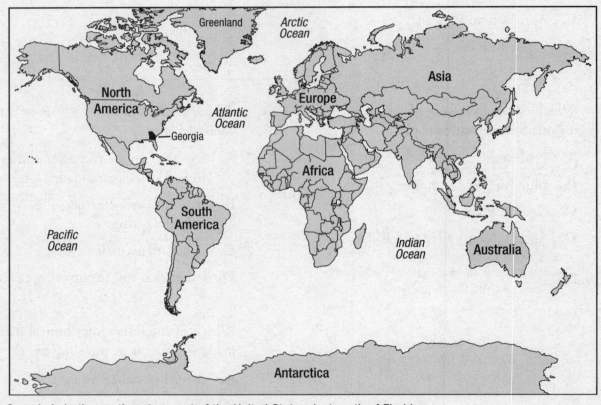

Georgia is in the southeastern part of the United States, just north of Florida.

Within the United States, you will find Georgia in the Southeast region, just north of Florida. Because it is in the South, the weather is mild, with hot summers and cool winters.

## The Impact of Climate on Georgia's Development

Georgia has a mild climate with cool winters and warm summers. The mild climate makes Georgia both a good farming area and a good tourist spot. The temperature averages 50 degrees in the winter and 80 degrees in the summer.

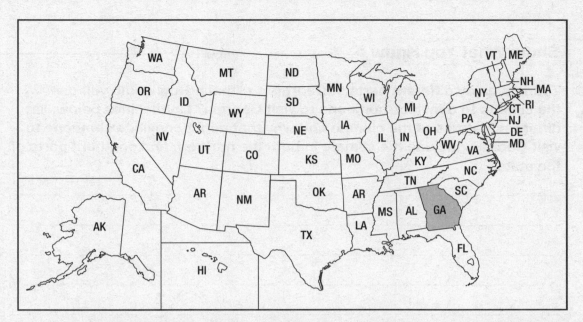

These are average temperatures. It is usually cooler in the northern part of the state than the southern. Summer is usually hot and humid and the winters are usually short. In the northern part of the state, there is some snow, but not very much.

The Coastal Plain and Piedmont regions are more humid and tropical than the other regions. Because they are between the warm waters of the Gulf of Mexico and the Atlantic Ocean, the summers tend to be long and hot. Summers in the Appalachian regions are cooler and less humid. Winters are also cooler, but are still considered mild when compared to the rest of the country.

The Blue Ridge Mountain region gets the most rain. When the humid ocean air rises over the mountains, it meets the cooler air and causes rain to fall. The Appalachian regions are well known as a vacation spot for people who enjoy outdoor sports. Hiking, fishing, and canoeing are popular. Hotel, restaurant, and other service jobs are available because of the many visitors in the mountains.

Across Georgia, the rainiest seasons are winter and summer. Precipitation in the state averages 50 inches a year. **Precipitation** is moisture in the form of rain, melted snow, and ice. This precipitation helps the agriculture, or farming industries. If an area does not get enough rain, the crops can die. Georgia is one of the leading growers of chickens and eggs. Chickens are Georgia's number one farm product. More peanuts are grown in Georgia than in any other state. Cotton is an important crop that grows in Georgia's mild climate. In the 1800s, Georgia's economy was based on cotton farming. Forestry is another business where climate is important. Forestry is growing trees that will be used to make paper and other wood products.

Georgia's mild climate has helped it become a favorite vacation spot for many people. Tourists help the economy by spending money at the beaches, in the mountains and in cities like Atlanta. The climate also makes it a good place to live and work. Many businesses and families are brought to the area because of the climate.

## Show What You Know

**Tourists enjoy different parts of Georgia's climate. How could you use the climate to convince someone to visit Georgia? On the lines below, list different features of the climate and why that might convince someone to visit Georgia. Include the climate in both the northern and southern parts of the state.**

_____

_____

_____

_____

_____

_____

_____

_____

_____

_____

_____

_____

_____

_____

_____

_____

_____

_____

_____

_____

# Lesson Practice

**DIRECTIONS**
**Circle the letter of the best answer for each item.**

## Thinking It Through

1. All of the following statements describe Georgia's climate EXCEPT

   **A.** the Coastal Plain is humid.

   **B.** summers in the Appalachians are cooler than in the Piedmont region.

   **C.** the Piedmont region gets the most precipitation.

   **D.** winters are mild when compared to the rest of the country.

*When warm, humid air rises over the mountains, it meets cooler air. This causes rain to fall in the region with the most precipitation.*

2. Which statement is true based on the phrases in the box below?

   > • The climate makes Georgia a fun vacation spot.
   >
   > • The climate is good for farming.
   >
   > • Georgia's climate is different in the mountains and at the coast.

   **A.** Climate can affect the economy.

   **B.** Climate is not important to people looking for a place to live.

   **C.** Winter in the Appalachians is the same as in the Coastal Plain.

   **D.** The cold winter temperatures make most people visit in the summer.

   **HINT** *The information given shows that people like Georgia's climate all year and that it is a good place to live or visit.*

3. Which of the following states borders Georgia?

   **A.** Mississippi

   **B.** Virginia

   **C.** Louisiana

   **D.** Florida

4. One reason people might want to live in Georgia is that

   **A.** the climate is the same throughout the state.

   **B.** the winters are mild.

   **C.** there is little rain in the Blue Ridge Mountains.

   **D.** the summers are cold.

# 32 Transportation Systems and the Economy

SS8G2.a, b, c

## Interstate Highway System

Georgia's transportation systems are important to the state's economy. Without the highways, it would be hard to move goods and people around the state. Many people use the interstate highways daily to get from their homes to their jobs. The highways join the state's major cities and join the state with the rest of the country. Georgia, which ranks tenth in the United States in number of superhighways, has fifteen interstate highways. The interstate highways were built to make it easier for the military to move soldiers and vehicles. It also allowed businesses to grow. Interstates 20, 75, and 85 all go through Atlanta helping to make it a center for transportation in the state.

Georgia's highways move people and goods through the state. Several highways cross in Atlanta, helping to make it a business center for the state.

Two very important north-south highways also pass through the state. I–95, which runs from Florida to Maine, goes through Georgia's coastal area. Traveling on I–75, one can go from Miami northwest into Michigan. On these highways, you will find people traveling to their jobs or on vacation and many semi-trucks bringing goods across the country.

## Hartsfield-Jackson International Airport

Hartsfield-Jackson International Airport is one of the busiest airports in the world. It is named after two former mayors of Atlanta: *William B. Hartsfield* and *Maynard Jackson*. Hartsfield founded the airport in 1925 and became its first commissioner. Maynard Jackson's name was added to the airport's name in 2003, following his death. He was first elected mayor in 1974 and served three terms. He was the first African American mayor of a major southern city.

Daily, more than 1,000 airplanes pass through the airport. Flights leaving the airport go to every continent except Antarctica and Australia. You can even fly to Johannesburg, South Africa, which is a fifteen hour and twenty-five minute flight, the longest flight departing Hartsfield-Jackson International Airport.

The airport covers 4,700 acres and has five runways. The fifth was opened in May 2006, to handle the growing air traffic through the city. Another control tower was added for the air traffic controllers. Air traffic controllers are responsible for aircraft that are taking off, landing, or are in the surrounding air space.

Hartsfield-Jackson International Airport is an important part of Georgia's economy. Thousands of business travelers pass through every day. Not only people fly from the airport. Mail and other cargo are sent, too. Twenty different companies send goods through the airport. The airport itself employs over 55,000 people and is the largest employer in Georgia. There are over 200 shops and restaurants located in the airport.

## Georgia's Deepwater Ports

Georgia's economy is driven in part by its two deepwater ports which are managed by the Georgia Ports Authority (GPA). Located in Savannah and Brunswick, the ports open up the state for trade and commerce with the world. Goods that are made in Georgia can be easily moved to world markets through its different ports.

Savannah is the site of two terminals, the Garden City terminal and the Ocean terminal. A **terminal** is a freight station where a ship can be loaded or unloaded. The Garden City terminal is a site for major container operations. A large container is packed with goods made in another country. It is loaded on a ship and brought to the United States. After the ship arrives, the containers are taken off the ship and taken to companies in the U.S. Goods made in the U.S. are taken to other countries in the same manner. The Garden City terminal handles general cargo from around the world. Toys made in Japan might come through the Garden City terminal. The Ocean terminal handles automobiles and other wheeled equipment.

Brunswick has three terminals: Mayor's Point, Colonel's Island, and Marine Port terminals. Mayor's Point terminal handles general cargo like the Garden City terminal in Savannah. Automobiles and dry bulk commodities come through the Colonel's Island terminal. **Commodities** are economic goods such as products of agriculture or mining when delivered for shipment. Marine Port terminal also handles bulk and general goods, however, it is run by a private company. The others terminals are run by the Georgia Ports Authority.

In addition to the deepwater ports, the GPA controls river transportation in the western part of the state. Two terminals are important parts of the river transportation system: Bainbridge Inland Barge terminal and Columbus Inland Barge terminal. The Columbus Inland Barge terminal handles liquid commodities like crude oil and petroleum products. The Bainbridge Inland Barge terminal is on the Flint River which joins the Chattahoochee River forming the Apalachicola River which flows into the Gulf of Mexico. This terminal handles all kinds of goods and lets these goods move down river, into the oceans and across the world.

These three transportation systems work together to keep Georgia's economy working. The highways, airports, and deepwater ports keep goods and people moving through the state.

## Show What You Know

**Make a prediction of what would happen to business in Georgia if Hartsfield-Jackson International Airport closed. Include at least two examples of how it would affect the state.**

_____

_____

_____

_____

_____

_____

_____

_____

_____

_____

_____

_____

_____

_____

_____

_____

_____

_____

_____

_____

_____

_____

# Lesson Practice

## DIRECTIONS
**Circle the letter of the best answer for each item.**

### Thinking It Through

1. Hartsfield-Jackson International Airport is

   A. home to three busy runways.

   B. named after a former governor of Georgia.

   C. the state's largest employer.

   D. an airport for passengers, not cargo.

*Hartsfield-Jackson International Airport had another runway added in 2006, to handle the air traffic. Many people work for its 200 shops and restaurants, and for the airlines. Two companies that fly planes through Atlanta are Delta and FedEx.*

2. Georgia's interstate highway system was built to

   A. help move the military through the state.

   B. bring tourism to the state.

   C. move goods through the state.

   D. make it the state's transportation leader.

   **HINT** *The federal government started the interstate highway system to help protect our country.*

3. Airplane traffic through Hartsfield-Jackson International Airport

   A. is for human passengers, not cargo.

   B. goes to every continent in the world.

   C. has been slowing in the past ten years.

   D. numbers more than 1,000 planes daily.

4. Georgia's deepwater ports

   A. might close because air traffic is more important.

   B. open the state for trade with the world.

   C. are only for goods coming into the state, not leaving.

   D. are mainly for automobiles.

**Choose the best answer for each question. Fill in the circle of the spaces provided on your answer sheet.**

1. In the Appalachian Mountains, there are

   A. many crops.

   B. long, cold winters.

   C. hot, humid summers.

   D. some areas of snow.

2. Which statement BEST explains the location of Georgia in relation to the South American continent?

   A. Georgia is located in the South American continent.

   B. Georgia is located east of the South American continent.

   C. Georgia is located west of the South American continent.

   D. Georgia is located north of the South American continent.

3. Which of the following statements BEST describes how Georgia's transportation systems provide jobs for Georgians?

   A. Cruise ships come through the deepwater ports.

   B. Many highways connect in Atlanta.

   C. Hartsfield-Jackson International Airport is growing to allow more planes daily.

   D. The transportation systems allow goods and people to move through the state.

4. Which of the following is now protected by the federal government?

   A. Okefenokee Swamp

   B. barrier islands

   C. Appalachian Mountains

   D. Chattahoochee River

5. Which two documents had the greatest impact on the end of the county unit system and reapportionment?

   A. the Declaration of Independence and the Thirteenth Amendment

   B. the Fourteenth Amendment and the Neill Primary Act

   C. the Fourteenth Amendment and the Voting Rights Act of 1965

   D. the Constitution and the Thirteenth Amendment

6. Which term is BEST described by the phrases in the box below?

   ┌─────────────────────────────────────┐
   │ • The Supreme Court forced Georgia  │
   │   to complete this reorganization.  │
   │                                     │
   │ • Congressional districts were      │
   │   changed so all people were        │
   │   represented fairly.               │
   │                                     │
   │ • More people of color were elected │
   │   after this was done.              │
   └─────────────────────────────────────┘

   A. the Voting Rights Act

   B. two-party politics

   C. primary elections

   D. reapportionment

7. Which of these statements MOST LIKELY describes the economic impact of the two-party system in Georgia?

   A. Jimmy Carter was elected governor of Georgia.

   B. More African American voters registered to vote.

   C. Industry began to grow in the urban areas.

   D. The Georgia Legislative Black Caucus (GLBC) began in 1975.

8. In which of the following geographic regions do the most people live?

   A. Appalachian Valley and Ridge

   B. Coastal Plain

   C. Blue Ridge Mountains

   D. Piedmont

9. In which of the following ways did the Olympics help the state of Georgia?

   A. more traffic and more people

   B. better roads and more jobs

   C. sports venues remained the same

   D. more commercialism

10. Jimmy Carter improved the state government by

   A. giving tax breaks to farmers.

   B. reorganizing over 300 organizations into 30.

   C. increasing the money given to education.

   D. reapportioning the counties in Georgia.

11. Which of the following is an example of how the three transportation systems work together to bring a product to people in Georgia?

   A. Vacationers travel by boat to the barrier islands and bring back souvenirs to their families.

   B. Semi-trucks deliver peanuts grown in the Coastal Plain to a town in the Blue Ridge Mountains.

   C. A video game comes to the U.S. on a ship, is taken by truck to the airport, and is sent to a store.

   D. Goods are moved down the Chattahoochee River to the Gulf of Mexico, then to ports in other countries.

12. Who made the statement, "I say to you quite frankly that the time for racial discrimination is over. No poor, rural, weak, or black person should ever have to bear the additional burden of being deprived of the opportunity of an education, a job, or simple justice"?

   A. Martin Luther King, Jr.

   B. President Jimmy Carter

   C. James Gray

   D. President Ronald Reagan

# CHAPTER 6

## Civics and Government

#  State Constitution and Powers

 SS8CG1.a, b

A constitution establishes the relationship between a government and its people. Some constitutions are unwritten traditions, while others are written documents. The ideas, or philosophy, behind a constitution may be written in a preamble. A preamble is an introduction. Georgia's Constitution, like the United States Constitution, has a preamble that states the purpose of the government and the Constitution. A constitution may also list the peoples' rights, and limit the government's power. A section where individual rights and government limits are written is often called a bill of rights. The United States Constitution and the Georgia Constitution both have a Bill of Rights. Constitutions may also establish the structure of government, and rules for running the government.

## Separation of Powers

Like the government of the United States, Georgia's government is divided into three different parts, or branches. The legislative branch makes the rules, or laws, that people must obey. The executive branch is the head, or leader, of the government. The executive branch also enforces the laws. If someone has been accused of breaking the law, the judicial branch decides whether they are guilty or not guilty. They interpret the laws. The judicial branch also acts as a go-between in cases of disagreement. Giving different branches of government different roles is called **separation of powers**. Separation of powers makes sure that the government does not become too powerful.

## Checks and Balances

The three branches of government also put limits, or checks, on each other. If one branch makes an error, another branch, it is hoped, will set it right, or balance it. For example, a law passed by the legislative branch can be turned down, or vetoed, by the executive branch. The members of the legislative branch can then try to keep the law alive by overriding the veto with a vote. In addition, the judicial branch may decide that a law goes against the state constitution. It will rule that the law should be changed.

This system of limiting the roles of each branch, and setting right another branch's error, is called **checks and balances**. Checks and balances, and separation of powers, help to secure people's freedom.

## Basic Structure of the Georgia State Constitution

| | |
|---|---|
| Preamble | A short paragraph that gives reasons for the Constitution |
| Article I: Bill of Rights | The first section lists individual rights. The second section mentions the separation of powers as well as the separation of church and state. The third section touches on property rights. |
| Article II: Voting and Elections | Made of three sections concerned with voting and elections—the first section says elections must be by secret ballot and law-abiding. This section also tells who is allowed to vote in Georgia. The second section mentions steps to take in case of a run-off election. The third section lists steps to take if a public official is found guilty of a serious crime. |
| Article III: Legislative Branch | Made up of ten sections—It outlines the structure and function of the two houses that make up Georgia's General Assembly. This article also explains how bills are passed into laws. |
| Article IV: Constitutional Boards and Commissions | Provides for the following: a Public Service Commission that oversees utilities such as electricity and water; a State Board of Pardons and Paroles that deals with people in Georgia's prisons; a State Personnel Board that ensures the rights of people who work for the state of Georgia; a State Transportation Board; a Veterans Service Board; and a Board of Natural Resources |
| Article V: Executive Branch | Sets out the qualifications and terms of office for both governor and lieutenant governor—this article also explains the duties and powers of the governor. In addition, another section lists other elected positions in Georgia's executive branch of government. |
| Article VI: Judicial Branch | Outlines Georgia's unified court system; gives the purposes and limits of each of Georgia's seven types of courts: magistrate courts, probate courts, juvenile courts, state courts, superior courts, Court of Appeals, and Supreme Court |
| Article VII: Taxation and Finance | Lists reasons why the state of Georgia may tax its citizens—the article also explains the methods and limits of taxation. |
| Article VIII: Education | Explains how Georgia's public school system is paid for by taxes—this article also outlines the structure of the school system at the state and local levels. |
| Article IX: Counties and Municipal Corporations | Outlines the roles and functions of county and city governments |
| Article X: Amendments to the Constitution | Explains how changes, or amendments, to the Constitution can be made |
| Article XI: Miscellaneous Provisions | These provisions deal mostly with historical and legal continuity—that is, how Georgia's different constitutions have been changed over the years. |

## Show What You Know

The first article of Georgia's Constitution is the Bill of Rights. Section II, Paragraph III of the Bill of Rights says, "The legislative, judicial, and executive powers shall forever remain separate and distinct; and no person discharging the duties of one shall at the same time exercise the functions of either of the others, except as herein provided."

In the space below, explain why the writers of Georgia's Constitution wrote this paragraph.

_____

_____

_____

_____

_____

_____

_____

_____

_____

_____

_____

_____

_____

_____

_____

_____

_____

_____

_____

# Lesson Practice

## DIRECTIONS
Circle the letter of the best answer for each item.

### Thinking It Through

1. A person wanting to know about school funding in Georgia would look at which two articles of the state constitution?

   A. Articles II and III

   B. Articles IV and V

   C. Articles VII and VIII

   D. Articles X and XI

*One way that schools get funding is through taxes. One of the articles directly addresses Georgia's education system.*

2. Article III of Georgia's Constitution says, "All bills for raising revenue, or appropriating money, shall originate in the House of Representatives." This statement expresses the idea of

   A. the Bill of Rights.

   B. constitutional boards and commissions.

   C. checks and balances.

   D. the separation of powers.

   **HINT** *The statement says that one branch has the power to do a particular action.*

3. The term "checks and balances" describes the relationship between

   A. the executive branch, judicial branch, and the legislative branch of government.

   B. the education system and the state's ability to tax the people.

   C. the Preamble and the Bill of Rights.

   D. the people's right to vote and freedom of speech.

4. In which part of the Georgia Constitution would the statement in the box below MOST LIKELY be found?

   "To perpetuate the principles of free government…we the people of Georgia, relying upon the protection and guidance of Almighty God, do ordain and establish this Constitution."

   A. Article VI: Judicial Branch

   B. Preamble

   C. Article VIII: Education

   D. Article II: Voting and Elections

# Voting and Political Parties

 SS8CG1.c, d, e

## The Rights and Responsibilities of Citizens

**Rights** are standards that keep institutions from harming people's freedom. Such institutions may be governments, police forces, businesses, or other groups. The Bill of Rights in Georgia's Constitution lists the rights of the citizens. Along with these rights come certain responsibilities. **Responsibility** involves knowing that actions have consequences. People and institutions must control their actions, as their actions might harm other people.

For example, the Constitution grants the right to freedom of religion. People cannot be turned down from jobs because of their religion. The practice of religion, however, must obey the laws of the state. Worship should not be immoral or harm the peace or well-being of anyone.

Other rights include the right to keep and bear arms, and the right to freedom of speech. People must obey the laws that deal with owning and carrying guns. People must know that if their words hurt another person, the hurt person might take legal action. People might also be called to account for the truth, or the falsity of what they say or write.

In addition, the Constitution says that all citizens are equally protected by the laws of the state. It is the state's responsibility to protect its citizens no matter who they are. People have the right to life, liberty, and property. But if a person is found guilty of breaking certain laws, these rights may be taken away.

To make sure that the state does not abuse its power, the Constitution grants other rights. All people have the right to the courts, and a right to trial by jury. People also have the right to a lawyer. People may also gather together to get their voices heard by the government, but this must be done in a peaceful manner.

Georgia's Bill of Rights also protects the citizens of Georgia against unreasonable searches and seizures. This makes sure that people are safe from the government, unless there is evidence that they have broken the law.

Thousands of people from various organizations march in downtown Atlanta, Georgia, on August 6, 2005. Some 2,000 civil rights activists, lawmakers, and celebrities marched in Atlanta to mark the 40th anniversary of the Voting Rights Act.

# Voting Requirements and Elections in Georgia

Article II of Georgia's Constitution lists voting requirements. To register and vote in Georgia, people must be 18 years old or older, be a citizen of the United States, and live in the county of Georgia where they wish to vote.

People who have been convicted of certain crimes may not vote while they are serving their sentence of punishment. Once their sentence is over, though, they may register to vote. Also, if a judge decides that a person has certain mental disabilities, that person cannot vote.

Georgia's citizens register to vote on a county-by-county basis. It is the responsibility of citizens to notify their county whenever they move. Every four years, Georgians vote for officers in their county government. In addition, people living in cities and towns vote for members of their city council. They may or may not vote for their mayor, depending on the form of their local government.

Every two years, Georgians vote for members of the state's General Assembly. Depending on where they live, Georgians elect representatives from among 56 districts. Except for the Atlanta metro area, most districts are made up of more than one county. Georgians also vote for members of the House of Representatives. These legislators represent 180 districts in Georgia.

Furthermore, every four years, there are elections to choose the governor and lieutenant governor of the state. In this election, Georgia's voters also select other state executive officers, such as the secretary of state and the attorney general.

At the national level, voters registered in Georgia vote for the president and the vice president. They also vote for members of the United States Congress. The people of Georgia elect 13 people to the House of Representatives and two people to the Senate.

# Role of Political Parties in Government

Voters do not have to join a **political party**. The people they vote for, however, usually are members of political parties. Political parties are groups of people that join together because of shared ideas and interests. Voters identify a particular set of interests and ideas with a particular political party. Identification with a political party makes it easier for voters to know what the candidate stands for. Candidates try to make the party's ideas and interests part of government policy.

There are two main political parties in the United States. They are the Democratic Party and the Republican Party. These are also the main political parties in Georgia. Sometimes people feel that neither party represents their ideas or interests. People may then try to form a third party.

In primary elections, voters choose from among several people with different ideas. **Primary elections** select candidates who will represent a political party at the **general election**. People running in a primary election are all from the same political party. The general election is where candidates from different political parties run against each other for a spot in government. All registered voters in all states can vote in general elections. In some states, though, voters must register as either a Democrat or a Republican to be able to vote in primary elections. Registered Democrats can only vote in Democratic primaries. Registered Republicans can only vote in Republican primaries. People who register as Independent, Green, Libertarian, or some other political party, cannot vote in a primary election. In Georgia, this is not the case. Any voter may vote in any party's primary election at the state level.

## Show What You Know

**Every citizen has basic human rights. However, with these rights come responsibilities. Write a paragraph discussing the relationship between rights and responsibilities as U.S. citizens. Do you think that if we are not responsible citizens we do not deserve our basic rights?**

_____

_____

_____

_____

_____

_____

_____

_____

_____

_____

_____

_____

# Lesson Practice

## DIRECTIONS
Circle the letter of the best answer for each item.

### Thinking It Through

1. In Georgia, people are not allowed to register to vote if

   A. they have spent time in prison.

   B. they have a physical disability.

   C. they are more than 18 years old.

   D. they are currently in prison.

   *People must meet three requirements to register to vote in Georgia. These requirements have to do with age, U.S. citizenship, and Georgia residency.*

2. Which of the following BEST describes a role of a political party?

   A. Puts limits on government institutions.

   B. Ensures the freedom of religion.

   C. Helps voters know what a candidate stands for.

   D. Votes for candidates in a primary election.

   HINT *Political parties are groups centered around a set of shared ideas and interests.*

3. A company fires an employee who believes that God is a frog. Which two rights granted by Georgia's Constitution would the employee MOST LIKELY use in a court case against the company?

   A. right to life, liberty, and property; right to keep and bear arms

   B. right to a trial by jury; right to freedom of speech

   C. right to a lawyer; right to freedom from unreasonable searches and seizures

   D. right to freedom of conscience; right to freedom of religion

4. In Georgia, a person who registers to vote as a member of the Green Party

   A. cannot vote in either general or primary elections at the state level.

   B. can vote only in general elections, but not in primary elections.

   C. must vote as a Democrat in primary elections at the state level.

   D. can vote in both primary and general elections at the state level.

# 35 Legislative Branch

 S8CG2.a, b, c

The **legislative branch** of government is the branch that makes the laws. Georgia's legislative branch is called the General Assembly. Two houses make up Georgia's General Assembly—the House of Representatives and the Senate. There are 180 representatives in the House of Representatives, and 56 senators in the Senate.

## Qualifications of Legislators

Senators must be at least 25 years old and citizens of the United States. In addition, they must be a legal resident of the district they represent, and have lived in Georgia for at least two years.

Representatives must be at least 21 years old. They too must be legal residents of Georgia for at least two years, and live in the district they represent. They also must be citizens of the United States. Someone who is currently serving in the military is not allowed to be either a senator or a representative.

## Terms and Elections

Members of both houses of the General Assembly serve two-year terms. The voters of Georgia elect members of both houses in general elections. Elections for members of the General Assembly occur in even numbered years. These elections, like many elections in the United States, take place on the Tuesday after the first Monday in November.

The Georgia State Capitol in Atlanta is home to Georgia's General Assembly.

# Duties

Starting on the second Monday of January of each year, the General Assembly meets for its regular session. This regular session usually lasts for about two months or less. For the rest of their two-year terms, the duties of senators and representatives take place in special sessions and committees. The General Assembly's most important duties include making Georgia's laws and passing Georgia's budget. Although Georgia's governor is responsible for distributing money in the state, the General Assembly makes the bills that actually raise the money. In addition, any change, or amendment, to the Constitution must first pass a **two-thirds vote** in the General Assembly. Georgia voters then vote on the final decision.

# Organization of the General Assembly

Much of the work done in Georgia's General Assembly takes place in committees. Committee membership reflects the balance of powers in each house. Each house has a majority party and a minority party. The **majority party** is the political party that has the most members in the house. The minority party has the fewest members. This difference comes about because voters voted for more candidates from one political party than from the other. Leaders, or chairs, of committees tend to be members of the majority party. In addition, members of the General Assembly try to join committees that deal with issues important to the people who elected them.

# House of Representatives

There are about 36 regular committees in the House of Representatives. Each representative sits on two or three committees. These committees deal with things such as education, transportation, agriculture, public safety, and so on. Representatives are assigned to committees by their political party leader.

The majority party tends to control the House. This is because the majority party has at least two leaders in the House. The most important leader is the **speaker of the House**. Since the speaker is elected by a majority vote in the House, he or she comes from the majority party. The speaker can say which representative should be assigned to which committee. The speaker can also decide when a topic needs to be discussed or debated in the House. In addition, the speaker chooses who will lead, or chair, each committee. Committees, thus, tend to be chaired by members of the majority party. The other leader from the majority party is the majority leader. The **majority leader** makes sure that the ideas and interests of the majority party get heard in the House.

The **minority leader** is the leader of the minority party in the House. He or she tries to get the minority party's ideas and interests heard in the House. The other leader in the House tries to get the ideas and interests of the governor heard. This promoter of the governor's cause is called the floor leader. The **floor leader** will most likely be from the same party as the governor.

# Senate

The leader of the Senate is called the **president of the Senate**. Georgia's lieutenant governor serves as president of the Senate. Since the lieutenant governor is elected by Georgia's voters, the president of the Senate may or may not be a member of the Senate's majority party. In addition, there is a **president pro tempore** of the Senate. The president pro tempore is the leader of the Senate's majority party. Yet like in the House, there is also a majority leader in the Senate who promotes the program of the majority party. Likewise, a minority leader does the same for the minority party. Since the president and the president pro tempore may be from different political parties, the balance of power in the Senate is sometimes less one-sided than it is in the House.

There are about 26 committees in the Senate. Each Senator is a member of at least three committees. Each committee is chaired by a Senator chosen by the president of the Senate.

# The Legislative Process

The Georgia Constitution states that, "All bills for raising revenue, or appropriating money, shall originate in the House of Representatives." This means that all bills for taxes start out in the House of Representatives. Bills that will become other kinds of laws can start out in either the House or the Senate. A **bill** is a text that calls for a change or an addition to the law. For a bill to become law, it must go through the following steps:

1. Drafting—With the help of lawyers from the Office of Legislative Counsel, legislators write the text of the bill.

2. Introduction—Only senators or representatives are allowed to introduce bills. They submit bills to the house they belong to. If the bill is submitted by a member of the House of Representatives, the Clerk of the House takes charge of the bill, makes copies of it, and reads it aloud to the House. If the bill is submitted by a senator, the Secretary of the Senate does the same.

3. Committee Consideration—The bill is assigned to a committee depending on its subject matter. The committee studies the bill. The committee may invite other legislators or state officials, the public, the bill's author, or lobbyists to comment on the bill. The committee may make changes to the bill. If the committee decides that the bill should not go forward, it will stamp it with a "do not pass" report. The committee may also decide to just do nothing, thus killing the bill. If the committee thinks that the bill should go on to the next step, it will stamp it with "do pass." The committee could also stamp it with "do pass with amendments." In this case, the committee has made changes to the bill. The committee could also stamp it with "do pass by substitute." This means that the committee has drafted a different bill to replace the original bill.

4. Floor Consideration—A bill that passes through committee is read aloud in either the House or the Senate during the regular session. A vote is called. If a majority of Representatives (91 out of 180) approve the bill, it goes on to the Senate. The Senate must also approve the bill by **majority vote** (29 votes out of 56). Legislators may debate the bill, and make changes to it, in either house. Both houses, however, have to approve identical copies of the bill for it to go on to the next step.

5. Governor Consideration—A bill that passes both houses is sent to the governor. The governor can sign the bill into law. Or the governor can veto the bill, thus sending it back to the General Assembly. The General Assembly can try to override the governor's veto with a two-thirds vote in both houses. Or the governor may do nothing. In this case, the bill automatically becomes law after forty days.

## Show What You Know

There are about 36 committees in the House of Representatives. There are about 26 in the Senate. In addition, leaders of House committees always belong to the majority party. In the Senate, this is not always the case. In the space below, explain why you think there are more committees in the House than in the Senate. Also, explain why the chairs of Senate committees may be from the minority party.

_____
_____
_____
_____
_____
_____
_____
_____
_____
_____
_____
_____
_____
_____
_____
_____
_____
_____
_____
_____

# Lesson Practice

## DIRECTIONS
**Circle the letter of the best answer for each item.**

### Thinking It Through

1. Which step in the legislative process and its description are matched correctly?

   **A.** introduction—signs bill into law

   **B.** committee consideration—invites public to comment on bill

   **C.** floor consideration—approves bill with "do pass" stamp

   **D.** governor consideration—submits bills to be considered

   *Only legislators are allowed to submit bills. When committees study bills, they often seek input from other people. Bills must be approved by majority vote in both houses to continue.*

2. The leaders of committees in the House of Representatives are members of the majority party because

   **A.** they are elected by the people of Georgia.

   **B.** they are appointed by the governor.

   **C.** they are selected by the speaker of the House.

   **D.** they are appointed by the lieutenant governor.

   **HINT** *The majority party is the party with the most members.*

3. The duties of the General Assembly include

   **A.** making bills to fund the state budget.

   **B.** signing bills into law.

   **C.** choosing the lieutenant governor.

   **D.** enforcing Georgia's laws.

4. The minimum age for a person to be a senator in the Georgia General Assembly is

   **A.** 18

   **B.** 21

   **C.** 25

   **D.** 35

# Executive Branch

 SS8CG3.a, b

Every four years, Georgia voters elect the state's head, or governor. The governor is leader of the state's executive branch. Georgia voters also elect the state's lieutenant governor. The qualifications for both of these offices are identical. The Georgia Constitution, however, puts different limits on their terms of office and defines the duties of governor and lieutenant governor in different ways.

| | Governor | Lieutenant Governor |
|---|---|---|
| **Qualifications** | • 30 years old or more<br>• U.S. citizen for at least 15 years<br>• Georgia resident for at least 6 years | • 30 years old or more<br>• U.S. citizen for at least 15 years<br>• Georgia resident for at least 6 years |
| **Term of Office** | • 4 years<br>• May run for and serve a second term | • 4 years<br>• No limit on number of terms |
| **Election** | • Elected by the citizens<br>• Does not run on same **ticket** or need to be in same party as lieutenant governor | • Elected by the citizens<br>• Does not run on same ticket or need to be in same party as governor |
| **Duties** | • Head of state and leader of executive branch<br>• Commander-in-chief of Georgia's military<br>• Can veto legislation put forward by the state legislature<br>• Signs bills into law<br>• Can use the floor leader of the House to suggest legislation<br>• Appoints people to lead many executive offices<br>• Addresses the GA legislature in a State of the State speech<br>• As director of the state budget, gives a report to the GA legislature with suggestions as to where and how state money is to be spent. | • Serves as governor if current governor dies or gets too sick to work<br>• As president of the Senate, decides committee memberships and chooses committee chairs |

# Organization of the Executive Branch

The executive branch is made up of many different offices, or departments. The leaders of some departments are chosen directly by Georgia's voters. Others are appointed, or chosen, by the governor. The table below shows three departments whose leaders are chosen by Georgia's voters.

The Georgia governor's mansion

### Departments with Elected Commissioners

| Office | Purpose |
|---|---|
| Department of Agriculture | Helps farmers; informs the public about matters related to food and animals |
| Office of the Commissioner of Insurance | Oversees programs related to health, safety, and life insurance for the public and various companies |
| Department of Labor | Offers various services related to jobs, taxes, wages, unemployment benefits, on-the-job training, and so on |

The following table shows a few of the departments whose leaders are appointed by the governor.

### Departments with Appointed Commissioners

| Office | Purpose |
|---|---|
| Department of Corrections | Runs the state's prisons; supervises people on probation |
| Department of Defense | Oversees the Georgia National Guard and State Defense Force |
| Department of Education | Oversees Georgia's public school system and how it is funded; provides information to students, parents, and teachers about the schools and programs |
| Department of Natural Resources | Runs programs to help protect Georgia's beaches, mountains, forests, and other natural resources, as well as keep Georgia's air and water clean |
| Department of Transportation | Oversees work and construction on roads and bridges; provides traffic, traveler, and transportation information; issues drivers licenses |

## Show What You Know

As president of the Senate, the lieutenant governor has a strong say in the make-up of Senate committees. Many decisions about Georgia's laws take place in committees. However, the lieutenant governor is not a senator. He or she cannot vote on legislation or introduce legislation. The governor, also, cannot vote on legislation or directly introduce legislation. Despite these limits on their powers, both the governor and the lieutenant governor can influence legislation. In the space below, write two ways the governor and lieutenant governor can influence Georgia's laws.

| Governor | Lieutenant Governor |
|---|---|
| Power 1. | Power 1. |
| Power 2. | Power 2. |

# Lesson Practice

## DIRECTIONS
**Circle the letter of the best answer for each item.**

### Thinking It Through

1. In which department of the executive branch would Georgia voters MOST LIKELY be able to make a change?

   A. Department of Transportation

   B. Department of Labor

   C. Department of Defense

   D. Department of Corrections

   *The leaders of some executive departments are appointed by the governor. In other departments, the leaders are chosen in a general election. General elections are ways people can choose their leaders.*

2. Georgia's governor and lieutenant governor are sometimes said to be political opponents. Which statement below BEST explains why the governor and the lieutenant governor might be political opponents?

   A. The governor and the lieutenant governor do not have the same qualifications.

   B. The governor and the lieutenant governor do not have the same duties.

   C. The governor and the lieutenant governor do not serve for the same terms.

   D. The governor and the lieutenant governor do not run on the same ticket.

   **HINT**  *The governor and the lieutenant governor can be members of different parties.*

3. The governor of Georgia

   A. has the power to veto bills passed by the General Assembly.

   B. is the president of the Senate.

   C. has the power to appoint committee chairs in the General Assembly.

   D. is the speaker of the House.

4. To be elected lieutenant governor of Georgia, how old does a candidate have to be?

   A. 21

   B. 35

   C. 25

   D. 30

# 37 Judicial Branch

SS8CG4.a, b, c, d

The judicial branch of government interprets the laws of the state. It makes decisions, or judgments, in courts.

## Trial Courts and Appellate Courts

There are two main kinds of courts. One kind of court is a **trial court**. In trial courts, people's actions and intentions are measured against the law. These actions and intentions may be judged to be against the law or not against the law. The judgments are made in one of two ways: either by a jury—which is a group of citizens—or simply by a judge. Georgia's trial courts are split into five classes. Of these five, three have jury trials, while two have judge trials only. The courts with jury trials are the superior, state, and probate courts. The courts without jury trials are the magistrate and juvenile courts.

The second kind of court is an **appellate court**. Appellate courts look over judgments made by trial courts. For example, if someone judged by a trial court thinks that a mistake was made in the trial, they may make an appeal. The appeal goes to an appellate court, which decides if the trial court has made a mistake or not. There are no juries in appellate courts, and facts about people's actions and intentions are not judged. Instead, appellate courts make sure that trials are fair and do not go against Georgia's Constitution. The state of Georgia has two appellate courts. These are the Supreme Court and the Court of Appeals.

## Jurisdiction

Each kind of court has its own jurisdiction. **Jurisdiction** includes the geographical area a court controls as well as the kinds of cases it can judge. For example, the jurisdiction of Georgia's Supreme Court includes the entire state and cases involving the death penalty. The jurisdiction of each magistrate court, however, is limited to its county and minor instances of breaking the law.

## Selection of Judges

At the head of every court is a judge, or group of judges. People can become judges in one of three ways. A judge can be elected in a **partisan election**. This means that the candidate for judge runs as a member of a political party. Or a judge can be elected in a nonpartisan election. In **nonpartisan elections**, candidates are not associated with political parties. The elections may be at the state, county, or local level. The third way that judges are chosen is by being appointed. Higher judges appoint some judges, while local legislators appoint others.

# Civil Cases and Criminal Cases

Trial courts oversee two types of cases. One is called a civil case. In a **civil case**, a person or group of people says that another person or group of people has somehow done them wrong. The person or group of people who complains about another person or group is called the **plaintiff**. The person or group who has supposedly done something wrong is called the **defendant**. The plaintiff brings their complaint to the court's attention. The plaintiff must then try to convince either a judge or a jury that their complaint has a real basis. If the plaintiff succeeds in this, the defendant may have to pay money to the plaintiff. These kinds of rules that apply to civil cases are called **civil law**. Most civil cases are resolved out of court, and people found guilty in civil cases never have to go to jail.

The second kind of case is a **criminal case**. In a criminal case, the government—at either the local, state, or national level—claims that a person or group has committed a crime. Committing a crime means breaking the law. The government is called the **prosecutor**. The person accused of breaking the law is called the defendant. If the prosecutor can convince a judge or jury that the defendant both committed a crime and wanted to commit a crime, the defendant is found guilty and punished. The guilty

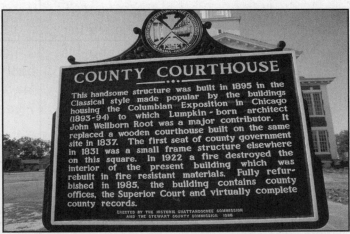

County courts form the center of Georgia's court system as well as Georgia's county governments.

defendant can be punished by being put in jail or made to pay a fine, or both. This set of rules that applies to criminal cases is called **criminal law**. In addition, criminal law defines two classes of crimes. Crimes for which the punishment is less than one year in jail are called **misdemeanors**. Crimes with punishments of one year or more in jail are called **felonies**. A felony is a serious crime, while a misdemeanor is a less serious crime. The punishment for very serious felonies such as murder may be death.

To ensure that different cases in all jurisdictions are treated fairly, Georgia's judicial branch is split among different classes of courts. The table on pages 216 and 217 shows the structure of the Georgia court system.

## The Georgia Court System

| | | Jurisdictions | Judges and Qualifications | Selection of Judges and Terms |
|---|---|---|---|---|
| Appellate Courts | Supreme Court | Georgia's highest court; reviews civil and criminal cases in trial courts and in Court of Appeals; handles appeals involving the death penalty; makes sure that elections are fair | 7 judges, called justices; have been lawyers for 7 or more years | Judges chosen by people in state-level, nonpartisan elections; serve 6-year terms; every 2 years, 1 of 7 justices is elected by the others to serve as chief justice |
| | Court of Appeals | Handles appeals concerning civil and trial cases from superior, state, and juvenile courts | 12 judges; each have been lawyers for 7 years or more | Judges chosen by people in state level, nonpartisan elections to serve 6-year terms; every 2 years, 1 of 12 judges is elected by the others to serve as chief judge |
| Trial Courts | Superior Courts Jury Trials | 49 circuit courts (circuits are made of one or more counties); handle many kinds of civil and misdemeanor cases; handle felonies, including serious violent felonies committed by juveniles | 193 judges; each have been lawyers for 7 years or more; are at least 30 years old; Georgia residents for at least 3 years | Nonpartisan elections within a circuit; serve 4-year terms |
| | State Courts Jury Trials | 71 county-level courts; handle misdemeanors, civil cases, and traffic violations | 110 judges; have been lawyers for 7 years or more: are at least 25 years old; Georgia residents for at least 3 years | Nonpartisan elections within a county; serve 4-year terms |

| | | **Jurisdictions** | **Judges and Qualifications** | **Selection of Judges and Terms?** |
|---|---|---|---|---|
| **Trial Courts (con't)** | **Probate Courts** Jury Trials (only in counties with more than 96,000 people) | 159 county courts; handle wills and inheritances, marriage and firearm licenses | 159 judges; must be high school graduates, at least 25 years old, and have lived in county for 2 or more years; in counties with more than 96,000 people, must have been a lawyer for at least 7 years | Partisan elections within county; serve 4-year terms |
| | **Magistrate Courts** No Jury Trials | 159 county courts; issue arrest warrants and search warrants; judge small civil cases | 159 chief magistrates; 354 magistrates; must be high school graduates, at least 25 years old, and have lived in a Georgia county 1 year or more | Majority of chief magistrates chosen by people in county level; nonpartisan elections to serve 4-year terms; some elected in partisan elections; others appointed by county legislators; magistrates appointed by chief magistrates |
| | **Juvenile Courts** No Jury Trials | 159 county courts; judges all children 18 years old and younger who are determined to be deprived and neglected; judges unruly and delinquent behaviors of 17-year-olds and younger | 120 judges and associate (part-time) judges; must be 30 years old; lawyers for at least 5 years; Georgia residents for at least 3 years | Appointed by judges in superior courts; serve 4-year terms |

# Conflict Resolution

Many civil cases are settled out of court. The two sides in a conflict often resolve their problem without lawyers or judges. They may be able to negotiate themselves, or use a mediator. A **mediator** is a third person who has no interest in the problem. The mediator helps two sides in a conflict come to an agreement or resolution. The mediator does not punish one side, and reward the other. Instead, the mediator helps both sides use their problem solving and communication skills to come to an agreement. The importance is using words and imagination to solve conflicts, not force or weapons.

## Show What You Know

In a civil case, a plaintiff tries to convince a judge or jury that their complaint is true. To do this, a plaintiff usually needs to show that just more than half the evidence is on their side. This notion is called "preponderance of evidence." In a criminal case, the prosecutor must convince a judge or jury that the defendant actually committed a crime and wanted to commit a crime. To do this, the prosecutor must show that, "beyond a reasonable doubt," every fact presented in court shows that the defendant is guilty. Is it more difficult to show that a defendant is guilty in a civil case, or in a criminal case? In the space below, use the notions of "preponderance of evidence" and "beyond a reasonable doubt" to explain your answer.

_____

_____

_____

_____

_____

_____

_____

_____

_____

# Lesson Practice

## DIRECTIONS
**Circle the letter of the best answer for each item.**

### Thinking It Through

1. The judges in some of Georgia's courts are selected in partisan elections. Partisan means

   A. not associated with a political party.

   B. associated with a political party.

   C. not associated with a particular county.

   D. associated with a particular county.

   *Most judges in Georgia are selected in nonpartisan elections. Some judges, though, must run as members of political parties.*

2. Which of the following is characteristic of an appellate court?

   A. trials

   B. juries

   C. decides if someone broke the law or not

   D. looks over decisions made by other courts

   **HINT** *Appellate courts review appeals.*

3. In a civil case, the defendant is accused of having wronged another person. The person who makes this accusation is called the

   A. plaintiff.

   B. prosecutor.

   C. judge.

   D. jury.

4. Which court and its jurisdiction are matched correctly?

   A. magistrate court—search warrants

   B. probate court—appeals from superior court

   C. juvenile court—violent felonies committed by adults

   D. state court—marriage and firearm licenses

#  38 Juvenile Justice System

 **SS8CG6.a, b, c, d**

Georgia's juvenile justice system has jurisdiction over children. By Georgia law, a child is anyone 17 years old or less. In addition, someone who is 18 years old, if deprived, is also considered a child. A deprived child is a child without the supervision of parents or other caregivers.

## Unruly Behavior

Juvenile courts in Georgia can decide that a child shows unruly behavior, which can be any of the following:

- The child frequently refuses to go to school.
- The child frequently disobeys his or her parents or caregivers.
- The child runs away from home.
- The child roams about on the streets between midnight and 5 A.M.
- The child goes to a bar without his or her parents or caregivers, and/or is caught with alcoholic drinks in hand.

Unruly behavior in children is also called a **status offense**. That means that the behavior would not be a crime if done by an adult. A child showing unruly behavior may be given appropriate supervision by adults. The child may also be given treatment, if the behavior involves drug or alcohol use. If the court decides that the unruly behavior is serious, the child may be committed to a place of detention run by Georgia's Department of Juvenile Justice. The child may have to stay there for up to two years.

## Delinquent Behavior

Juvenile courts may also judge that a child shows delinquent behavior. **Delinquent behavior** means committing a crime. A child who is less than 13 years old, though, cannot be tried for a crime in Georgia. On the other hand, children from 13 to 17 years old will be punished according to the law. This may include spending up to five years in a detention facility.

## Rights of Juveniles in Custody

Children accused of unruly or delinquent behavior have the following rights:

- Right to have a lawyer: If parents or caregivers can afford a lawyer, they are urged to hire one; if parents or caregivers cannot afford a lawyer, the court will appoint a lawyer for free. In addition, the juvenile court judge must tell the child and his or her parents or caregivers, that there may be dangers if they choose not to use a lawyer.

- Right to cross-examine witnesses

- Right to provide evidence to support one's own case

- Right to provide witnesses to support one's own case

- Right to remain silent: The child does not need to say anything about what they are charged with, and the judge cannot use this silence against them. However, if the child does choose to state their case in court, the judge can use what they say in order to judge the facts of the case.

- Right to appeal: If the accused child or his or her parents or caregiver think a mistake was made during the trial, they can appeal to an appellate court.

- Right to a transcript of the trial: The child, and his or her parents or caregiver, can ask for and receive a copy of all that was said and done in court during the trial.

## The Juvenile Justice Process

When children thought to be delinquent are arrested, the police notify their parents or caregivers. The police then decide whether to release the delinquents or detain them. To detain means to keep under arrest. Detained delinquents may be put in a Regional Youth Detention Center or in a community shelter or foster home.

For detained delinquents, the next step is a **probable cause hearing.** The probable cause hearing takes place in two days or less. A judge in the juvenile court looks over the case and decides whether the children should be released or detained further.

For released children, a petition will be filed 30 days or less if it seems likely that the children really were delinquent—or if the judge decided that they were unruly or deprived. For detained delinquent children, the petition will be filed in three days or less. For unruly and deprived children, it is five days or less. A petition is a text that outlines the charges against the child. The petition is filed by a member of the Department of Juvenile Justice known as a Juvenile Probation Parole Specialist.

The next step is called an **adjudicatory hearing.** This takes place in ten days or less for detained children. For released children, it takes place within 60 days or less. At the adjudicatory hearing, a judge in the juvenile court decides whether the charges in the petition are true or not. If the judge thinks that the charges are untrue, the case will be dismissed.

If the judge thinks that the charges in the petition are true, a **dispositional hearing** takes place. At the dispositional hearing, the judge decides the course of treatment, supervision, or rehabilitation that the delinquent, unruly, or deprived child should undergo. The judge may decide that probation is necessary. For instance, a child who frequently skips school will be ordered to go to school. The judge might also decide that the child should be put into a detention facility or youth development center. For certain serious crimes, the delinquent may be detained for up to five years. In certain cases, the judge may decide that the case should be transferred to a superior court where the child will be tried as an adult.

# The Seven Delinquent Behaviors

Seven delinquent behaviors are automatically outside the jurisdiction of juvenile court. Children between the ages of 13 and 17 who are thought to have committed any of these seven crimes will be tried as adults in a superior court. These seven crimes are:

- Aggravated child molestation
- Aggravated sexual battery
- Aggravated sodomy
- Murder
- Rape
- Voluntary manslaughter
- Armed robbery with a firearm

The consequences of being found guilty of any of these crimes are harsh punishments. The punishment for murder, for example, may be life in prison or even death.

## Show What You Know

**A juvenile taken into custody has the right to be represented by a lawyer. A juvenile also has the right to remain silent. In addition, the judge in a juvenile case is required to tell the juvenile and his or her parents or caregivers, that there may be "dangers" of not using a lawyer. Based on the right to have a lawyer and the right to remain silent, explain what you think these "dangers" might be. Use the space below for your answer.**

_____

_____

_____

_____

_____

_____

_____

_____

# Lesson Practice

## DIRECTIONS
**Circle the letter of the best answer for each item.**

### Thinking It Through

1. The term "delinquent behavior" describes

    A. criminal behavior by a person older than 18 years old.

    B. criminal behavior by a person less than 18 years old.

    C. unruly behavior by a person older than 18 years old.

    D. unruly behavior by a person less than 18 years old.

*Breaking the law means committing a criminal act. If an adult breaks the law, it is a crime. If a child breaks he law, it is a delinquent act.*

2. Unruly behavior is sometimes called a "status offense" because

    A. the behavior would be a crime if done by an adult.

    B. it is the same as delinquent behavior.

    C. it gives status to the person who does it.

    D. the behavior would not be a crime if done by an adult.

**HINT** *An important factor in unruly behavior is age.*

3. A judge says that a juvenile must spend 60 days in a youth development center. This judgment MOST LIKELY takes place in

    A. a dispositional hearing.

    B. a court with a jury trial.

    C. an appellate court.

    D. an adjudicatory hearing.

4. Which step in the juvenile justice process and its description are correctly matched?

    A. probable cause hearing—takes place within two days of being arrested

    B. petition—judge decides how long a juvenile will be detained in a detention facility

    C. adjudicatory hearing—a probation specialist outlines the charges

    D. dispositional hearing—takes place in ten days or less for detained children

# Local Governments

  SS8CG5.a, b, c

After the American Revolution, Georgia's parishes became counties. Counties serve as ways for people to be represented in state government. Also, through the sheriff, counties act to protect people. Additional county functions include keeping track of land ownership, marriage and automobile licenses, and elections at both the county and state levels. Today, there are 159 counties in Georgia, as determined by the Constitution.

## Municipal Governments

Georgia has some 535 cities and towns, which are also called municipalities. Municipalities have charters, which are similar to constitutions. They outline the form and structure of the municipality's government, and define the municipality's boundaries and powers.

The Georgia Constitution puts no set limit on the number of municipalities in the state. Citizens living in a particular area can form a municipality by asking the state legislature to grant them a charter. The legislature will grant the charter if 200 or more people live in the area, the area is more than three miles from another municipality, and at least 2/3 of the land is split into properties for either living or business purposes.

To remain as a city or town, the municipality must then hold regular elections, have at least six official meetings per year, and provide three or more services from an official list. If the city or town does not do these three things, its charter can be taken away. The municipality will then cease to exist as an independent municipal government.

## County Governments

Georgia is broken up into Senate and House districts as well as counties. The districts overlap county boundaries so that all counties are represented in the General Assembly. In addition, every county has a probate court, a magistrate court, and a juvenile court. While municipalities may have their own courts, they do not fill the same functions that the county level courts do. Furthermore, counties build and maintain roads. They also control licenses for cars and trucks, and run Georgia's welfare programs. Although Georgia residents vote at all levels of government, they register to vote in their counties.

At the county level of government, Georgians vote for county commissioner and/or a board of commissioners, clerk of superior court, judge of probate court, sheriff, tax receiver, and tax collector.

## Forms of Municipal Government

The forms of government of Georgia's counties are standard across the state. In towns and cities, though, there are three main forms of government. In all forms of municipal government, residents elect members to city council. The city council is the city's legislative branch. It makes the city's laws. The forms of city government differ according to the make-up of the executive branch.

**Services Offered by Georgia's Municipalities**

- Police and fire protection
- Garbage collection and disposal services
- Public health facilities and services
- Street and road construction and maintenance
- Parks, recreational areas, programs, and facilities
- Storm water and sewage collection and disposal systems
- Development, storage, treatment, purification, and distribution of water
- Public housing
- Public transportation
- Libraries, archives, and arts and sciences programs and facilities
- Terminal and dock facilities and parking facilities
- Codes, including building, housing, plumbing, and electrical
- Air quality control
- Creation, modification, and maintenance of retirement or pension systems for local government employees
- Planning, zoning, and community redevelopment
- Electric or gas utility services
- Street lighting

In the **council-manager** form of city government, the city council hires a city manager. The city manager is the head executive of the city. The city manager decides who is in charge of city services. The city manager also runs the city's budget. Council-manager cities do have mayors, however. Some council-manager cities elect their mayors, while in others, the city council chooses the mayor. In this form of city government, though, the mayor is a member of the legislative branch like the rest of the members of city council.

The **strong mayor-council** form of city government also has a powerful executive officer. This powerful executive officer is the mayor, who is elected by the voters in the city. In this form of government, the mayor can veto legislation passed by city council. The mayor can also choose people to run the city's various service departments. Like the city manager, the strong mayor also has the power to run the city's budget. In addition, strong mayors often influence the make-up of city council committees where the major decisions are made.

In the **weak mayor-council** form of city government, the mayor has no such power. Though elected by the city's voters, the weak mayor's office is more for show than for function. The weak mayor has no special executive powers—no power to veto, no power to choose committee members, and no overriding say in the budget.

# Special-Purpose Districts

The Georgia constitution allows **special-purpose districts** to be created. Special-purpose districts are also called special-purpose governments or local government authorities. City and county governments create special-purpose governments in order to meet specific needs of the people. They are administrative units which aim to accomplish a specific task. They are different from city and county governments, which have a wide range of functions. The following are some special-purpose governments in Georgia:

- Development Authorities: create jobs and increase business in specific counties

- Downtown Development Authorities: maintain and rebuild the downtowns of cities

- Recreation and Parks Authorities: maintain and develop land for parks and recreation areas in counties

- Housing Authorities: manage housing options in counties

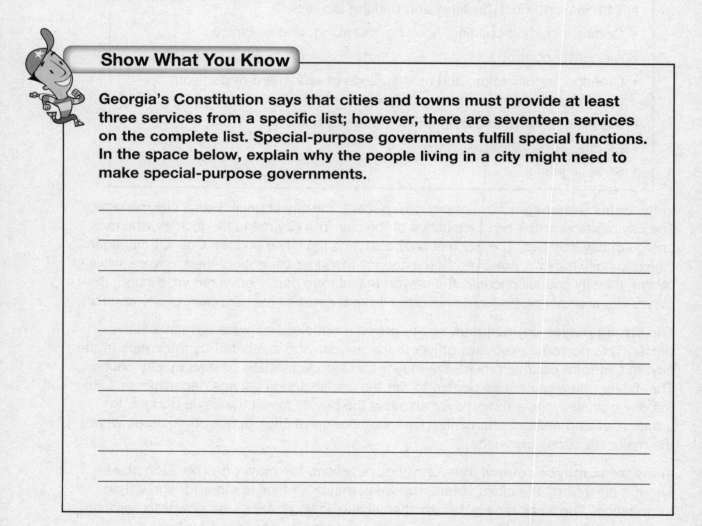

## Show What You Know

Georgia's Constitution says that cities and towns must provide at least three services from a specific list; however, there are seventeen services on the complete list. Special-purpose governments fulfill special functions. In the space below, explain why the people living in a city might need to make special-purpose governments.

_____

_____

_____

_____

_____

_____

_____

_____

_____

_____

# Lesson Practice

## DIRECTIONS
**Circle the letter of the best answer for each item.**

### Thinking It Through

1. Georgia law says that every city must

   **A.** provide public housing.

   **B.** have a sheriff.

   **C.** hold regular elections.

   **D.** pay for street lights.

   *Towns and cities in Georgia provide at least three services. In addition, they must hold at least six official meetings per year. Also, all cities in Georgia have an elected city council.*

2. There are 159 counties in Georgia. The number of cities and towns, though, varies over time. This is because

   **A.** new municipalities can be created and others dissolved.

   **B.** the Georgia Constitution states that new cities should be created.

   **C.** Georgia's declining populations causes cities to disappear.

   **D.** the Georgia Constitution puts a limit on the number of cities.

   **HINT** *The Georgia General Assembly can take away a municipal charter if certain basic rules are not met.*

3. Which of the following is a correct statement about municipal and county governments in Georgia?

   **A.** All counties have a probate court and all cities have a municipal court.

   **B.** All counties have a tax receiver and some cities have a city manager.

   **C.** All counties have a probate court and some cities have a municipal court.

   **D.** All counties have a county commissioner and all cities have a city manager.

4. The form of municipal government in which the mayor has no special executive powers is called

   **A.** council-manager.

   **B.** strong mayor-council.

   **C.** commission.

   **D.** weak mayor-council.

**Choose the best answer for each question. Fill in the circle of the spaces provided on your answer sheet.**

1. If a person found guilty of a crime thinks that a mistake was made in their trial, they may take their case to

   A. a magistrate court.

   B. a trial court.

   C. a state court.

   D. an appellate court.

2. To register to vote in the state of Georgia, a person must be at least how old?

   A. 30

   B. 25

   C. 21

   D. 18

3. Someone who is 14 years old and skips school twice a week without any sort of explanation may be charged with

   A. delinquent behavior.

   B. unruly behavior.

   C. juvenile behavior.

   D. adult behavior.

4. In a city without an elected mayor, the chief executive officer of the city will MOST LIKELY be

   A. an appointed mayor.

   B. a city manager.

   C. a judge of probate court.

   D. a county commissioner.

*Use the numbered list in the box below to answer question 5.*

> 1. adjudicatory hearing
> 2. probable cause hearing
> 3. dispositional hearing
> 4. petition

5. Which of the following lists the correct order of steps in the juvenile justice process?

   A. 1, 2, 3, 4
   B. 4, 3, 2, 1
   C. 2, 4, 1, 3
   D. 3, 1, 4, 2

6. The governor and lieutenant governor of Georgia

   A. are always members of the same political party.
   B. have no influence on legislation.
   C. might be members of different political parties.
   D. can both sign bills into laws.

7. One way that people solve conflicts is through a mediator. A mediator is someone who

   A. punishes one side and rewards the other.
   B. helps both sides come to an agreement.
   C. lobbies for the cause of one side against the other.
   D. decides between right and wrong.

8. Which of the following shows the correct order of events for a bill to become a law in the state legislature?

   A. introduction; floor consideration; committee consideration; governor consideration
   B. introduction; floor consideration; governor consideration; committee consideration
   C. introduction; committee consideration; governor consideration; floor consideration
   D. introduction; committee consideration; floor consideration; governor consideration

9. A city where the mayor can veto decisions made by the city council and hire and fire the heads of city services, has which form of government?

   A. commission

   B. council-manager

   C. weak mayor-council

   D. strong mayor-council

10. For a person accused by the county of having used a gun to rob a grocery store, which set of rules will MOST LIKELY apply to their court case?

    A. civil law

    B. trial law

    C. criminal law

    D. appellate law

11. The football and baseball fields and the outdoor basketball and tennis courts in the city of Rhodalia are in very bad condition. Which is the BEST way the citizens of Rhodalia could make these things better?

    A. create a local Parks and Recreation Authority

    B. appeal to the Supreme Court of Georgia

    C. bring a civil suit against the city manager

    D. write a letter to the lieutenant governor

12. Which of the following is a government authority figure found in Georgia counties?

    A. sheriff

    B. mayor

    C. council

    D. manager

# CHAPTER

# 7 Economics

#  40 Goods, Services, and Growth

 **SS8E1, SS8E3.a, b, c**

Throughout its history, Georgia's economy has been based on producing goods. Its first products were farm products. During the 18th century, common crops in Georgia were rice, sugar cane, and indigo. Cotton farming came later in the 1700s. Cotton was the main crop until the 1920s.

Today, farming is not the main source of Georgia's economy. The economy does still include crops including cotton, peaches, corn, tobacco, and peanuts.

Manufacturing is an important part of Georgia's economy today. The textile industry began in the 1830s and grew after the Civil War. Other products included cottonseed oil, cattle feed, and fertilizer. World War II increased the demand for goods. Manufacturing expanded, including the variety of goods. Today, Georgia products include textiles, transportation equipment, processed foods, chemicals, paper, and plastic.

Services are also part of Georgia's economy. These include legal advice, computer work, trade, finance, insurance, real estate, and construction.

## Entrepreneurs

Georgia began to industrialize in the early 19th century. Entrepreneurs emerged during this period. An **entrepreneur** is a person who takes the risk to start up a new business.

Expenses are the costs for a business to produce goods or services. The money a business receives from consumers is used to pay its expenses. Remaining money is called a profit. **Profit** is the main incentive, or reason, for starting a business. Entrepreneurs look for new businesses and ways to make a profit. They help expand and develop the economy.

Georgia manufacturing began with the textile industry in the 1830s. Risk is a part of starting a business. An entrepreneur is a risk taker. An entrepreneur invests money in a new business, but cannot know if it will be profitable. A business may lose money. An entrepreneur will research a new business idea to find out the chances of success.

Entrepreneurs and their businesses help Georgia's economy. Coca-Cola, Delta Airlines, Georgia-Pacific, and The Home Depot are examples of Georgia businesses that were started by entrepreneurs.

## Coca-Cola

The Coca-Cola Company makes many beverages, but best known for its namesake Coca-Cola. Coke is one of the most familiar products in the world. The company was started in the 1880s by a Georgian entrepreneur named *John Smith Pemberton*. Pemberton worked as a pharmacist. He created the cola formula and sold it as a health tonic. He had to compete with other tonics that were popular at that time.

Coca-Cola was advertised as a health tonic in the 1800s.

## Delta Air Lines

Delta Air Lines is one of the largest airlines in the country. Delta began as an aerial crop dusting service, which sprayed farm crops with chemicals and fertilizer. The company was started in the 1920s by an entrepreneur named *Collett E. Woolman*. Woolman worked to expand Delta to offer passenger and mail services. In 1929, Woolman bought three planes and started flying passengers between Texas and Mississippi. Today, Delta flies passengers all over the world.

When Woolman started Delta as a passenger service in the 1930s, his small company had to compete with major airlines. The U.S. government began controlling the airline industry during that time. The government set ticket prices, flight routes, and schedules. This government control helped Delta to compete and become successful.

## Georgia-Pacific

Georgia-Pacific is a paper company based in Atlanta. It is one of the world's top producers of tissue, pulp, paper, packaging, and building goods. The company was the idea of an entrepreneur named *Owen R. Cheatham*. Cheatham started the company in 1927 as a small lumber mill. He took the risk to expand his mill into a larger business. By 1938 the company was running five lumberyards in the South. In 1947, Georgia-Pacific bought a lumber mill on the Pacific Coast. The company continues to be successful and produce a wide assortment of goods.

## The Home Depot

The Home Depot is the world's largest chain of home improvement stores. It was started in 1978 by entrepreneurs named *Bernie Marcus and Arthur Blank*. Before The Home Depot opened, hardware stores were specialized. A consumer might have to visit many stores to buy the materials needed for one project. Marcus and Blank wanted their stores to sell all of the possible materials a person might need. Operating on a large scale allowed prices to be low. The store employees were able to be experts in home improvement. These ideas had not been tried at the time when The Home Depot began. The Home Depot changed the way that home improvement stores are operated.

## Show What You Know

Imagine you are an entrepreneur. Create an idea for your new business. What product will you sell? It can be a good, like pies, or a service, like walking dogs. Who are your competitors? What type of consumers will buy your product? Write out a plan for how your business will make a profit.

_____

_____

_____

_____

_____

_____

_____

_____

_____

_____

_____

_____

_____

_____

_____

_____

_____

_____

_____

_____

_____

# Lesson Practice

## DIRECTIONS
**Circle the letter of the best answer for each item.**

### Thinking It Through

1. The term "entrepreneur" is best defined as

   A. someone who owns a business, but does not handle its operation or management.

   B. a buyer of goods and services.

   C. someone who takes on the operation, management, and risk of a new business.

   D. an employee of the airline industry.

   *John Smith Pemberton, the entrepreneur who started Coca-Cola, created the formula for Coke and sold it as a health tonic, even though there were other, similar tonics already available.*

2. Georgia-Pacific is a company known for manufacturing

   A. tissues, pulp, paper, and packaging.

   B. automobiles.

   C. processed meats and cheeses.

   D. computers and software.

   **HINT** *The company that would become Georgia-Pacific started in 1927 as a small lumber mill.*

3. Which one of these ideas are BEST associated with The Home Depot business model?

   A. stores that sell only local, specialized home improvement goods

   B. store employees who are new to home improvement

   C. lower prices due to a large-scale operation

   D. stores that are opened only on the weekends

4. World War II helped Georgia's economy because

   A. jobs were created in other countries.

   B. it resulted in a limited variety of goods manufactured.

   C. cotton stopped being grown as a result of the war.

   D. the demand for goods increased, and manufacturing grew as a result.

#  41   Trade

 **SS8E2.a, b**

Trade is the act of buying and selling goods. When nations agree to trade with each other without charging tariffs, the act is called **free trade**. Free trade makes cheap foreign goods available to consumers. It also allows industries to use their resources for production and import what they cannot produce cheaply.

## Trade History of Georgia

People have been trading in Georgia for hundreds of years. Long before Georgia was a state, Native American groups traded with each other. Trade makes a much wider variety of goods available to people.

When Europeans came to the Americas, international trade came to Georgia. In the early 18th century, Europeans took huge amounts of resources from the region for export back to Europe. Timber, plant products, and animal pelts from Georgia were all sold in Europe.

Large numbers of Africans were enslaved and brought to the Americas by way of Savannah, Georgia. They were traded for agricultural goods such as cotton, rice, and tobacco, which were then exported to Europe.

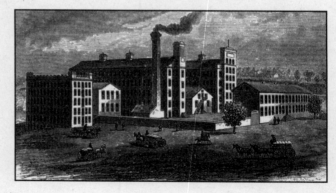

Georgia's plant products were in high demand in the 18th and 19th centuries. Slavery made goods cheap to produce and quite profitable. In 1793, the invention of the cotton gin made textile production easier. "King Cotton" then became the most important export from Georgia.

In the 19th century, the textile industry also grew in Georgia. From 1840 until the Civil War, Georgia was the largest producer of cloth in the southern states. Other industries followed, such as foundries and paper mills.

In the 19th century, Atlanta, Georgia became a center of trade. During the Civil War, Atlanta's industries grew. Railroads increased trade in Georgia, and linked the region to many markets.

After the Civil War, leaders in Georgia wanted to make a "New South." They believed that for the New South to succeed, a number of goals had to be met. These goals included making peace with the North, increasing industry, and growing a wider variety of crops.

Cotton was the backbone of Georgia's economy until the mid-20th century. In 1915, boll weevils ruined much of the cotton crop. World War I followed, causing a weakened foreign market. Low cotton prices forced farmers to grow other crops. Farming stayed important to Georgia's economy, however, even with the decrease in cotton sales.

Georgia invited many large companies to base their southern offices in Atlanta. Many did, such as Sears and General Motors. These companies created more jobs and caused the city to grow even more. Atlanta's well-developed highway system also helped trade.

Like most southern cities in the mid-20th century, Atlanta was racially segregated. Nevertheless, more blacks owned businesses there than in other parts of the U.S. Auburn Avenue was a street in a black area of Atlanta. It was a center of black culture and education. It became a heart of business for the country.

## Georgia in Today's World Economy

World War II changed the South forever. The federal government spent billions of dollars on war industries and military installations all over the region. Atlanta in particular grew as a result of World War II. Many people moved to Atlanta from rural areas. They provided a work force for Atlanta's growing industries.

Millions of federal dollars were also spent on housing, schools and roads. Georgia-based companies such as Coca-Cola grew quickly due to the war. Atlanta in particular and Georgia as a whole emerged from World War II connected, thriving, and ready to do business with the world. Georgia is still a leading state in production of farm products, but agriculture is only a small part of today's Georgian economy.

Since World War II, Georgia's prominence as a center of international trade and commerce has continued to grow. Georgia had long been a key in regional land transport. It became a center for air traffic as well. Today, Hartsfield-Jackson Atlanta International Airport is one of the busiest airports in the world.

Since the 1970s, tourism has been a key part of Georgia's economy. Travelers are attracted by the mild climate, state parks, and historical sites.

Atlanta continued its rapid growth. In the 1970s and 1980s, many people moved to the area from other states and countries. People are still moving to the Atlanta area looking for jobs, education, and opportunity.

Corporations continue to be attracted to Georgia's open and vigorous business climate. Today, Atlanta is one of the most important trade centers in the United States. It is widely recognized as the business capital of the Southeast and is home to companies such as CNN, Delta Airlines, and UPS.

### Georgia's Top Ten Publicly Owned Companies in 2006

| Company | Revenue (in billions of dollars) |
| --- | --- |
| The Home Depot, Inc. | $78.83 |
| United Parcel Service, Inc. | $40.47 |
| Coca-Cola Company | $22.98 |
| BellSouth Corporation | $20.45 |
| Coca-Cola Enterprises | $18.62 |
| Delta Airlines, Inc. | $15.69 |
| AFLAC, Inc. | $14.24 |
| Southern Company | $13.11 |
| Genuine Parts Company | $9.63 |
| SunTrust Banks | $7.4 |

## Show What You Know

Georgia's role in the world economy changed during World War II. First, make a list of some key trade items produced in Georgia before the war. Then list trade items produced after the war. How are they different? What changed in Georgia's economy during the war?

_____

_____

_____

_____

_____

_____

_____

_____

_____

# Lesson Practice

## DIRECTIONS
**Circle the letter of the best answer for each item.**

### Thinking It Through

1. How did the idea of the "New South" affect trade and industry in Georgia?

   A. Crops were diversified, ending the reign of "King Cotton."

   B. Industries grew in Georgia, preparing the area for the industrial expansion of World War II.

   C. Large numbers of people from the north settled in the Atlanta area.

   D. It caused the Civil War to drag on, hurting southern industry.

*After the Civil War, state leaders wanted Georgia to be a part of the national and world economy. They were convinced that prosperity lay in ending conflict and expanding industry.*

2. Which industry contributed the most to Georgia's economic growth in the 19th century?

   A. transportation

   B. textiles

   C. agriculture

   D. communications

   **HINT** *Early Georgia was mostly a rural society.*

3. Since World War II, which factor has helped expand industry the MOST in Georgia?

   A. agriculture

   B. education

   C. tourism

   D. technology

4. Which Georgia-based company grew the most during World War II?

   A. Coca-Cola

   B. Delta Airlines

   C. UPS

   D. CNN

# 42 State Revenue

 SS8E4.a, b, c

All governments require money. Running the government as well as providing services both cost money. The money that governments bring in is called **revenue**. The state of Georgia and its local governments have several ways of raising revenue.

## Taxes

Taxes in Georgia can be levied by the state as well as by counties and cities. A **tax** is a required payment to a government by a person or business. Taxes are the largest source of revenue for Georgia. There are many different kinds of taxes.

Income tax is a tax on money earned by people or businesses. Personal income tax is Georgia's largest single source of revenue. Personal income tax is a graduated tax, meaning the tax rate rises or falls depending on a person's income. People who make more money pay a larger percentage of their income than those making less.

Corporate income taxes are usually flat rate taxes based on the money a company makes in Georgia. Money made outside of the state is not taxed. Income taxes are collected only by the state, not by local governments.

Sales taxes may be collected by state and local governments. A sales tax is a tax levied on most retail goods and services. The amount of sales tax is calculated as a percentage of price. Sales taxes are Georgia's second largest revenue source. Currently, Georgia has a 4% state sales tax. Local governments also have the option of levying sales taxes with voter approval. With combined state and local sales taxes most purchases in Georgia have a tax of 7 to 8%.

Property taxes are a key source of funds for local governments in Georgia. A property tax is a tax placed on property such as land, homes, cars, boats, and business inventory. Property taxes are based on a percentage of the value of the property. Some properties are not taxed, such as churches. Personal property worth less than $500.00 is also not taxed. Property taxes do not contribute significantly to state revenues.

## Non-Tax Revenue Sources

The largest non-tax revenue source for the state of Georgia is the state lottery. Other sources include entry fees to state parks, and license fees for driving and hunting.

The federal government can also add to state and local funds. Federal money comes in the form of grants has many uses. These include building airports, preserving historical sites, and improving areas with poor economies.

Local governments get non-tax revenue through fees for services such as water and sanitation. Counties and cities may also borrow money, but this practice is limited by state law and must be approved by voters.

## Spending the Money

Georgia is required by its constitution to have a balanced budget. This means the state cannot spend more money than it brings in. It may not borrow money or operate under a deficit. Keeping a balanced budget keeps the state out of debt and fiscally strong. It also limits programs on which the state's money is spent.

In Georgia many groups compete for state funds. The process of deciding how and where to spend money is complex. It involves the governor, representatives from state agencies, the state legislature, and special interest groups. The governor submits a budget to the state legislature. This budget is then modified by legislators. It is signed by the governor, who can veto items in the budget. The bu

dget may be reviewed and changed if spending exceeds revenue.

| Georgia State Revenue Sources (2004) | |
|---|---|
| **Source** | **Amount** |
| Taxes, fees, and sales | $1,563,809,957 |
| Lottery funds | $691,795,656 |
| Tobacco settlement funds | $175,080,760 |
| Brain and spinal injury trust fund | $2,000,000 |
| Revenue shortfall reserve | $141,997,339 |
| TOTAL FUNDS | $16,174,683,712 |

| Georgia State Spending (2004) | | |
|---|---|---|
| **Program Budget** | **Funds Budgeted** | **Percentage of Total** |
| Education | $7,963,725,135 | 52.02% |
| Social services | $3,177,123,873 | 20.75% |
| Criminal justice | $1,618,182,395 | 10.57% |
| Debt service | $778,879,879 | 5.09% |
| transportation | $688,508,938 | 4.5% |
| All other state agencies | $701,387,076 | 4.6% |
| Property tax cut | $380,000,000 | 2.5% |

How revenue in Georgia is spent depends in part on how it is generated. Most taxes are put into a general fund from which many services are financed. State services include the public school system. School buildings must be maintained, teachers paid, and supplies bought to run the schools. The state also maintains roads throughout the state. State parks and conservation areas are also maintained and protected. All of these services and more are paid for by the general fund.

Some money is targeted for a specific purpose. Most park fees, for example, go to maintain parks. Lottery revenues must be spent on special programs such as scholarships and preschool programs. Georgia also has a fund collected from hospitals to help pay for healthcare for those that cannot afford it.

Local governments charge money for services like electricity. These fees go to maintain those services. Local governments also maintain local roads. This maintenance is paid for through license fees and traffic fines. Special taxes provide funds for facilities such as libraries.

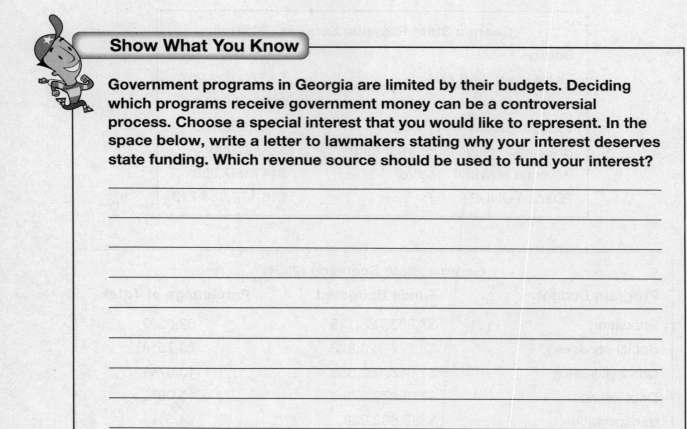

## Show What You Know

**Government programs in Georgia are limited by their budgets. Deciding which programs receive government money can be a controversial process. Choose a special interest that you would like to represent. In the space below, write a letter to lawmakers stating why your interest deserves state funding. Which revenue source should be used to fund your interest?**

# Lesson Practice

## DIRECTIONS
**Circle the letter of the best answer for each item.**

### Thinking It Through

**1.** In Georgia, both the state government and local governments share the power to

    **A.** impose taxes.

    **B.** operate military bases.

    **C.** establish schools.

    **D.** build interstate highways.

*The state of Georgia imposes a 4% sales tax on goods statewide. Most Georgians actually pay between 7% and 8% sales tax.*

---

**2.** Which revenue source BEST contributes to Georgia's state revenues?

    **A.** personal income taxes

    **B.** corporate income taxes

    **C.** sales taxes

    **D.** federal grants

**HINT** *In Georgia, local governments do not have the right to collect income tax.*

**3.** Which revenue source contributes the most to Georgia's local revenues?

    **A.** income taxes

    **B.** utility fees

    **C.** park entry fees

    **D.** property taxes

**4.** Which is the largest non-tax revenue source for the state of Georgia?

    **A.** bank loans

    **B.** license fees

    **C.** federal grants

    **D.** the state lottery

# 43 Personal Money Management

 SS8E5

For most people, their income is what they get paid for doing work. Some people, however, are able to live off of income from savings or investments. Income may also come from gifts or from selling something.

The main goal of budgeting is saving money. Saving allows people to plan to buy something expensive in the future. By setting aside a small amount of money every week, it is possible to save a large amount of money over time. Saving also creates a store of money that can be used in an emergency.

There are many different ways to save money. It is best to save money in some type of bank. In a bank, money can earn **interest**. Interest is a charge that the bank pays you to use your money. Although you can get your money at any time, a bank uses your money in various ways. For this privilege, the bank pays you a percentage of the amount that you have saved. The amount of interest paid ranges from less than 1% to as much as 13 or 14%.

Interest rates at banks are based on the **prime lending rate**, which is set by the Federal Reserve. When the prices of goods and services become too high, the "Fed" raises the prime rate. When unemployment becomes high, or the economy needs to be stimulated, the "Fed" lowers the prime rate. The prime lending rate affects how much interest is paid for savings accounts. It also affects the amount of interest charged for credit.

If $10 is placed in a bank account that earns 5% interest, then 5% of the total balance of the account is added to it on a regular basis. Over time, this helps the money grow.

| Bank Balance | 5% Interest Added |
|---|---|
| $10.00 in May | $0.50 at the end of May |
| $10.50 in June | $0.51 at the end of June |
| $11.01 in July | $0.55 at the end of July |
| $11.56 in August | $0.58 at the end of August |

Notice that the bank balance started with $10 and no new money is put into the bank, except interest. If the person with the bank account does not take the money out and just lets the interest add up, the balance will continue to grow. This effect is called **compounding interest.** Compounding interest also affects both savings and credit accounts.

# Investing and Credit

**Investing** is spending money in the hope of earning more money than is spent. One example of an investment that many eighth graders might have is a set of collectible trading cards. A card that is bought for $1 may someday be worth $10. A **return on investment** of $9—which is 900%—is a very good investment. Almost no large investments provide such a generous return.

In almost every location, the value of homes increases over time. This increase is one of the reasons that homes are considered one of the best investments people can make. A home is also the largest investment that most people have.

Stocks and bonds are another kind of investment that many people make. Stocks and bonds are small investments in large companies. If the company does well, the stock makes money. If it does poorly, the stock loses money.

Many people invest in stocks and bonds through a retirement plan through their job. A small percentage of their paycheck is withheld and added to their retirement account. These accounts are managed by outside companies that specialize in investing. In most cases, these investments are pooled together in mutual funds. **Mutual funds** invest in many stocks at once.

Every kind of investment involves risk. A **risk** is the possibility of losing money that has been invested. Often, the greater the risk of losing the money, the greater the possible return will be if the investment does well.

**Credit** is money that borrowed from a bank. When the bank uses your money, the bank pays you interest. But when you use the bank's money, you must pay the bank interest. The same compounding interest that worked in your favor in a savings account will work against you when you borrow money. This fact is why it is important to only borrow when absolutely necessary and pay back borrowed money as quickly as possible. See below how the compound interest on a credit card quickly adds up:

| Balance Owed | 10% Interest Charge |
|---|---|
| $100.00 borrowed in May | $10.00 interest |
| $110.00 owed in June | $11.00 interest |
| $121.00 owed in July | $12.10 interest |
| $133.10 owed in August | $13.31 interest |

There are many different types of credit—credit cards, home loans, and student loans are just a few of the most common types. Even electricity service and phone service are types of credit because the service is offered before money is paid. Anytime money is owed, credit has been extended.

The key to personal finance is never to borrow more than you can pay off in a reasonable amount of time. Learning to control and understand personal finance is the job of every adult.

## Show What You Know

**Do you have a credit account? Remember, any account where you use a service before paying—such as a cell phone—is a credit account. How did you get the account? Do you pay on time or have you had problems with credit? If you have not had a credit account yet, are you planning to have one? Write a short essay about your experience or plans for credit.**

_____

_____

_____

_____

_____

_____

_____

_____

_____

_____

_____

_____

_____

_____

_____

_____

_____

# Lesson Practice

## DIRECTIONS
**Circle the letter of the best answer for each item.**

### Thinking It Through

1. When the Federal Reserve sets the national base interest rate it is called the

   A. prime lending rate.

   B. primary interest hike.

   C. centralized rate.

   D. central-controlled interest.

   *Banks base the interest that they pay on savings and charge on credit on this rate. Both savings and credit are a form of borrowing. In savings, the bank borrows from you. In credit, you borrow from the bank.*

2. For most people in the United States, what is the MOST LIKELY goal of saving money?

   A. buying stereo equipment

   B. buying a home

   C. retirement

   D. buying a car

   **HINT** *Most people have a portion of their paycheck set aside for this purpose.*

3. The system of using electricity before paying for it is a form of

   A. savings.

   B. investment.

   C. income.

   D. credit.

4. Which of the following is a correct statement about compounding interest?

   A. Compounding interest subtracts value from a savings account.

   B. Compounding interest plays a role in both savings and credit.

   C. Compounding interest plays a role in both savings and income.

   D. Compounding interest adds value to income.

# 7 CRCT Review

**Choose the best answer for each question. Fill in the circle of the spaces provided on your answer sheet.**

1. In Georgia's colonial era, both rice and cotton were

   A. common imports.
   B. grown in the North, but processed in Georgia.
   C. the main crops grown.
   D. blighted by disease.

2. Which statement BEST explains the importance of profit to an entrepreneur?

   A. Every entrepreneur makes a profit.
   B. Every entrepreneur takes a risk so that they might make a profit.
   C. Entrepreneurs rarely make a profit.
   D. Entrepreneurs are often able to save money.

3. Which statement BEST illustrates the term "risk"?

   A. A businessperson inherits money from their parents.
   B. A businessperson saves money in a bank account.
   C. A businessperson invests money in real estate.
   D. A businessperson spends money on dinner.

4. Coca-Cola was first sold in the 1880s. For what purpose was Coca-Cola originally sold?

   A. anti-bacterial soap
   B. automobile oil
   C. health tonic
   D. alcoholic beverage

5. Where were Georgia's agricultural products MOST LIKELY sold during the colonial period?

   A. Africa

   B. Canada

   C. Georgia

   D. Europe

6. Which of Georgia's cities is described by the phrases in the box below?

   - headquarters of CNN
   - business capital of the Southeast
   - new residents moving in from rural areas

   A. Macon

   B. Atlanta

   C. Savannah

   D. Athens

7. The term "graduated tax" describes

   A. a tax rate that rises or falls depending on a person's income.

   B. a tax rate that is the same for every person.

   C. a tax rate that rises or falls according to a person's age.

   D. an illegal type of taxation.

8. Which of the following sources contributes most to state revenue?

   A. lottery funds

   B. tobacco settlement funds

   C. taxes, fees, and sales

   D. revenue shortfall reserve

9. Which state service did Georgia spend the most revenue to operate?

   A. social services

   B. transportation

   C. criminal justice

   D. education

10. How are credit cards and cell phone services similar?

   A. They both involve saving money.

   B. They both involve paying interest.

   C. They are both forms of credit.

   D. They are both forms of income.

11. Which of the following statements BEST describes how decisions are made about spending state revenues?

   A. The governor decides how to spend state revenue.

   B. The legislature and local businesses work together to decide how to spend state revenue.

   C. The legislature, governor, state agencies, and citizens work together to decide how to spend state revenue.

   D. The governor asks permission from state agencies about how to spend state revenue.

12. What is the main savings goal of most people?

   A. buying cars

   B. retirement

   C. buying a home

   D. spending on luxuries

# Georgia CRCT Coach, GPS Edition, Social Studies, Grade 8

# POSTTEST

**Name:** _____

## General Instructions

Today you will be taking the Social Studies Criterion-Referenced Competency Test. The Social Studies test consists of multiple-choice questions. A sample has been included. The sample shows you how to mark your answers.

There are several important things to remember.

- Read each question carefully and think about the answer.

- Answer all questions on your answer sheet. Do not mark any answers to questions in your test booklet.

- For each question, choose the best answer, and completely fill in the circle in the space provided on your answer sheet.

- If you do not know the answer to a question, skip it and go on. You may return to it later if you have time.

- If you finish the section of the test that you are working on early, you may review your answers in that section only. You may not review another section or go on to the next section of the test.

Coach™®

## Sample Question

The sample test question below is provided to show you what the questions in the test are like and how to mark your answer to each question. For each question, choose the one best answer, and fill in the circle in the space provided on your answer sheet for the answer you have chosen. Be sure to mark all of your answers to the questions on your answer sheet.

## Sample

Who is responsible for writing laws in Georgia?

    A.   governor

    B.   Supreme Court

    C.   General Assembly

    D.   secretary of state

**PLEASE STOP! DO NOT GO ON TO THE NEXT PAGE.**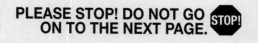

## Section 1

**Section 1 of this test has thirty questions. Choose the best answer for each question. Fill in the circle in the spaces provided for questions 1 through 30 on your answer sheet.**

1. At the Battle of Kettle Creek, during the Revolutionary War, why was Austin Dabney singled out by the state of Georgia?

   A. He led the victorious charge against the British.

   B. He was the only slave to fight in the battle.

   C. He was defeated by Elijah Clarke.

   D. He provided much needed arms to the Georgians.

2. Who was MOST responsible for promoting the Atlanta Braves and the city of Atlanta on a national basis?

   A. Ivan Allen, Jr.

   B. William B. Hartsfield

   C. Ted Turner

   D. Rankin M. Smith

3. In Georgia's Constitution, what is the BEST explanation of the idea of limiting one branch of government and correcting any errors?

   A. checks and balances

   B. separation of powers

   C. Bill of Rights

   D. judicial review

4. What is the BEST explanation of the motive of an entrepreneur to enter the business world?

   A. to capitalize on the growing market trend to establish a legacy

   B. to maximize profits with the risk of capital

   C. to reduce the budget deficit through investment

   D. to increase expenditure through balance of trade

**PLEASE GO ON TO THE NEXT PAGE.**

5. What was one of the major problems with the Articles of Confederation that left the colonial government short of money during the war?

   A. no power to wage war

   B. power of local postal services

   C. no power to tax the states

   D. power to control Native American affairs

6. Who can vote in a Republican primary election in Georgia?

   A. registered Republicans only

   B. either a Republican or a Democrat registered to vote

   C. registered voter without any party affiliation

   D. anyone registered can vote in a primary election

7. Which early explorer was MOST LIKELY responsible for introducing the diseases that devastated the Native American populations in Georgia?

   A. Ponce de León

   B. Hernando de Soto

   C. John Smith

   D. Jacques Cartier

8. What is the term used in a dispute settled peacefully?

   A. litigation

   B. arbitration

   C. negotiation

   D. subjection

9. In which industries are the new waves of immigrants from Latin America MOST LIKELY to fill the growing jobs?

   A. deep water shipping

   B. information technologies

   C. manufacturing

   D. agricultural

10. What are the qualifications to be elected to the Georgia General Assembly?

    A. age of 25 for a representative, 21 for a senator, both U.S. citizens, and residency in Georgia for 1 year

    B. age of 25 for a senator, 21 for a representative, both U.S. citizens, and residency in Georgia for 1 year

    C. age of 25 for a representative, 21 for a senator, both U.S. citizens, and residency in Georgia for 2 years

    D. age of 25 for a senator, 21 for a representative, both U.S. citizens, with a two-year residency in Georgia

**PLEASE GO ON TO THE NEXT PAGE.**

11. What is the BEST explanation for Congress passing the Lend-Lease Act in 1941?

    A. to offer arms to allies who could not pay

    B. to stoke the fires of America's economy

    C. to insure America's entry into the European Theater

    D. to stop Japanese aggression in the Pacific

12. Which is described by the list in the box below?

> • Southeastern United States
> • Western Hemisphere
> • north of Florida

    A. absolute location of Georgia

    B. GPS location of Georgia

    C. relative location of Georgia

    D. latitude and longitude for Georgia

13. Juveniles taken into custody are afforded which of the following rights?

    A. freedom from status offense

    B. right to object to unruly behavior

    C. right to have a lawyer

    D. freedom from delinquent behavior

14. Which Georgian, during his service in Congress, was instrumental in preparing the United States naval forces during the time of Lend-Lease, and also helped to expand the shipbuilding industries in Savannah and Brunswick that still feel the effects of his efforts today?

    A. Richard Russell

    B. Carl Vinson

    C. Franklin D. Roosevelt

    D. William B. Hartsfield

15. What was the major change that led to a more balanced two-party system in Georgia instead of one dominated by the views of a few in the Democratic Party?

    A. election of a Republican to the presidency in 1968

    B. *Miranda v. Arizona*

    C. Voting Rights Act in 1965

    D. *Plessy v. Ferguson*

**PLEASE GO ON TO THE NEXT PAGE.**

16. Which Georgian is BEST described by the phrases "accommodation," and "dignify and glorify common labor"?

   A. Booker T. Washington

   B. W. E. B. Du Bois

   C. Alonzo Hearndon

   D. Burns Hope

17. Georgia played an important part in the ratification of the Constitution, becoming the fourth state to do so. Which two Georgians were signers of the U.S. Constitution?

   A. Abraham Baldwin and W. E. B. Du Bois

   B. William Few and Richard Russell

   C. Francis Marion and Booker T. Washington

   D. William Few and Abraham Baldwin

18. To vote in Georgia, you must

   A. be 21 years of age or older.

   B. never have committed a crime.

   C. be of sound mind, if so designated by a judge.

   D. vote in two consecutive elections.

19. City and county governments cover different jurisdictions of control. Which of the following is characteristic of a county government?

   A. formed by a charter

   B. named a municipality

   C. provides electric or gas utilities

   D. home of voter registration

20. Where are most of the taxes and fees that are collected in the state of Georgia deposited to help pay the bills of the state?

   A. general fund

   B. educational fund

   C. special improvement districts

   D. governor's budget fund

21. Which group of early Georgian settlers was initially expelled from their home in the Austrian Alps?

   A. Malcontents

   B. Salzburgers

   C. Moravians

   D. Highland Scots

**PLEASE GO ON TO THE NEXT PAGE.**

22. When did Georgia officially become a British Crown colony?

    A. before the Trustee period

    B. after the Trustee period

    C. at the start of the French and Indian War

    D. after the Battle of Bloody Marsh against the Spanish

23. The county unit system was devised to give votes during the primary elections in each county. Which group was unfairly represented in the distribution of votes in the mainly rural state of Georgia?

    A. rural sector

    B. urban sector

    C. town sector

    D. all were equally represented

24. How is the concept of "separation of powers" BEST illustrated in relation to the legislative branch of government?

    A. They interpret the laws.

    B. They form public policy.

    C. They make the laws.

    D. They head the military.

25. A bill from the General Assembly may be presented to the governor for his consideration, and potentially be signed into law, after which of the following processes?

    A. introduction

    B. drafting

    C. committee consideration

    D. floor consideration

26. What act by Ellis Arnall led to Eugene Talmadge being elected to succeed him as governor?

    A. educational reforms in the university system

    B. revamping the penal system

    C. allowing blacks to vote in white primaries

    D. paying off Georgia's enormous debt

27. What would be an example of a special-purpose government?

    A. City Council

    B. Downtown Development Authority

    C. Attorney General

    D. Ways and Means Committee

**PLEASE GO ON TO THE NEXT PAGE.**

28. The juvenile justice system in Georgia has jurisdiction over

   A. all individuals 16 years of age or younger.

   B. all individuals 15 years of age or younger.

   C. all individuals 17 years of age or younger.

   D. all individuals 18 years of age or younger.

29. One of the chief responsibilities of the governor as head of the executive branch of Georgia's government is

   A. to decide if a law is constitutional.

   B. to make budgetary recommendations to the General Assembly.

   C. to write effective legislation.

   D. to review judicial decisions and veto judicial laws.

30. What was the basic premise behind the 1896 Supreme Court decision *Plessy v. Ferguson*?

   A. equal voting rights

   B. women's suffrage

   C. demise of Jim Crow laws

   D. separate but equal

**PLEASE STOP! DO NOT GO ON TO THE NEXT PAGE.** STOP!

# Section 2

**Section 2 of this test has thirty questions. Choose the best answer for each question. Fill in the circle in the spaces provided for questions 31 through 60 on your answer sheet.**

31. What made 1972 an important year for not only Andrew Young, but also for the African American community in Georgia?

    A. He was the first elected African American mayor of Atlanta.

    B. He was appointed the United Nations ambassador of the U.S.

    C. He was the first African American elected to Congress from Georgia since the 1860s.

    D. He followed Dr. Martin Luther King, Jr., as leader of the SCLC.

32. What was the main focus of the Jewish community in Georgia when the revelation of the atrocities in Europe against the Jewish community became known?

    A. forming a military division in the service of the U.S.

    B. raising money to fight discrimination abroad

    C. forcing lawmakers to adopt pro-Jewish legislation

    D. lobbying Congress to promote the establishment of a Jewish homeland

33. How did Eugene Talmadge begin his service to the great state of Georgia?

    A. secretary of state

    B. insurance commissioner

    C. lieutenant governor

    D. agricultural commissioner

34. President Roosevelt directed numerous war-time projects toward his home away from home. Which one of them is still used today, in Marietta ?

    A. Bell Aircraft

    B. Martin-Marietta

    C. The Home Depot

    D. IBM

35. Why did the Spanish concentrate their initial colonization along the barrier islands?

    A. The land inland was less fertile.

    B. There were too many Native Americans inland.

    C. It was easier for ships to access the shore.

    D. Rumors of malaria kept sailors close to the sea.

**PLEASE GO ON TO THE NEXT PAGE.**

36. In the early 1700s, the three main crops found in Georgia were

 A. cotton, tobacco, and sugar.

 B. sugar, rice, and indigo.

 C. tobacco, peanuts, and peaches.

 D. cotton, tobacco, and rice.

37. What two parties are MOST LIKELY to be found in a civil law trial?

 A. prosecutor and defendant

 B. defendant and plaintiff

 C. prosecutor and plaintiff

 D. jury and prosecutor

38. In Georgia, what was one of the main tasks undertaken by the Civilian Conservation Corps during the early years of President Roosevelt's New Deal?

 A. to restore the fisheries off Georgia's coast

 B. to provide jobs to restore the inner cities

 C. to build many of Georgia's state parks

 D. to capitalize on Georgia's mineral resources

39. According to the Georgia Bill of Rights, Georgians have the right to bear arms. What does this specifically mean?

 A. the right to vote

 B. the right to criticize government

 C. the right to possess property

 D. the right to possess firearms

40. Which ideal did the 1956 adoption of the Georgia state flag promote?

 A. link to legalized slavery

 B. equality for all

 C. unity with the North

 D. dissolution of the Confederacy

41. The Trail of Tears was the forced relocation of the Cherokee Nation from their homeland to land designated by the federal government. It resulted in the death of many people. Where did this forced march take place?

 A. Georgia to Tennessee

 B. Oklahoma to Georgia

 C. Georgia to Oklahoma

 D. South Carolina to Ohio

**PLEASE GO ON TO THE NEXT PAGE.**

42. At the end of World War II, Georgia was a farming state. What percentage of Georgia's population is involved with farming today?

    A.   2%

    B.   10%

    C.   25%

    D.   50%

43. Why do most of Georgia's people live along the fall line?

    A.   because of the rich sandy soil

    B.   because of a milder climate

    C.   because of the rivers and waterfalls

    D.   because it is near the coast

44. How is the election and term of office for the lieutenant governor different than that of the governor?

    A.   The lieutenant governor does not run on the same ticket.

    B.   The lieutenant governor must belong to the same party.

    C.   The lieutenant governor must be 30 years old or older.

    D.   There are no term limits for the lieutenant governor.

45. Why was the Yazoo land sale reversed in the 1796 Rescinding Act?

    A.   Fraud and bribery were involved.

    B.   The western frontier was unsafe.

    C.   It was Cherokee land.

    D.   Land was too expensive.

46. Which major interstate highway connects Georgia with buyers and sellers in the Midwest?

    A.   I-95

    B.   I-75

    C.   I-20

    D.   I-85

47. What was the result of the end of the county unit system and the eventual reapportionment?

    A.   Segregation increased, as a result.

    B.   Conservatives remained in control.

    C.   Rural areas won more legislative power.

    D.   Blacks and urban dwellers won more legislative power.

**PLEASE GO ON TO THE NEXT PAGE.**

48. After the Eastern Woodlands people began to settle down and live in villages instead of living as hunter-gatherers, the "Three Sisters" became very important to their lives. What are the Three Sisters?

   A. sun, moon, and the stars

   B. maize, beans, and squash

   C. fish, water, and potatoes

   D. sun, gods, and water

49. Which Georgian and his or her description is correctly matched?

   A. Jimmy Carter—urban U.S. senator

   B. Martin Luther King, Jr.—Georgia representative to Congress

   C. Mary Musgrove—peacekeeper who represented and protected Native Americans

   D. Andrew Young—first presidential cabinet appointee from Georgia

*Use the table below to answer question 50.*

### Georgia State Revenue Sources (2004)

| Source | Amount |
| --- | --- |
| Taxes, fees, and sales | $15,163,809,957 |
| Lottery funds | $691,795,656 |
| Tobacco settlement funds | $175,080,760 |
| Brain and spinal injury trust fund | $2,000,000 |
| Revenue shortfall reserve | $141,997,339 |
| TOTAL FUNDS | $16,174,683,712 |

50. According to the table, what accounts for the 3rd largest source of revenue for Georgia in 2004?

   A. Lottery funds     B. Tobacco settlement funds

   C. Revenue shortfall reserve     D. Brain and spinal injury trust fund

51. What was the stated purpose of the General Assembly Committee on Schools, also known as the Sibley Commission?

   A. to gather information on how people felt about desegregation

   B. to speed up school desegregation

   C. to increase segregation of schools

   D. to re-certify the University of Georgia

**PLEASE GO ON TO THE NEXT PAGE.**

52. One of the stated reasons that Atlanta wanted to host the 1996 Olympics was to show the world that Georgia and Atlanta were ready for worldwide business. How did the federal government help in the effort to get the state and city of Atlanta ready for the nearly 72 million visitors during the Olympics?

    A.  built all new sports arenas

    B.  replaced sidewalks and planted trees

    C.  donated money to sponsor companies

    D.  convinced the international Olympic committee

*Use the table below to answer question 53.*

### Georgia State Budget

|  | General Funds Budgeted | Percentage of Total Budget |
| --- | --- | --- |
| Board of Education | $7,189,516,840 | 40.77% |
| Regents | $1,917,240,948 | 10.87% |
| Technical and Adult Education | $336,788,064 | 1.91% |
| Medicaid | $2,142,863,566 | 12.15% |
| PeachCare | $62,188,968 | 0.35% |
| Human Resources | $1,394,958,349 | 7.91% |
| Department of Corrections | $997,756,694 | 5.66% |
| Debt Service | $867,362,612 | 4.92% |
| Department of Transportation | $664,032,462 | 3.77% |

53. According to the table, what is the second most costly line item in the part of the 2007 Georgia budget shown?

    A.  Education funding

    B.  Department of Corrections

    C.  Medicaid

    D.  Human Resources

54. In which form of local government would the office of mayor be little more than ceremonial?

    A.  special improvement district

    B.  council-manager

    C.  strong mayor-council

    D.  weak mayor-council

**PLEASE GO ON TO THE NEXT PAGE.**

55. Through which of Georgia's deepwater ports run by the Georgia Port Authority might you find an automobile being shipped?

A. Ocean terminal

B. Garden City terminal

C. Marine Port terminal

D. Mayor's Point terminal

56. Because of the drought, overuse of farmland, and the arrival of the boll weevil, what is the BEST term to describe Georgia's farm economy leading up to the 1930s?

A. booming

B. depression

C. inflation

D. recession

57. How is a judge selected to serve in Georgia?

A. must be elected in a partisan election

B. must be elected in a nonpartisan election

C. must be appointed by another judge or legislator

D. can be appointed by another judge or legislator

58. What was the ultimate objective of General Robert E. Lee when he was stopped at the Battle of Antietam?

A. recapture of Atlanta

B. avenge of Gettysburg

C. capture of Washington, D.C.

D. defense of Richmond

59. Who is the largest employer in the state of Georgia?

A. Georgia government

B. Hartsfield International Airport

C. The Home Depot

D. Coca-Cola

60. Which of the following lists the correct order of events of official acts of Congress?

1. voting rights not allowed to be denied by race

2. grants citizenship to all African Americans

3. voting rights extended to women

4. abolition of slavery

A. 1, 2, 3, 4

B. 2, 4, 3, 1

C. 4, 2, 1, 3

D. 3, 4, 2, 1

**PLEASE STOP! DO NOT GO ON TO THE NEXT PAGE.**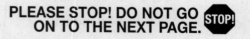

# Glossary

**abolitionist** person opposed to slavery and in favor of ending it (Lesson 12)

**accommodationism** viewpoint that compromises or adapts to the viewpoint of the opposition (Lesson 17)

**adjudicatory hearing** situation in juvenile court where judge decides if charges in petition are true or not (Lesson 38)

**affirmative action** policy or program that seeks to undo past discrimination through active measures to ensure equal opportunity in education and employment (Lesson 25)

**agriculture** the practice of cultivating the land or raising stock; farming (Lesson 1)

**Allied powers** a group of countries (Britain, France, and eventually the United States and the Soviet Union) that led one side of World War II (Lesson 22)

**ally** person, group, or nation that is associated with another or others for a common cause or purpose, often in war (Lesson 22)

**amendment** change made to the Constitution of the United States (Lesson 7)

**anthropologist** scientist who studies human life and culture (Lesson 1)

**anti-Semitism** violence or unfairness to Jewish people (Lesson 15)

**appellate court** court that determines if a trial court has made mistakes; may also determine if laws agree with constitution or not (Lesson 37)

**archaeologist** scientist who learns about ancient cultures by studying their remains (Lesson 1)

**Articles of Confederation** early version of constitution approved by Continental Congress; lasted from 1781 to 1789 (Lesson 7)

**artifact** physical remnant of an ancient culture (Lesson 1)

**Atlanta Compromise** statement on race relations by Booker T. Washington, made in a speech at the Atlanta Exposition in 1895, in which he asserted that vocational education was more valuable than social equality or political office (Lesson 17)

**Austro-Hungarian Empire** multi-ethnic configuration of territories, which is significantly larger and more ethnically homogeneous than present-day Hungary, that lasted from 1000 to 1526 (Lesson 18)

**Axis powers** a group of countries (Japan, Italy, and Germany) that led one side of World War II (Lesson 22)

**barrier island** island that blocks the mainland from the ocean (Lesson 30)

**BCE** Before the Common Era (Lesson 1)

**Beringia** Bering land bridge that connected Asia to North America during the Ice Age (Lesson 1)

**bill** legislation that calls for additions or changes to a law (Lesson 35)

**black codes** state laws in the South during Reconstruction that were meant to limit the freedoms of African Americans (Lesson 14)

**blitzkrieg** military tactic used by Germany in World War II designed to create psychological shock to enemy forces through the use of surprise, speed, and military superiority; means "lightning war" in German (Lesson 22)

**Boston Tea Party** Dec. 16, 1773; patriots dumped British tea into Boston Harbor in protest of taxes (Lesson 5)

**Bourbon Triumvirate** group comprised of Alfred Colquitt, Joseph Brown, and John Gordon that led the Bourbon Democrats in Georgia, after the end of Reconstruction; encouraged industrialization in Georgia (Lesson 15)

**carbon-14 dating** determination of the age of an ancient object by measuring the amount of carbon-14 it contains (Lesson 1)

CE Common Era (Lesson 1)

**charter** document similar to a constitution that outlines a municipality's powers and borders, and the form and structure of its government (Lesson 3)

**checks and balances** system in which different branches of government limit and correct each other (Lesson 33)

**chiefdom** small society in which one person makes most decisions (Lesson 1)

**civil case** court case where one person or group, called the plaintiff, claims that another person or group, called the defendant, has done them wrong in some way which does not involve committing a crime; in civil cases; the defendant never has to go to jail or pay a fine to the government, but may have to pay money to the plaintiff (Lesson 37)

**civil law** set of rules that apply to civil cases (Lesson 37)

**civil rights** the rights of a person regardless of race, color, or gender by the Bill of Rights, amendments to the Constitution, and acts of Congress (Lesson 26)

**clan** group of people with common ancestry (Lesson 1)

**Cocking Affair** 1941; Georgia Governor Eugene Talmadge fired professors, administrators, and members of the Board of Regents of the university system of Georgia, including Walter Cocking, dean of the College of Education at the University of Georgia (Lesson 20)

**commercialism** overly concerned with how much money can be made from something (Lesson 29)

**Commission on Interracial Cooperation** group formed in the South in 1919 to work at preventing race riots and to provide the African American population of the South with schools (Lesson 17)

**commodities** bulk products, such as metals, grains, and foods, that are bought, sold, or traded (Lesson 32)

**compounding interest** interest which is added to the original principal; when money grows by allowing the principal's monthly interest to add up over time (Lesson 43)

**Compromise of 1850** series of bills that were fought over in Congress for eight months made to keep the balance between slave and non-slave states (Lesson 12)

**congressional district** area of land represented by one member in the House of Representatives (Lesson 26)

**council-manager** form of municipal government with an elected city council and an appointed city manager; city council is legislative branch, city manager is chief executive, and mayor is member of city council (Lesson 39)

**county unit system** Georgia system of giving votes in primary elections where each county was assigned a set number of unit votes, those unit votes won by the candidate who won the popular vote in a given county (Lesson 15)

**credit** arrangement for deferred payment of a loan or purchase (Lesson 43)

**crest** the highest part of a hill or mountain range (Lesson 30)

**criminal case** court case where the government, called the prosecutor, accuses someone, called the defendant, of committing a crime; a person found guilty in a criminal case may have to pay a fine to the government, go to jail, or both (Lesson 37)

**criminal law** laws that apply to criminal cases (Lesson 37)

**culture** patterns of behavior and thinking shared by people in social groups (Lesson 1)

**Declaration of Independence** document that stated the separation of the thirteen colonies from Great Britain; approved on July 4, 1776 (Lesson 7)

**defendant** in a civil case, a person who is complained about; in a criminal case, a person charged with committing a crime (Lesson 37)

**delinquent behavior** behavior that would be a crime for an adult, but is committed by a child (Lesson 38)

**democracy** government by the people (Lesson 28)

**depression** severe and prolonged recession characterized by inefficient economic productivity, high unemployment, and falling prices (Lesson 19)

**diplomatic relations** managing the relationship between nations (Lesson 27)

**disenfranchisement** revocation of, or failure to grant, the right to vote to a person or group of people (Lesson 16)

**dispositional hearing** situation in juvenile court where judge decides on course of supervision, treatment, and rehabilitation of delinquent; or chooses to transfer case to superior court (Lesson 38)

**ecosystem** a system formed by the interaction of a community of organisms with their environment (Lesson 30)

**Eighty-second All-American Division** division of the U.S. army formed on March 5, 1917, at Camp Gordon, Georgia, given the nickname "All-Americans" since members of the division came from all 48 states (Lesson 18)

**Emancipation Proclamation** proclamation issued by President Abraham Lincoln declaring freedom for all slaves in states still in rebellion against the federal government; took effect on January 1, 1863 (Lesson 13)

**entrepreneur** someone who takes on all aspects of a new business, including the operation, management, and risk (Lesson 40)

**ethnic group** sizable group of people sharing a common and distinctive racial, national, religious, linguistic, or cultural heritage (Lesson 18)

**executive order** principle, rule, or law designed to control or govern conduct (Lesson 20)

**federal** relating to the central government of a country (Lesson 29)

**felony** serious crime for which the punishment is a year or more in jail (Lesson 37)

**Fifteenth Amendment** ensures that the right to vote cannot be denied to any U.S. citizen on account of "race, color, or previous condition of servitude" (Lesson 14)

**floor leader** promotes the governor's position in the House of Representatives (Lesson 35)

**Fort Frederica** fort on Georgia's southern boundary where the British made their military headquarters (Lesson 3)

**Fourteenth Amendment** grants equal rights to every person born in the U.S. regardless of race (Lesson 14)

**free trade** trade between nations without restrictive barriers such as tariffs (Lesson 41)

**Freedmen's Bureau** government agency set up during Reconstruction that helped poor people and freed slaves with clothes, food, employment, and education (Lesson 14)

**freedom rider** one of an interracial group of civil rights activists in the early 1960s who rode buses through parts of the southern United States for the purpose of challenging racial segregation (Lesson 25)

**French and Indian War** North American phase of a war between France and Britain to control colonial territory from 1754 to 1763 (Lesson 4)

**Fugitive Slave Act** law declaring that all states must help return runaway slaves to their owners (Lesson 12)

**general election** election where candidates from different political parties run against each other for government office (Lesson 34)

**Georgia Platform** the North would support the Fugitive Slave Act and not ban slavery in new states in order to uphold the Compromise of 1850 (Lesson 12)

**governor** chief executive of a state in the United States of America (Lesson 27)

**grandfather clause** clause which stated that if a man had an ancestor who had been allowed to vote before 1867, he was permitted to vote; since African American men weren't allowed to vote until 1867, this clause deliberately excluded them (Lesson 16)

**Great Compromise** also called Connecticut Compromise; the establishment of a bicameral legislature; the Senate would only have two representatives per state and the House of Representatives would have state representatives based on population (Lesson 7)

**Great Depression** longest and most severe economic depression ever experienced by the Western world, which began in the U.S. soon after the New York Stock Market Crash of 1929, lasting until about 1939 (Lesson 19)

**headright system** system under which land was granted to the heads of families (Lesson 9)

**Holocaust** systematic killing of European Jews, Gypsies, homosexuals, and political dissenters by the Nazis during World War II (Lesson 22)

**human rights** rights of all human beings to justice and to basic needs, such as food, shelter, and education (Lesson 27)

**ideology** organized collection of ideas (Lesson 18)

**"I have a dream" speech** historic speech by Dr. Martin Luther King, Jr., about his desire for a future where blacks and whites coexist harmoniously as equals; King gave his speech on August 28, 1963 from the steps of the Lincoln Memorial at the March on Washington for Jobs and Freedom (Lesson 25)

**immigrant** person who moves to another country, usually to stay (Lesson 29)

**impeachment** formal document charging a public official with misconduct in office (Lesson 14)

**inaugural address** speech delivered at an inaugural ceremony (Lesson 27)

**industry** business, trade, and/or manufacture of goods (Lesson 28)

**inequalities** not equal; unjust (Lesson 26)

**interest** charge for a loan, usually a percentage of the amount loaned (Lesson 43)

**Intolerable Acts** four laws passed by the British to punish the colonies (Lesson 5)

**investing** spending money in the hope of earning more money than is spent (Lesson 43)

**Iranian hostage crisis** Americans citizens were held by a terrorist organization in Iran from November 4, 1979 to January 21, 1981 (Lesson 27)

**isolationism** national policy of abstaining from political or economic relations with other countries (Lesson 22)

**Jim Crow laws** laws that enforced racial segregation in the South between 1877 and the 1950s (Lesson 16)

**jurisdiction** geographic and legal range over which a court has control and can pass judgments (Lesson 37)

**Kansas-Nebraska Act** law that divided the Kansas territory into two states (Lesson 12)

**land lottery** system under which ordinary Georgians could purchase cheap land (Lesson 9)

**legislative branch** branch of government that makes the laws (Lesson 35)

**Lend-Lease Act** passed on March 11, 1941, this law provided U.S. military aid to foreign nations during World War II (Lesson 22)

**literacy test** government practice of testing the literacy of potential citizens at the federal level, and potential voters at the state level (Lesson 16)

**loyalists** American colonists who stayed loyal to Britain (Lesson 5)

**majority leader** promotes the ideas and interests of the majority party in the legislature (Lesson 35)

**majority party** political party that has the most members in the legislature (Lesson 35)

**majority vote** vote that requires slightly more than half the voters to approve something; in Georgia's House of Representatives, it requires 91 out 180 members; in the Senate, it requires 29 out of 56 (Lesson 35)

**Malcontents** wealthy colonists of Scottish descent; not as loyal to the Trustees or Britain (Lesson 3)

**manufacturing** making something by hand or machine (Lesson 28)

**mediator** person who helps two sides in a conflict come to an agreement or resolution (Lesson 37)

**minority leader** promotes the ideas and interests of the minority party in either the Senate or House of Representatives (Lesson 35)

**minority party** political party that has the fewest members in the legislature (Lesson 35)

**misdemeanor** less serious crime for which the punishment is less than a year in jail (Lesson 37)

**missionary** sent by a church to a foreign country to spread their religion (Lesson 2)

**Mississippian culture** after the Woodland period, begin from about 900 CE until the late 15th century; Native American Farmers who lived in the Southeast; known for chiefdoms, trading, and temple mounds (Lesson 1)

**Missouri Compromise** 1820 agreement between the North and South about slavery in new states (Lesson 12)

**Moravians** Protestants who came from Bohemia, present-day Czech Republic, to Georgia in 1735 (Lesson 3)

**mutual fund** continually offers new shares and buys existing shares back at the request of the shareholder and uses its capital to invest in diversified securities of other companies (Lesson 43)

**National Association for the Advancement of Colored People (NAACP)** founded in 1909 to ensure that all people have equal rights; founders included W .E. B. Du Bois and Ida Wells-Barnett (Lesson 17)

**National Association of Colored Women (NACW)** formed in 1896 by two national African American women's organizations that joined under the leadership of Josephine Ruffin, Margaret Murray Washington, Mary Church Terrell, and Victoria Earle Matthews (Lesson 17)

**Neill Primary Act** law which made the county unit system of voting legal in Georgia in 1917 (Lesson 26)

**New Deal** programs and policies to promote economic recovery and social reform introduced during the 1930s by President Franklin D. Roosevelt (Lesson 21)

**Niagara movement** influential civil rights group organized by W. E. B. Du Bois in 1905 to split with the philosophy of Booker T. Washington (Lesson 17)

**Nobel Peace Prize** annual prizes given by the Nobel Foundation for achievement in physics, chemistry, economics, medicine, physiology, and promoting peace (Lesson 27)

**nomadic hunter-gatherer** ancient people who moved from place to place annually, in search of food (Lesson 1)

**Non sibi sed aliis** Latin motto of Georgia's Trustees, which means "Not for self, but for others" (Lesson 3)

**nonpartisan election** election in which candidates do not run as members of political parties (Lesson 37)

**nullification** belief that a state has the right not to follow a federal law (Lesson 12)

**one-party system** one political party has the power to make rules (Lesson 28)

**partisan election** election in which candidates run as members of political parties (Lesson 37)

**patriots** people who rebelled against British rule during the American Revolution (Lesson 5)

**plaintiff** person or group who complains about another in a civil case; must convince a judge or jury that their complaint has a true basis (Lesson 37)

**political party** group of people that represents particular ideas and interests and tries to make these ideas and interests part of government policy (Lesson 34)

**poll tax** tax levied on people often as a requirement for voting (Lesson 16)

**popular sovereignty** vote by the people of each state to decide the issue of slavery (Lesson 12)

**popular vote** majority of individual votes given to the winning candidate in an election (Lesson 26)

**populism** movement of southern farmers and other people against the elite (Lesson 15)

**precipitation** moisture in the form of rain, melted snow, and ice (Lesson 31)

**president of the Senate** leader of the senate; lieutenant governor of Georgia (Lesson 35)

**president pro tempore** leader of the Senate's majority party; becomes leader of Senate if president gets ill or dies (Lesson 35)

**Presidential Medal of Freedom** highest civilian award given in the United States (Lesson 27)

**primary election** individuals from the same political party try to become their party's candidate for a general election (Lesson 34)

**prime lending rate** lowest rate of interest on bank loans at a given time and place, offered to preferred borrowers (Lesson 43)

**probable cause hearing** situation in juvenile court where a judge decides, based on the facts of the case, whether a child should be detained or released (Lesson 38)

**profit** in business, the money remaining after expenses are paid, and the main incentive for starting a business (Lesson 40)

**prosecutor** in a criminal case, a government body that charges a group or person of committing a crime (Lesson 37)

**racism** discrimination, segregation, domination, or persecution based on race (Lesson 27)

**Radical Republicans** group of anti-slavery activists who tried to kick President Andrew Johnson out of office (Lesson 14)

**reapportionment** changing the boundaries of a congressional district (Lesson 26)

**Reconstruction** period after the American Civil War when the Southern states were reorganized and reintegrated into the Union; 1865–1877 (Lesson 14)

**responsibility** knowledge that actions have consequences, and that these consequences effect other people (Lesson 34)

**return on investment** profit made from money spent (Lesson 43)

**revenue** income (Lesson 42)

**revival** meeting intended to reawaken interest in religion, usually includes emotional preaching and public testimony (Lesson 8)

**right** standard or law that ensures that governments and other institutions protect people's freedom and treat people equally in society and politics (Lesson 34)

**risk** chance that an investment's actual return will be less than expected (Lesson 43)

**royal colony** colony overseen by the crown of England (Lesson 4)

**rural** country or farming area (Lesson 26)

**SALT II** treaty between the U.S. and the Soviet Union to reduce the amount of nuclear arms in both countries (Lesson 27)

**Salzburgers** Protestants who came from Salzburg to Georgia in 1734 (Lesson 3)

**secession** withdrawal of a state from the Union (Lesson 12)

**segregation** intentional separation of races (Lesson 14)

**separation of powers** system in which government is broken up into different parts or branches, and each branch has a different role (Lesson 33)

**service industry** industry that provides services to others; includes medical care, food, and entertainment businesses, law firms, and private schools (Lesson 28)

**sharecropping** farming method in which a land owner loans farmers housing, seeds, and tools in return for a share of the crop's profits (Lesson 14)

**sit-in** organized protest demonstration in which participants seat themselves and refuse to move (Lesson 25)

**Spanish Armada** Spanish naval fleet that attacked England (Lesson 2)

**speaker of the House** leader of the House of Representatives; member of the majority party; decides what should be debated in House; chooses committee chairs (Lesson 35)

**special-purpose district** special purpose government or local government authority created by cities or counties to meet a specific purpose such as housing, development, or environmental resources (Lesson 39)

**Stamp Act of 1765** tax on all documents, permits, commercial contacts, newspapers, pamphlets, and playing cards (Lesson 5)

**Stamp Act Congress** representatives from nine colonies who met to oppose the Stamp Act (Lesson 5)

**status offense** unruly behavior in children that would be a crime if done by an adult (Lesson 38)

**strong mayor-council** form of municipal government with an elected city council and an elected mayor; city council is legislative branch and mayor is a powerful executive officer (Lesson 39)

**suffrage** right to vote (Lesson 15)

**tabby** mixture of mortar and lime used in home building throughout the southeast U.S. during the colonial period (Lesson 4)

**tariff** tax on foreign goods (Lesson 12)

**tax** a fee that individuals and businesses must pay to government (Lesson 42)

**terminal** location where goods are loaded or unloaded from its mode of transportation (Lesson 32)

**textile** any cloth or goods produced by weaving, knitting, or felting (Lesson 30)

**Third Reich** official designation for the Nazi Party's regime in Germany from January 1933 to May 1945 (Lesson 22)

**Thirteenth Amendment** amendment to the Constitution that abolished slavery as a legal institution (Lesson 14)

**Three Sisters** corn, beans, and squash; the three most important crops in Native American agriculture (Lesson 1)

**ticket** list of candidates who are members of the same political party, and who are running together for different offices (Lesson 36)

**tourism** the business of serving tourists, individuals traveling through the state (Lesson 28)

**Trail of Tears** forced relocation of the Cherokee to present-day Oklahoma; thousands died along the way (Lesson 11)

**treaty** contract between two or more countries (Lesson 27)

**trial court** court that determines if a person's or group's actions and intentions are against the law or not, decided by judge or jury (Lesson 37)

**tribe** group of people who share language, customs, and territory (Lesson 1)

**trust** a legal title showing ownership of property for the benefit of another (Lesson 3)

**trustee** someone who oversees a property on behalf of someone else (Lesson 3)

**Trustee period** time when Georgia was ruled by a group of trustees, from 1732 to 1752 (Lesson 3)

**two-thirds vote** requires two-thirds to approve; in Georgia's House of Representatives, it requires 120 out of 180 members; in the Senate, it requires 37 out of 56 (Lesson 35)

**urban** characteristic of a city or town; the opposite of rural (Lesson 26)

**venue** the scene or locale of any action or event (Lesson 29)

**weak mayor-council** form of municipal government with an elected city council and an elected mayor; most decisions made by city council, which is the legislative branch; mayor is weak (Lesson 39)

**welpolitik** "world politics" in German (Lesson 18)

**white primary** practice that began in the 1920s when southern states used the white primary as a way of limiting the ability of African Americans to play a part in the political process (Lesson 16)

**Yazoo land sale** sale of 35 million acres in a corrupt Georgia land deal (Lesson 9)